SAGGISTICA 32

Cesare Pavese's Long Journey

A Critical-Analytical Study

Cesare Pavese's Long Journey

A Critical-Analytical Study

By
Giose Rimanelli

Edited with an introduction by Mark Pietralunga

Bordighera Press

Library of Congress Control Number: 2018964450

Printed in the United States.

Published by
BORDIGHERA PRESS
John D. Calandra Italian American Institute
25 West 43rd Street, 17th Floor
New York, NY 10036

SAGGISTICA 32
ISBN 978-1-59954-133-4

Dedicated to the memory of Giose Rimanelli,
an "Honoray" Piedmontese.

TABLE OF CONTENTS

EDITOR'S NOTE

The monograph on Pavese is found in the Rimanelli Collections at the State Archive of Campobasso. In the Collections there are four typewritten drafts of the study: two in English and two in Italian. The transcription of the manuscript printed here is drawn from the more complete of the two English versions. It is comprised of 284 typewritten pages and bears the title *Cesare Pavese. A Critical-Analytical Study.* The following pages are missing from the manuscript: 223-225; 229-230; 232-233; 235-237. These missing pages pertain to the notes for Chapters I, III, IV, V, and VII respectively. The handwritten annotations and corrections in this copy are limited.

In anticipation of the publication of the monograph in English, several chapters appeared in North American journals during the 1960s and 1970s:

1) "The Conception of Time and Language in the Poetry of Cesare Pavese," *Italian Quarterly* 13 (1964): 14-34. This publication reproduces in its entirety Chapter II ("The Conception of Time").

2) "Pavese's Journey," *Forum Italicum* 1.2. (1967): 67-78. With some variation at the beginning and end as well as to the translations of Pavese's poems, the article reproduces the first section ("Problems of Form") of Chapter III ("The Cyclical Development") and the second section ("Relation with the Hero") of Chapter IV ("Ab Initio"). At the end of the article, Rimanelli adds his translations of selected poems from *Lavorare Stanca.*

3) "Pavese's Mythical Theatre of the Mind," *The Theatre Annual* 25 (1969): 1-19. With the exception of the first paragraph, the article reproduces, with few modifications, Chapter VI ("The World of Myth") in its entirety.

4) "Myth and De-Mythification of Pavese's Art," *Italian Quarterly 3.49 (1969): 3-39.* This essay reproduces, with some modifications, the first three sections ("The Misunderstanding with the Neorealists," "The Misunderstanding with Proust," and "The Misunderstanding with the Existentialists") of Chapter

1 ("Introduction: Maturity is Defeat") and all of Chapter IV ("Ab Initio").
5) An expanded and revised version of Chapter VIII ("The *Burning Brand*") that bears the title "Pavese's *Diario*: Why Suicide? Why Not?" is included in the volume *Italian Literature. Roots and Branches. Essays in Honor of Thomas Goddard Bergin,* edited by Giose Rimanelli and Kenneth John Atchity, New Haven: Yale University Press (1976): 383-405. This article and the Italian version of the manuscript have allowed me to reconstruct the missing notes from the above-mentioned chapters.

In the transcription of the text, I have attempted to remain faithful to the original version in English. Typographical and other editorial adjustments have been made in order to create greater consistency, and inadvertent misspellings have been corrected.

I wish to acknowledge my indebtedness to Sebastiano Martelli, who initially proposed this project to me and has been an important source of information in the various stages of this endeavor. His edition of the Italian version of the Pavese monograph is forthcoming. I am also deeply grateful to Sheryl Postman for her generous support and encouragement. Many thanks to Anthony Tamburri of Bordighera Press for his thoughtful counsel and continued helpfulness. I wish to extend my appreciation to Matteo Mario Socci, who graciously agreed to allow me to use his art work for the cover of this volume. A final expression of gratitude to Karen Myers for her ongoing patience and aesthetic advice.

INTRODUCTION
An Important Chapter of Rimanelli's Life Journey

Mark Pietralunga

In a letter of February 7, 1964, Giose Rimanelli informs Davide Lajolo, the author of the influential biography on Cesare Pavese *Il vizio assurdo: Storia di Cesare Pavese* (Milan: Il Saggiatore, 1960) and then deputy to the Italian Parliament, that he plans to begin work on a monographic study on the Piedmontese writer later that year.[1] As part of his research for the study, in the early months of 1964 Rimanelli contacts Italo Calvino, then managing editor at the Einaudi Publishing House, asking for suggestions of recent critical studies on Pavese. After complimenting Rimanelli for his thriving academic career across the Atlantic, Calvino writes that so far the only critical book that is diligent, well-documented, and does not say a "load of rubbish" is Lorenzo Mondo's *Cesare Pavese*

---

[1] See Appendix for entire letter, which first appeared in *Rimanelliana*, ed. Sebastiano Martelli (Stony Brook: Forum Italicum Publishing, 2000) 104-108. Martelli, the editor of the forthcoming Italian version of the monograph on Pavese, writes in his essay on the role Pavese played in Rimanelli's artistic and life journey, that his research of the Rimanelli Collections at the State Archive of Campobasso has led to the discovery that the news shared in the Lajolo letter surrounding the preparation of the study was not entirely accurate. Martelli indicates that a large part of the material, despite not yet being in a complete organic volume, had already been collected. According to Martelli, these contributions are the result of Rimanelli's "longstanding loyalty" to Pavese and are now motivated by academic demands of professional development as a professor of Italian and Comparative Literature. In his essay, Martelli notes that the drafting of the book on Pavese is preceded by a number of other professional and academic activities, dating back to his first lecture in the United States at the Library Congress in 1960. For further information regarding the dating of the manuscript material see S. Martelli, "Rimanelli e Pavese: Dall'Italia in America con uno 'scrittore nella valigia," *Leucò va in America. Cesare Pavese nel centenario della nascita. An International Conference Stony Brook, NY, 13-14 marzo 2009*, ed. Mario Mignone (Salerno: Edisud: Stony Brook, NY: Forum Italicum Publishing, 2010) 192-193.

(Ugo Mursia Editore, 1961).[2] Nearly two years later, on March 15, 1966, Rimanelli announces to Calvino that his book-length critical study of Cesare Pavese, contracted with an American publishing house, was complete and was scheduled to appear in the fall of that year. In his letter he tells Calvino that, although it was originally written in English, he had also prepared an Italian version, which he hoped to have published in Italy.[3] Rimanelli encloses in his letter a copy of a chapter from the manuscript, which was published both in Italy and the United States, in the hope of receiving some feedback from Calvino.[4] Though impressed by the essay, Calvino informs Rimanelli on April 7, 1966 that, because of Pavese's affiliation with Einaudi Publishers, it was the company's policy to publish only works by the Piedmontese writer, preferring that critical works on him appear elsewhere (Pietralunga 321). A year later, on June 22, 1967, Rimanelli sends Alberto Mondadori, whose company had already published three of his previous novels,[5] a copy of the Italian version of his study titled "Il lungo viaggio di Cesare Pavese" ("Cesare Pavese's Long Journey") and, in the accompanying letter, quotes the following epigram that the Piedmontese writer had sent to the Turin publisher Carlo Frassinelli when he submitted his translation of Sherwood Anderson's

---

[2] Calvino's letter is found in the Rimanelli file of the Einaudi Archive at the State Archives of Torino. See also Mark Pietralunga, "*Tiro al piccione* di Giose Rimanelli e il ritorno agli inizi: la corrispondenza completa tra lo scrittore molisano e l'editore Giulio Einaudi," in *Campi immaginabili* 46-47 (2012): 319.

[3] Ibid, 320. In his essay "Pavese e Rimanelli," Martelli, notes that the book was scheduled to appear in the Italian authors series (approximately 30 volumes) for Twayne Publishers, planned by a group of Italianists at UCLA headed by Carlo Golino. Evidently the project never materialized and the study remained unpublished even though, as Martelli observes, there are indications among Rimanelli's papers that other attempts were made to publish the manuscript, the last of which in 1974 with the Editorial Fundamentos di Madrid, thanks to the interest of a colleague at the University of Albany (194-195).

[4] Rimanelli's essay appeared in the following publications: "Il concetto di tempo e di linguaggio nella poesia di Pavese," *Terra rossa terra nera*, Laurana Lajolo and Elio Archimede, eds., Asti: Presenza Astigiana (1964): 37-51; and "The Conception of Time and Language in the Poetry of Cesare Pavese," (see "Editor's Note").

[5] Rimanelli's previously published works with Mondadori were *Tiro al piccione* (1953), *Peccato originale* (1954), and *Biglietto di terza* (1958).

Dark Laughter: "To You/ this book/ translated during a sad peri-od/ of decline of Italian letters/when/ not even one bum of a publisher/ wanted it/ now everyone wants to read and publish/ I offer/ for only twenty lire."[6] Rimanelli chooses to send Mon-dadori what he deems to be "the 'only' important critical book on Pavese's work" because the Milanese firm had published, in his view, "the only important biography on Pavese," Lajolo's *Il vizio assurdo*. In his letter to Alberto Mondadori, Rimanelli writes that both Lajolo and critic Giacomo Debenedetti, the latter being a con-sultant at the time for Mondadori, had read the study and liked it very much. Shortly thereafter, Alberto Mondadori passed the manuscript on to editorial consultant Franco Fortini, whose as-sessment was much less favorable; consequently, the Italian ver-sion, like the original English, remained unpublished.[7]

In his essay "Rimanelli e Pavese: Dall'Italia in America con uno 'scrittore nella valigia,'" Sebastiano Martelli offers an enlightening overview of Pavese studies in the early 1960s when Rimanelli was preparing his monograph on the Piedmontese writer (Martelli 195). Martelli indicates that these are years in which there are a number of significant developments in Pavese studies, most nota-bly in the transition from militant criticism to a more far-ranging approach to the author's works (Martelli 195). Martelli speaks of a "critical and methodological impasse" concerning Pavese and his works about a decade after the writer's death in 1950 and refers to

---

6 Rimanelli's letter is found in the Rimanelli file of the Fondo Autori at the Archi-vio Storico of the Fondazione Arnoldo and Alberto Mondadori in Milan. Pave-se's letter to Frassinelli is dated May 1932 (Cesare Pavese, *Lettere 1924-1944* [Tu-rin: Einaudi, 1966]: 335).

7 In his negative reader's report, Fortini deemed the study to be "a type of long graduation thesis on Pavese." The letter is located in the Rimanelli file of the Fondo Autori at the Fondazione Arnoldo and Alberto Mondadori. In another internal letter, Vittorio Sereni, literary director at Mondadori, writes that the de-cision to publish the manuscript "evidentemente è un No" ("evidently it is a NO"); however, he adds that the subject of Rimanelli is a "global" one and, con-sequently, the decision must be global. Before making any final decisions regard-ing Rimanelli, he would like to receive opinions and decisions regarding his nar-rative works. This letter is also located at the Fondo Autori of the Fondazione Arnold and Alberto Mondadori.

a "need to follow other paths" compared to those pursued up to that point in time (Martelli 195). Among the critics who voiced such a shift was Italo Calvino, who promoted a close reading of the text versus the generic nature of the "closed-book" criticism, which continued to dominate in Italy. Calvino shares his opinion on the state of Pavese critical studies in a letter of 25 January 1965 to Michele Tondo, who had sent him a book-length manuscript on the Piedmontese writer (Martelli 195). After complimenting Tondo for "being the first critic to have studied the development, one might almost say, day by day, of the poetics versus works nexus in Pavese," Calvino then points to the gap that his book would fill in the "inadequate" bibliography of the writer:

> It re-establishes the link between Pavese the poet and Pavese the intellectual that a certain kind of criticism (Moravia, Salinari) had destroyed, and at the same time it defines Pavese's historic "commitment" as an internal fact inside his literary oeuvre, something which cannot be judged on the basis of an assessment of the activism in his political behavior (*pace* Lajolo), but on the contrary something that was historically useful precisely in its establishment of an impossibility. It puts the biographical moments back in their appropriate place (again *pace* Lajolo), giving us once more the outline of Pavese's life in his itinerary as a writer. Furthermore it underlines how Pavese's creative experience is indivisible, dictated as it is by an aesthetic-ethical-existential quest which is certainly far removed from any concern of a naturalistic representation of society [...] but also substantially different from other examples of twentieth-century lyrical-ethical prose writing [...]. (Calvino 284)

Martelli suggests that had Rimanelli's monograph on Pavese been published at the time of its completion between 1964 and 1965, it would have been a "point of reference" in Pavese studies not only in America but also in Italy. He argues that 1964 signals a new phase in Pavese studies with the publication of a special issue of the journal *Sigma*, dedicated to the Piedmontese writer (Martelli 195). Calvino also viewed the issue of *Sigma* to be a watershed

moment in Pavese scholarship in which "specialist studies conducted with scholarly rigor" explored, along with the writer's literary text, the technical and structural aspects of his language as
well as the culture of "myth" and Pavese as translator (Calvino
572). At the time Rimanelli was completing his monograph on Pavese, the groundbreaking issue of *Sigma* had not yet appeared.
Martelli underscores the originality of Rimanelli's critical analysis
and perspective when compared to the developments of Pavese
criticism in the 1950s and early 1960s. He recognizes, among the
most significant of Rimanelli's critical inquiries, a modern approach
strongly focused on the texts; a comparatist and world literature
apparatus that distances itself from somewhat outdated debates,
such as neorealism/decadentism and the questions of *engagement*
and existentialism (Martelli 195-196). Instead, continues Martelli,
Rimanelli gives special attention to Pavese's poetry and insists on
drawing from the writer's diary *Il mestiere di vivere* as an important point of reference for the conception of his novels (196).

Rimanelli's journalistic pieces on Pavese date back to his 1955
article, "Ricordo di Pavese," which appeared in the Turin newspaper the *Gazzetta del popolo* in commemoration of the fifth year of
the writer's death.[8] In this article, Rimanelli refers to Pavese as his
"padrino" and recalls seeing him at the "Caffè Greco" in Rome towards the "end of 1949" in the company of the American actress
Constance Dowling.[9] In that brief encounter, Pavese warns Rimanelli not to be captivated by the world of cinema and to keep writing novels. Reflecting upon the writer's personal tragedy, Rimanelli
points to the importance of myth (i.e. "a return to the origins of
human poetry") in Pavese's literary discourse, beginning with his
first published novel *Paesi tuoi* and ending with the shaping of his
last work *La luna e i falò*.

---

[8] Giose Rimanelli, "Ricordo di Pavese," *Gazzetta del popolo* (2 Settembre 1955): 3.
[9] Pavese met Constance Dowling for the first time during a week long trip to
Rome over the New Year, 1949-50. The meeting Rimanelli is referring to here
most likely occurred in January 1950.

Pavese also holds a position of significance in Rimanelli's high-ly controversial collection of essays, *Il mestiere del furbo*, which is a sharp denouncement of the patronage, lobbying barriers, and po-litical machinations of the contemporary Italian literary *milieu* and its cliques.[10] The title of Rimanelli's "scandalous" work, which leads to his emigration to North America and to a new life in academia, appears to allude ironically to Pavese's *Il mestiere di vivere*. In his commentary on Pavese, Rimanelli begins by focusing on the writ-er's interest from an early age in the discovery of American au-thors. With this discovery, Rimanelli asserts that Pavese, along with Vittorini, introduced to Italy "the pionieristic and messianic novel, bard of strong and raw passions"[11] declaring implicitly that it was time to discard the "fiorentinismo" and "strapaese" and to look beyond its restrictive artistic boundaries.[12] For Rimanelli, it is by this discovery "from within" of the Americans that Pavese found his vocation. Consequently, Rimanelli observes that with his early novel *Paesi tuoi*, Pavese succeeds in realizing his artistic conviction: "objectification, dialect, provincial, rediscovery of primordial and elementary instincts" (Rimanelli, *Il mestiere* 34).

In the chapter of *Il mestiere del furbo* entitled "La lente sporca" (the dirty lens), Rimanelli highlights the centrality of Pavese in

---

[10] Before appearing in book form, Rimanelli's essays were published in a fea-tured column titled "Letteratura" in the Italian weekly *Lo specchio* from March 30, 1958 to December 1959 under the *nom de plume* A.G. Solari. Shortly before the collection of essays was to go to press, the editors of the volume announced that they had received a letter from Giose Rimanelli informing them that he was in fact A. G. Solari (A.G. Solari, *Il Mestiere del Furbo. Panorama della narrativa italiana contemporanea* [Milan: Sugar Editore, 1959]: 8-9). A second edition of the volume, edited by Eugenio Ragni, has been published (Giose Rimanelli, *Il mestiere del fur-bo. Panorama della narrativa italiana contemporanea [1930-1959]* [New York: Bor-dighera Press, 2016]). Ragni also published an enlighting, detailed study of the collection of essays titled *"Il mestiere del furbo. Un 'suicidio annunciato,'" Rimanel-liana*: 37-96 (Rev.ed. *Giose 1959 un 'suicidio' annunciato* [New York: Bordighera Press, 2016]).

[11] Translations of quotes from *Il mestiere del furbo* are mine.

[12] Quotes are from Ragni's edition of *Il mestiere del furbo*: 39. All translations are mine.

this volume and the celebrated author's influence on the young Italian writers of the 1950s:

> The lesson of Pavese was a lesson of intelligence, of new research and inner torment. His work opens up into two directions: an essentially realistic literature, and an essentially individualistic literature. Pavese had declared two principles of research: one that aims toward subjective ecstasy, the other toward objective knowledge. He found and realized his personality in the first. The novels *Il carcere, Il diavolo in colline* and the poetry of *Lavorare stanca* define the nature of his art. The same country-city dualism, the first originating from memory, childhood, the hills—the mythic age—the second from the road, from relationships, from socialization—the intellectual age- testify to his idea of seeing the world. However, only when Pavese sits in his mythical universe, and in an almost whispered tone shares with us the truth of his intimate "being," in particular, his solitude, made of memory and semi-madness, grows enormous to our eyes and becomes the incorruptible poet who will have a long lasting voice in the literary processes. (79)

While recognizing the key role Pavese played in introducing the major voices of nineteenth and twentieth century American literature to Italian letters, Rimanelli identifies the prominent place that American writers, beginning with Herman Melville and Walt Whitman, held in the Piedmontese author's early works. One need only mention Pavese's poem "I mari del sud" to appreciate the influences of Melville and Whitman in its rhythm and in the adventurous life at sea. For Rimanelli, Pavese's role as a "maestro" to many in the postwar years is a result of a search to avoid the beaten track as a writer, unlike many of his contemporaries. While noting that he has no plans to do a more in depth study of Pavese's writings, Rimanelli believes he has succeeded in highlighting his importance as a writer. Rimanelli further sustains that a study on Pavese's work would require an entire volume. What interests Rimanelli is Pavese's legacy and the opportunity to make clear that after his life and death no other "violent personality" has come forth "to slap our reconstructed literary conformism and the mediocre attempts of its youngest voices in the face as he has" (80).

In February of 1960, Rimanelli's review of Pavese's *Racconti*, which Einaudi published in the same year, appeared in the weekly *Rotosei*."[13] In his review, Rimanelli observes that the fixed idea of man's solitude and of man's carnality remains the cornerstone of an unresolved quest for a painful liberation. For Rimanelli, Pavese's short stories live as in a perpetual threat of a primordial and untamed ("selvaggio") drama that reveals itself in the "unanchored" man, the so-called *outsider,* and that remains an indispensable constant in the life of these stories (Martelli 191-192). Martelli appropriately observes that this review marked the end of Rimanelli's Italian phase as both a critic and writer and the beginning of his new American chapter. In doing so, adds Martelli, Rimanelli is obliged to move from militant and social criticism to academic criticism, with Pavese becoming a familiar subject of analysis in this new critical methodology (192). Martelli also reminds us that the years 1960-1964 correspond to Rimanelli's first academic lectures and teaching assignments in various North American universities, including Sarah Lawrence College, Yale University, the University of British Columbia, and the University of California at Los Angeles (UCLA).

It is from Los Angeles that Rimanelli enters the date of September 1965 at the end of his Acknowledgements to the completed English manuscript on Pavese.[14] In lieu of a Preface to his study, Rimanelli, in his Acknowledgements, directs his readers to the Appendix which contains his correspondence with Davide Lajolo, the above-mentioned author of the biography on Pavese *Il vizio assurdo*, and Elio Archimede, literary editor of the Asti weekly *La nuova provincia*. These letters serve as valuable material concerning the process of writing the book and its objectives, along with

---

[13] Giose Rimanelli, "I racconti di Cesare Pavese," *Rotosei* 9 (26 February 1960).
[14] On the cover page of the manuscript, Rimanelli writes: "Address: Professor Giose Rimanelli, Italian Department, University of California, Los Angeles, California 90024."

offering insight into the "the Italian public's interest in the personality and work of Cesare Pavese." Moreover, these letters shed light on the figure of Rimanelli and the impact that Pavese and his works have had on him as a writer, academic, emigrant, expatriate, and outsider.

Before we highlight some observations from the author's Appendix, we might consider points raised by Rimanelli in the Preface to the Italian version of his study on Pavese.[15] Here Rimanelli notes immediately that Pavese "is not an easy writer to accept, to ignore, or to classify." By virtue of the quality of his writing and the range of his perspectives, Rimanelli recognizes that Pavese may seem to some "a writer of social facts" and to others "a stylist who is constantly concerned with intellectual questions of form." To others, continues Rimanelli, Pavese is an artist who works with archetypes. However, Rimanelli is quick to assert that Pavese eludes any categorical definitions and he offers as a point of comparison the restricted scope of the early critics of Melville's *Moby Dick* and of the works of James Joyce. Rimanelli observes that *Moby Dick* was simply seen as a sea adventure, while Joyce's writings were merely considered "philological questions that often lead to puzzles and charades." Instead, Rimanelli argues that their works possess a "mythical time that renders the past present or the present already forgone and nevertheless statically sacred, current, active, not frozen, because they constantly offer a new way to explain reality."

Rimanelli informs readers that his study on Pavese intends to investigate those directions that the writer's poetics suggest. He adds that these directions may appear somewhat adventurous to an Italian sense of criticism, which has a more realist cultural tradition. Even though Pavese seems so attached to his region of Piedmont, Rimanelli suggests that "he is only apparently a product of his culture and of Italian sensibilities" and, like Italo Svevo, Pavese is difficult to explain with Italian critical measures. Rima-

---

15 For further details of the Preface to the forthcoming Italian version, see Martelli 193.

nelli also feels compelled to point out that we should be cautious when referring to Pavese's "American cultural experiments"; instead, we must clarify and insist that America acted "as a catalyst, as a pretext, and as a dimension of memory." Even though he by no means rejects the significance of such writers as Whitman and Melville on the young Pavese, Rimanelli declares that there comes a time that one must learn to walk on one's own, stand on one's own two feet, think with one's own mind, and suffer in one's own flesh. Consequently, for Rimanelli, "one does not arrive at Pavese, as it were, but one could very well begin from him."

As mentioned above, Rimanelli's correspondence with Davide Lajolo and Elio Archimede, included in the Appendix to the English version, highlights the aims of Rimanelli's study on Pavese and the process in which it came into being. In the first of the letters, dated November 3, 1960, Lajolo attempts to re-establish his friendship with Rimanelli, who by then had relocated to the United States, and shares with him the success of his biography of Pavese. Lajolo also notes in his letter that, at the time he was writing his biographical study, he had in mind what Rimanelli had said about Pavese in his controversial book *Il mestiere del furbo*, namely that he was worthy of a comprehensive study. In his response to Lajolo on November 24, 1960, Rimanelli's confession-like reflections offer key insights into the influence of Pavese on his life experiences as a young writer, particularly those circumstances surrounding the manuscript of his first novel *Tiro al piccione*. Rimanelli expresses his gratitude to Lajolo for his friendship and informs him of his "new life" as a professor at New York University and at Sarah Lawrence College.

On February 7, 1964, four years after the first exchange of letters, Rimanelli resumes his correspondence with Lajolo. In this letter, Rimanelli offers an overview of the state of Pavese studies in the United States and informs Lajolo of his unsuccessful attempts to have *Il vizio assurdo* published in the United States. Based on Pavese's lack of name recognition, the publishers believed it would be difficult to market the biography. While criticizing "the absurd American vice of weighing things in terms of the 'forseeable' profit from the sale of a consumer's item," Rimanelli also suggests that the Italians, as a result of their "defeatist character," bear some of the responsibility for the difficulty of publishing a translation of *Il vizio assurdo* because they have not known how to validate Pavese's work and protect it. However, for Pavese to gain the attention of a serious reading public, Rimanelli suggests that it is important to follow the lead of the French and Anglo-American critics who are "excellently organized on the critical front regarding their writers." It is in this spirit of establishing a critical front that Rimanelli declares Pavese to be one of those few Italian contemporary writers who deserves critical attention. Nevertheless, Rimanelli recognizes that, except for articles by Leslie Fiedler and John Freccero, there exist no critical studies on Pavese.[16] Rimanelli intends to remedy this void and closes his letter by announcing to Lajolo his plans of a book-length study on Pavese.

In his letter of February 27, 1964 to Elio Archimede, Rimanelli applauds the cultural initiative of the newspaper *La nuova provincia* dedicated to Pavese and asserts that Pavese criticism "is still minimal and not at all satisfactory." Rimanelli observes that, like Lajolo, he was first drawn to Pavese for sentimental and personal reasons and only later did his interest become critical in nature. He recounts that an important moment in this transition occurs when he was lying in a hospital bed in Mexico City and read Pavese's poetry collection *Lavorare stanca*, which contains all of the dominant themes of the Piedmontese writer's artistic production: the juxtaposition of the two contrasting landscapes of the city and country, the relationship between youth and maturity, the return to one's roots, escapism, work, misogyny, and solitude. The fact of being in Mexico, observes Rimanelli, "signified participation in the *fiesta*, that is to say in a cosmic experiment in disorder, a journey into the unconscious which brings one back to the beginnings

---

[16] See Leslie Fiedler, "Introducing Cesare Pavese," *Kenyon Review* 16.4 (1954): 536-553 (Reprinted in *No! In Thunder Essays on Myth and Literature* [Boston: Beacon Press, 1960: 135-150]) and John Freccero, "Mythos and Logos: *The Moon and the Bonfires*," *Italian Quarterly*, 4.16 (Winter 1961): 3-16.

and hence to a new start, a re-vivification." It was this experience of the Mexican *fiesta* that offered insight into Pavese's lyrical sensitivity and his fascination with mythology and anthropology, which engender the multidimensional levels inherent in his works and contribute to the writer's uniqueness in the landscape of contemporary Italian literature. Rimanelli concludes his letter to Archimede with the encouraging observation that Italian literature is emerging from its isolation in academic circles and that "Italian poets and prose-writers are being translated more diligently, and are appearing in newspapers and journals." It is Rimanelli's hope that Pavese, as well as other Italian contemporary writers, will benefit from future studies and translations.

A brief overview of the translations, or translatability, of Pavese's works into English may help shed light on possible reasons for the limited critical and popular recognition of the Piedmontese writer in the years that lead up to and immediately follow Rimanelli's study. As Lawrence G. Smith has observed in his essay "Pavese in America: A New Beginning?," Leslie Fiedler's observation in his pioneering 1954 essay "Introducing Cesare Pavese" that the translations of Pavese's works did not succeed in stimulating a general interest or understanding of the Piedmontese author has remained valid over the years.[17] Smith suggests that this is in part the result of the "overall problem of translated literature in America and in part due to the particular history of translations of Pavese" (168). In the preface to his 1968 volume *Three Italian Novelists: Moravia, Pavese, and Vittorini*, Donald Heiney states that one of the reasons he chose to translate all the excerpts in his study was that "in some cases the authors have been wretchedly translated."[18] Heiney adds that "translation is terribly hard work and rather badly paid, and in order to translate a novel adequately it is necessary for the translator not only to be an expert linguist, but to

---

[17] Lawrence G. Smith, "Pavese in America: A New Beginning," *Incontro con Cesare Pavese. Un giorno di simpatia totale*, Quaderno 3 (Turin: Liceo Classico Dazeglio, 2010) 168.

[18] Donald Heiney, *Three Italian Novelists: Moravia, Pavese, Vittorini* (Ann Arbor, The University of Michigan Press, 1968) x.

have something like a novelist's talent in his own right" (x). In a letter of October 4, 1964 to Davide Lajolo, William Arrowsmith, the translator of *Dialoghi con Leucò* and *Lavorare stanca*, reinforces Heiney's observations when he refers to the unfortunate quality of Pavese's translations into English and how British and American publishers handle the Piedmontese writer's works:

> Pavese, by the way, has suffered enormously in English translation. The British publisher, Peter Owen, persists in bringing out versions which are infelicitous in the extreme—clumsy, heavy, stilted English prose, without a trace of Pavese's virtues—and copyright law, of course, products [sic] these wretched versions from competition. In America, it is just as bad, if not worse, since the publishers simply import Owen's versions and republish them. It was for this reason that my collaborator, DS Carne-Ross, and I spent most of a year working on the Dialogues. Whether we were successful is of course open to question, but I think we made every effort to create an English Pavese as eloquent and forceful as the Italian Pavese.[19]

Other critics have referred to Pavese's translations as "serviceably enough,"[20] "not so much technically bad as *critically* wrong,"[21] "hasty workmanship,"[22] and "so full of errors as to be unrealiable" (Smith 169).

During his lifetime and at the time of his death in 1950, no work by Pavese was translated into English. In a January 1951 piece for the *New York Review of Books* treating the contemporary literary landscape in Italy, Paolo Milano introduces Pavese in the following terms: "Cesare Pavese, in many ways the most promising of the new Italian writers and the only significant one still unknown

---

[19] The letter is located at the Lajolo Archives in Vinchio d'Asti.
[20] Glauco Cambon, "Truth as Fiction: Pavese's Diary," *Michigan State Quarterly Review* 16.1 (1977): 1.
[21] Fiedler, *Kenyon Review*, 536.
[22] Lionel Casson, "Night Thoughts from Olympus," *Saturday Review* (June 5, 1965): 25.

to the American reader, killed himself in the fall."[23] In 1952 Louis Brigante published in his review *Intro* a "letter" written to him by translator and critic D. D. Paige which provides an overview of the Italian contemporary narrative. In his letter Paige asserts that, despite its general high level, the contemporary Italian narrative "doesn't travel well." He holds firm to the opinion that contemporary Italian literature is either boring, lacks an experimental capacity, or finds itself lost among seemingly disparate linguistic options: a lofty, archaic, and strictly literary vocabulary or colloquial and vernacular style. Among those authors spared by Paige is Pavese, who remains for him "the most interesting of the younger group of writers," despite the "revolutionary (and therefore objectionable) quality of his prose."[24]

The question of translatability of Pavese's works is a common topic in the correspondence between Sanford Greenburger, the American literary agent who represented Einaudi Editore in the postwar years, and American publishers. The correspondence confirms that the strictest economy of the American publishing houses is reserved for the translation. In a letter of April 10, 1950, Arthur Ormont, Associate Editor at Farrar, Straus and Company, informs Greenburger of the refusal of Pavese's *La bella estate*. While Ormont speaks to the author's talents and originality, the primary concern is one of translatability.[25] And in a letter of October 31, 1950, Ormont writes Greenburger of Farrar, Straus and Company's serious interest in *La luna e i falò* (The Moon and the Bonfires); however, he raises concerns about the translatability of the novel and how Pavese would be introduced to an English speaking public (Greenburger, Box 13). Nevertheless, the strong incentive of a cost share option with the English publisher Lehman would eventually lead to the publication of *La luna e i falò* in English.

---

[23] Paolo Milano, "A Literary Letter abut Italy," *New York Times Book Review* (21 January 1951): 28.
[24] D. D. Paige, "Italian Letter," *Intro*, I, 1952: 21.
[25] Sanford J. Greenburger Literary Agency Records, 1921-1977, Box 13, University of Oregon Libraries Special Collections and University Archives.

In his 1954 introduction to the English translation of the novel *The Moon and the Bonfire*, Paolo Milano addresses the question of why the delay in translating Pavese's works:

> Whenever I have found myself with an Italian friend, discussing the lively interest of Americans in contemporary Italian fiction — in the work of Alberto Moravia, Carlo Levi, Vasco Pratolini, Giuseppe Berto, Elio Vittorini, Elsa Morante, and the rest — invariably I have been asked, "Why hasn't Pavese been translated yet?" A natural enough question, because Italians consider Pavese's novelettes to be the finest, if not the most colorful, fruit of the postwar literary crop. "Of course," my Italian friends usually add, "how could Pavese's elliptic and allusive style bear translation of any kind?"[26]

In his 1954 essay, Fiedler suggests that Milano's brief introduction is not enough "to offset the effect of the translation itself, which seems not so much technically bad but *critically* wrong in the writer it finds and tries, without much grace, to English; just another young Italian exploiter of sex and violence and the sentimental myth of the Resistance" (Fiedler 537).

Despite Fiedler's championing of Pavese, Frances Keene, in her introduction to the English translation of the Piedmontese author's *Il mestiere di vivere* which appeared several years later in 1961, speaks to a general unfamiliarity with the writer's life and works in the United States:

> [...] in this country Pavese's novels have been published haphazardly and the myth of his personality has been imperfectly documented. In Italy and France he is, with Elio Vittorini and Alberto Moravia, established in the front rank of contemporary Italian authors, and he is read increasingly in England. We have

---

[26] Cesare Pavese, *The Moon and the Bonfires*, New York, Signet Book (1954): vii. Milano's essay first appeared under the title "Pavese's Experiments in the Novel," *The New Republic* (4 May 1953): 17-23.

yet to have a coherent view of Pavese in the United States, and the publication of this journal should be a step in that direction.[27]

In her 1962 essay "The artist as an exemplary sufferer," Susan Sontag writes that Pavese deserves a "good deal more attention in England and America" than he has received thus far and, in welcoming the recent publication of Pavese's diary into English, observes that it can be read "without any acquaintance" of his novels.[28]

While the publication of Pavese's diary was a step in the right direction in providing a more "coherent view" of the writer, Stanley Edgar Hyman, as late as 1968, would write in his review of R. W. Flint's edition *The Selected Novels of Cesare Pavese* that "Cesare Pavese is still not very well known in this country, but he is the most prominent postwar novelist."[29] In the same year of the publication of his edition of Pavese's novels, R. W. Flint published the essay "Translating Cesare Pavese" in which he explored in detail the question of why such quality as Pavese's writings had to wait so long for recognition outside of Italy. In his essay, Flint reflects on the versions of the early translators: "the first translators, all presumably young men, had overlaid the text with often amusing, sometimes hilarious, record of breezy enthusiasm, snuffy timidities, and general miscomprehension with which the Anglo-American world had first greeted a prostrate Italy when the war was over."[30] Flint is quick to point out that these early translators "were not equally or uniformly bad," however, what appeared unsettling to them was "Pavese's novel combination of gentility and profanity, mildness and rigor, saturnine subversive humor and high poetic elevation" (157).

---

[27] Pavese, *The Burning Brand: Diaries 1935-1950* (New York: Walker & Company, 1961) 7.
[28] Susan Sontag, "The artist as an exemplary sufferer," *Against Interpretation and Other Essays*, New York: Farrar, Straus & Giroux (1961):41.
[29] Stanley Edgar Hyman, "Sad Encounters," *The New Yorker* 44.27 (August 24, 1968): 114.
[30] R.W. Flint, "Translating Cesare Pavese," *Delos* 1 (1968): 156.

Publishing obstacles such as those above may have ultimately played a role in Rimanelli's decision to shelve his manuscript on Pavese. With this decision, Rimanelli abandoned his hope of helping to promote a major voice of contemporary Italian literature and to pay tribute to a man to whom he was bound for personal and sentimental reasons.[31] Despite the over a half century since Rimanelli's initial attempts to have the manuscript published both in English and in Italian, there is much to learn from this study not only as it pertains to Pavese but also as it relates to its author. It seems appropriate that Bordighera Press would choose to publish this study on Pavese on the heels of bringing back in print Rimanelli's controversial book *Il mestiere del furbo* after over fifty years. Eugenio Ragni's observations in his introductory remarks to the recent re-release of *Il mestiere del furbo* strike us as applicable to Rimanelli's book-length study on Pavese. Ragni refers to *Il mestiere del furbo* as an example of intellectual independence and whose analysis is still critically valid after so many years.[32] The same holds

---

[31] An unpublished manuscript titled "Gli occhi chiusi di Pavese" (Pavese's Closed Eyes), originally written for a lecture he gave at Southern Connecticut State College in Spring 1974, may offer additional insight into why Rimanelli chose to abandon this project. In his lecture, Rimanelli declares that he had decided not to write anymore about Pavese. He adds that this decision signifies a liberation from Pavese, from his death in 1950 that had weighed on him from the time of their first meeting in Rome in March of 1950 and had impacted the greater part of his life. Rimanelli observes that Pavese's death in August 1950 became his life: "In his death was my life, because I accompanied him, and he maintained and accompanied me. As a writer I know him all too well; therefore, he did not possess me. As a man, however, he nourished me with all his magic. He made me strong. Pavese was my village." Drawing from the words of Anguilla, the protagonist of Pavese's final novel ("A village means that you're not alone, that you know that in those people, those trees, and that soil, there is a part of you; that even when you aren't there it stays there waiting for you."), Rimanelli announces his separation from Pavese: "Pavese was my village and my myth. But now the time for a separation has arrived. If maturity means solitude, maturity means other duties. Ciao, Pave." The manuscript of this lecture, originally titled "Il libro rubato" (The Stolen Book) is found in the Rimanelli Collections at the State Archive of Campobasso. There are three drafts of the essay, the second draft (14 pages typewritten and dated "April 1974") is the most complete and contains a number of handwritten revisions.

[32] Rimanelli, *Il mestiere del furbo*: xvii.

true for Rimanelli's study of Pavese, as does a similar careful reading of the texts combined with a balanced philological and narratological approach. Moreover, a distinguishing feature of both *Il mestiere del furbo* and *Cesare Pavese's Long Journey: A Critical-Analytical Study*, particularly from other criticism in the 1950s and early 1960s, are Rimanelli's enlightened references to foreign works and authors. Finally, the publication of this book-length study of Pavese brings to light an important chapter of Rimanelli's own life journey. It highlights a strong sense of tradition, a loyalty to place and to one's roots, and the idea of America as a metaphor for one's literary substance, one's myth, and one's destiny.

Cesare Pavese's Long Journey

A Critical-Analytical Study

By
Giose Rimanelli

For
Dennis M. Healy
and Carlo L. Golino
and Salvator Attanasio
in affectionate remembrance
of those
days
in British Columbia
Chicago
and New York

TABLE OF CONTENTS

Acknowledgments

Instead of writing a Preface, which is bound to say too little or too much about the intentions in dealing in a subject, I refer the reader to the Appendix which contains some useful (hopefully) material concerning Cesare Pavese, his friends, and the making of this book.

I wish to express my thanks to the authorities of the University of British Columbia, for haven (and my mind goes to the kind Miss Rachel Giese and Mrs. Stefania Ciccone, the brilliant Dick and Jane Friedeman, the sober and deserving Edro Signori, Earle Birney the poet), books and research funds; to the *Italian Quarterly*, University of California at Los Angeles; *Comparative Literature*, University of Oregon, Eugene; *Presenza Astigiana*, Asti, Italy; and to the publishing house Giulio Einaudi, in Turin, to Alfred A. Knopf, Inc., publishers, in New York, to Peter Owen Ltd., publishers, in London, and to The University of Michigan Press, Ann Arbor, for permission to quote from the works of Cesare Pavese in Italian and in English. In many cases I have taken the liberty of modifying the translations only for the purpose of putting my inter relations in bold relief.

Even if I cannot thank all those friends and pupils who, in one way or another, contributed to the making of this book, it goes without saying that I remember them fondly and that I am immensely grateful to them. I must, however, mention two students and good friends of mine in particular, Frank Donovan, Jr. and Franco Loriggio who were helpful during my research and who, by their enthusiastic participation in the seminar discussions helped to clarify and bring to light many obscure points. I also wish to extend my heart-felt thanks to Hon. Davide Lajolo for his valuable suggestions, and to Laurana Lajolo and Elio Archimede for graciously allowing me to make use of a certain part of the Pavesian Bibliography which they published in *Terra rossa terra nera*. I am also especially grateful to Professors Giovanni Gullace of Harpur College and Giovanni Cecchetti of Stanford University for encouragement and criticism, and to the gentle and patient Mrs. Nancy Perri who succeeded in typing my almost illegible manuscript.

G. R.

Los Angeles, California
September, 1965

CHRONOLOGY

September 9, 1908	Cesare Pavese born in Santo Stefano Belbo, Cuneo.
1914	His father dies.
1923-26	Studies at the Liceo Massimo D'Azeglio in Turin.
1927-30	First Translations.
1930	Receives his degree in Letters with a thesis on Walt Whitman which creates a sensation.
1931	His mother dies. He publishes the translation of *Our Mr. Wrenn* by Sinclair Lewis. First poems of *Lavorare stanca* (Work Wearies).
1933	Founding of the Giulio Einaudi publishing house.
1934	Assumes the direction of the review *La Cultura* published by Einaudi.
1935	Arrested for anti-fascist activity, tried and sentenced to three years to a place of confinement at Brancaleone Calabro. Sentence remitted, he is released in 1936.
1936-38	Writes the short stories later to be collected in *Notte di festa* (Festival Night).
1938-39	*Il carcere* (The Political Prisoner) and *Paesi tuoi* (The Harvesters).

September 8, 1943	After the signing of the armistice, he finds refuge in Serralunga, Cuneo.
1945	Returns to Turin and reorganizes the Einaudi publishing house. Writes *La terra e la morte* (Earth and Death).
1945-47	*Dialoghi con Leucò* (Dialogues with Leucò).
1946	*Il compagno* (The Comrade).
1947-48	*La casa in collina* (The House on the Hill).
1948	Writes *Il diavolo sulle colline* (The Devil in the Hills).
1949	*Tra donne sole* (Among Women Only) and *La luna e i falò* (The Moon and the Bonfires).
1950	Meets the American movie actress Constance Dowling. Wins the prestigious literary prize, Il Premio Strega, for his 1949 literary triptych, *La bella estate* (The Beautiful Summer)
August 27, 1950	Commits suicide in a room of the Hotel Roma in Turin.

We live in a world of things, facts, deeds, which is the temporal world. Our ceaseless, unconscious effort is to reach out beyond time towards the ecstatic moment when our liberty will be realized.

Pavese, *The Burning Brand*

PART ONE

POETRY
(1930 - 1940)

Chapter I

INTRODUCTION: MATURITY IS DEFEAT

1. THE MISUNDERSTANDING WITH THE NEOREALISTS

"Cesare Pavese bore the imprints of all the somatic characteristics of a peasant people in his face, in his curved nose and in his thin lips, in his stature, tall and lean as a pruned elm tree, in his long and knotty hands, even if he had never wielded a hoe, but only the pen."[1]

This is how Pavese is described by his most authoritative biographer, Davide Lajolo. And this is how I remember him on those (two) occasions when I ran across him in Rome (January 1950). At that time he was already a kind of myth, particularly for those who knew and understood very little about him. On the one hand there was a man of culture who under fascism kept open the dialogue — prohibited by fascism — against every form of chauvinist autarchy in the realm of culture; on the other hand there was the Pavese of legend, woven of petty nature, which defined him as an acute but harsh man, all of one piece, distant, ungenerous, and even envious[2] like a discontent God, and extremely severe especially in regard to young writers.

---

[1] Davide Lajolo, "Cesare Pavese, un contadino sotto le grandinate," *La nuova provincia*, 16 (April, 29, 1954); reprinted in the volume *Terra rossa terra nera*, 7.

[2] See Alberto Moravia's article "Pavese decadente," *Il corriere della sera* (December 22, 1954): 3; reprinted in the volume *L'uomo come fine*, Milan: Bompiani (1964). Among other things he states: "In these last few days I have for the first time read *Il mestiere di vivere* by Cesare Pavese. It is a painful book. This pain, upon careful scrutiny, derives above all from the singular combination of a constant, deep, and acerb sorrow with the wretched, solitary and almost delirious characters created by a professional man of letters. These characters of Pavese are placed in their proper light if, outside any question of quality, we compare *Il mestiere di vivere* with Leopardi's *Zibaldone*. Leopardi too was a professional literary man besides being a poet. But in Leopardi poetry and life communicated and

3

But this legend for which the Roman literati (whom Pavese criticized),[3] are mainly responsible, attacked only one aspect of the man—that of appearances—and it was not based on facts. The facts are that Pavese was not indulgent to the stupidities of the young or of the old, just as he was unsparing towards himself.

It was Pavese who discovered, launched and encouraged a writer of such subtle intelligence as Italo Calvino. And it was he who, during one of his sojourns in Rome, got his hands on my first manuscript and published it.[4]

At that time, the fact that Pavese had taken an interest in my work did not make me altogether happy because—like many of my contemporaries—I felt the Pavesian literature to be alien to my approach to reality. Pavese, who soon thereafter was to have a great influence on young writers, was not involved with the neorealists even if critics often confused him with them. The neorealists still based their art on 19th century canons: action in the novel

---

mutually balanced and purified each other. In Pavese, instead, there is a literary man first of all and only, in his life as well as in his work. And that sorrow which, as has been said, does not seem to find expression neither in life nor in the work, remained without the outlet of action and without poetic purification, finally drove him to suicide."

In addition, Moravia identifies the "wretched characters" whom he attributes to Pavese with "childish, measureless, megalomanic vanity," "envy, it too of a childish character." An irascible lack of generosity and of charity towards friends and colleagues.

[3] *The Burning Brand: Diaries 1935-1950* (*Il mestiere di vivere*), translated by A.E. Murch (with Jeanne Molli), New York: Walker & Company (1961) 320. We read: "The Roman school—that meeting place of journalists, adventurers, writers, painters—has invented a reflexed art of the type associated with Alexandria, a taste for remodeling a given style, technique, world, exercising their intelligence without becoming involved. Longanesi and *Omnibus*, Cecchi and Praz, Cardarelli and Bacchelli, Moravia and Morante. Outside of Rome, Landolfi and Piovene. This substantially was fascist art; what was alive and true—and cynical—in the fascist period. Only the two extremes stayed free of it, Sicily and Piedmont, which were not fascist, and discovered 'barbarian' culture across the sea—Vittorini and Pavese. For them, you need another formula."

[4] The novel was *Tiro al piccione* (Milan: Mondadori, 1953). Pavese read and accepted the book for the Einaudi publishing house, who printed it for their series "I Coralli." After Pavese's suicide it was returned to me in galley sheets. Three years went by before its acceptance and publication by another publisher.

and a minute development of situations, whereas Pavese developed his themes on static essences, in an aura of facts that have already occurred and which nevertheless are present now. In short Pavese, playing with sensations and atmospheres, created an intellectual rhythm which transformed narrative action and narrative events into "symbols of a given reality."[5] Therefore he was already outside, and at the antipodes, of that neorealistic process of the Italian literary renaissance which had characterized our second post-war period, and which he himself had anticipated years before, at least on the formal plane, with the novel *Paesi tuoi*.

The neorealists, speaking of the objective world, spoke of science and thought that they could regenerate mankind through the work of art. At bottom they were optimists and "engagés" in the Sartrean sense. But by so doing they were avoiding consciousness, the true nature of human suffering. They gave full value to the reality *of man*, whereas Pavese gave full value to the reality *in man*, and not, in short, to phenomenological reality. The neorealists, in practice, situated themselves between two experiences: that of the Cubists, for example, who studied the reality beyond appearances, and that of Pavese himself who studied the ambience as reality.

The equivocation of the neorealists lay in their search for the real, for individuals, in not imposing their view of reality, that is to say their morality. Pavese's characters, instead, are individuals

---

[5] On June 12, 1950, hardly two months before taking his own life, Cesare Pavese replied to several questions put to him in the following manner: "When Pavese begins a story, a fable, a book, it never happens to him to have a socially determined ambience in mind, a character or characters, a thesis. What he has in mind is almost always an indistinct rhythm, a play of events which, more than anything else, are sensations and atmospheres. His task lies in grasping and structuring these events, according to an intellectual rhythm that transforms them into symbols of a given reality." At this point, Fabio Carpi (*La nuova provincia*," 18, April 29, 1964, Asti) reveals that Pavese "has implicitly fixed the principles of a new cinematic language, formulating its premises through a type of new narrative in which the characters simply serve the function of fashioning intellectual fables whose theme is the rhythm of that which happens." Examples: the films of Michelangelo Antonioni before *Blow-Up*.

who exist only by virtue of their essence, of their realities, not as phenomena of a given reality. Here Pirandellian dualism once again poses itself between theatre and life. But this dualism did not exist for Pavese. Between subject and object there is only one reality, that one which comes to light in the consciousness of the individual.

Neorealism has had a deep and positive influence on post Second World War Italian literature; yet this movement did not suggest an indispensable self-criticism to the writers who practiced it, because at bottom it was a reaction to the culture of the period of twenty years under fascism. In consequence it exhausted itself in letting off steam. By his *a priori* acceptance of some schemes and some attitudes as acquired and justified, that is to say without a personal exploration of the material common to all, the neorealist writer has fallen into the same error of his predecessors, namely into mannerism. Moreover, his investigation of the real, and his posing of the historicity of a situation as an absolute, made him lose sight of those premises which moved him to action. In short, they caused him to lose sight of the individual. Taking man as his point of departure, the neorealist writer ended up by creating summary characters, devoid of inwardness or singularity. If the writer of "prosa d'arte" etherealized his style into an exasperating preciosity, the neorealist writer gradually ended up in an exasperating and often superficial psychologism.

Now the very recent tendency to couple Pavese with the writers of his generation, and to establish parallels which are intended to reshape the myth Pavese is (not always) very productive. True, Pavese's characters do not always have a countenance that is uniquely theirs. And Pavese himself knew this. "The characters in these stories are delineated in a summary fashion, they are names and types, nothing else: they stand on the same plane as a tree, a house, a storm or an air-raid."[6] Nevertheless these characters differ from those created by the neorealists. The psychological anonymity of the characters is replaced by the language, by the narra-

---

[6] *La letteratura americana e altri saggi*, 295.

tive rhythm, and adroitly exploited in relation to the fundamental thematic line. Anguilla, for example, who evokes the past does not make use of the interior monologue because he does not reveal details that can contribute to an eventual definition of his personality. Recollections are never motivated by unconscious associations or by other psychological mechanisms. It is not at all a case, as we shall soon see, of an involuntary memory that presents fragments of the past to the consciousness. Rather, it is a question of a linear narrative whose development does not depend on contingencies or on external facts. Anguilla already knows all that which will be of interest to him. As a boy, when the others used to call him bastard, "the rage of being a nobody"[7] drives him to set out for the fabulous world of his dreams, where he hopes to define himself and to create a name and an individuality for himself.

Now, upon returning home, he would like to find a society where existence would not be over-individualized and thereby becoming "terra e paese" (385). Talking with the share-croppers he reveals his identity by having recourse to the nickname that they had once given to him, and he recalls to them the times of la Mora. Thus, at one and the same time he sees himself objectivized in places. "A homeland means not to be alone, to know that there is something of yourself in the people, in the plants, in the earth, which remains waiting for you even when you are not there" (387). Anguilla wants to discover whether there is a continuity in his existence, whether a moment just lived can be connected to an immobilized past, and return as something still present. In other words he aspires to a condition of perfect metaphysical equilibrium: to be free and at the same time fixed, subject and object, rooted in historicity and yet outside time. Anguilla wants to possess himself, coincide with himself, as it were. In fact, Nuto tells him, "Your father... it is you" (390).

Pavese, therefore, even though he tells a story with the immediacy of his contemporaries, imposes structures on all the events that he narrates. The result is that under-play of rhythm and at-

---

[7] *La luna e i falò*, in *Romanzi*, vol. II, 482.

mospheres that so deeply mark his style. At bottom his ambition was to reconcile the conflict that had arisen on the plane of narrative technique with the labels of naturalism and symbolism. As a test of this after the experience of *Paesi tuoi* he tries (with the exception of *Il Compagno* which called for the expressiveness of a dialect-phraseology) to control the tendency toward the *parlato*, and to purify language. At any rate, reality in itself does not interest Pavese. He is primarily interested in the relationship between man and his emotions. "We always confuse what we are with the truth. This is the historical error—idealistic relativism,"[8] he writes on March 11, 1949. It seems to me that the difference between Pavese and the neorealists is first of all one of a philosophical rather than a literary character. Neorealistic novels are lacking in that ontological measure, the past-present-future dimension, that structuring of characters encased in the very fabric of language.

For the neorealists representation signifies *analysis*, further the imposition of an external structure on the narrative. For Pavese analysis is an aimless procedure. Representation alone has value. But for him representation signifies to *represent* "in a vivid way, with analysis implied; present *another* reality on which new analysis can be based, new standards, a new ideology."[9] Obviously, Pavese also imposes an external structure on the narrative in the sense that some of his novels unfold along the pre-established line, the myth of return. Nevertheless the external return and the internal rhythm achieve the proper proportions and mutually sustain each other. For, in Pavese's view, representation signifies grasping the very rhythm of life—childhood, adolescence, maturity etc.—in other words, not only historical situations but also the psychic process. In fact the "I" in his novels tells about action only, and grasps only palpable objects, while the snatches of dialogue, the language itself, add the mythic dimension with correspondences which subtly interpret reality. This is why Pavese, in

---

[8] *The Burning Brand*, 336.
[9] *Ibid*, 335.

that famous radio interview in 1950,[10] states that he made no distinction between narrative fiction and theatre, whereas in the *Diary* he explains why he admires both the Greek and the Elizabethans who, by presenting action above all did not concern themselves with the staging and didactic asides.[11]

According to Mario Bonfantini, Pavese once confided to their mutual friend, Enzo Giachino, that "having dedicated the first ten years of his activity to poetry and the second ten to narrative, he would be able, perhaps, to dedicate the next decade to theatre."[12] On the critical plane, Michele Tondo was the first to perceive that "the study of Shakespeare and of the Elizabethans offered a sheet anchor to him (Pavese): the *image*, understood not historically as metaphor, but as a fantastic relation ... which itself was the subject of the tale."[13] Thus the theatre, as representation, is always present in Pavese. Inherent in his novels, beyond the naturalistic development of an action, there is a symbolic, psychic progression on various levels which—always interconnected—in the end produce a multidimensional effect. In Pavese's novels then, as in the archetypical theatre, the plot, the imitated action—as Aristotle suggests—becomes also a ritual celebration.

It is especially possible to apply the Greek "tragic rhythm," the phases *Poiema, Pathema, Mathema*, which, according to Kenneth Burke, constitute the structure of every representation with a ritualistic basis, to the novel *La luna e i falò*. The three psychic phases could be summarized as follows: 1) Anguilla's departure for the purpose of creating a name, an individuality for himself; 2) discovery of the myth in America and the subsequent doubt concerning his own subjectivity; 3) return, and the awareness of solitude as an inevitable human condition. Moreover this novel exemplifies the rhythm *hubris-dike*, which is the implicit structure of many Greek tragedies. In fact, after departing as if to escape his fate, and

---

[10] *La letteratura americana e altri saggi*, 225.

[11] *The Burning Brand*, February 19, and April 1 (1943), 237.

[12] *Terra rossa terra nera*, 55.

[13] "L'esperienza poetica di Cesare Pavese," *Annals of Faculty of Letters and Philosophy*, vol. VIII (1962), ed. Bari: Cressati, 12.

after committing the sin of pride in order to assert his freedom, Anguilla returns to begin anew, in order to renew himself when now it is already too late.

When Pavese accepted my first novel for publication, I thought that he was motivated by considerations of a neorealistic or political character. In fact, that novel in its objective reality is neorealist and political. I became aware of the Pavesian world (and of my error in judgment) only many years later when I re-read Pavese's comments on *Tiro al piccione* (The Day of a Lion): "It is not a political book—there exists no case of the fascist who becomes disgusted or converts—but that of the misled youth, caught up in the whirlpool of blood, without an idea, who escapes by a miracle, and then begins to listen to other voices. This is a remarkable thesis and one to interest the whole world, not only Italians."[14]

The emphasis here is on "... and then begins to listen to other voices." This is tantamount to saying that the emphasis is on that reality of character which is intimate and unique, which belongs to him alone, perhaps unrepeatable, and which cannot be taken as an example of a phenomenological reality.

Now in speaking of characters such as Valino, Nuto, Anguilla, Clelia, Corrado, etc. Pavese's intention is not merely to project them against their environment. Environment merely defines them. They are only symbols of a "given" reality to which the writer has arrived through a process in which the narrative action and the narrative events are transformed into static substances.

It is by virtue of this process of intellectual creation that the Langhe, Asti, Canelli, Santo Stefano, the Belbo etc., the entire Piedmont region cease to be simple geographical points of reference for Pavese (and also for us), and become part of that mythic history that belongs to man's soul.

2. THE MISUNDERSTANDING WITH PROUST

Pavese's poetry, and hence all his work, offers different planes and levels. They are layers piled upon layers, like those very an-

---

[14] The original letter is found in the Einaudi Archives.

cient stones which bear the signs of their different formation. The successive strata never erase the previous accumulations. They merely conceal them. Pavese had this concept in mind when he wrote that the fixed, imperturbable observation of the same object ultimately will lead to an almost miraculous transformation of the object which, of course, will disclose itself in its unique essence only after having nullified its primitive multiplicity.

Pavese writes: "The surest, and the quickest, way for us to arouse the sense of wonder is to stare, unafraid, at a single object. Suddenly — miraculously — it will look like something we have never seen before."[15]

At this point the mind recalls the Proustian predilection for immobilizing object and observation. The individual who observes, for example, the "roses of Bengal," and the immobile object. Giacomo Debenedetti comments on the dual observations as follows:

> Here the immobility of the observation is augmented by an immobility of the objects which, by not moving, never make way for other objects to intervene and replace them, and thus arouse the observer's attention. We are in the presence of a dual immobility, derived from a state and concentrated vigil so that things may open up themselves in order to reveal the essence peculiar to them.[16]

The observation is correct. Proust's search, and his immobility in front of the Bengal rose-bush, is motivated by the senses. Proust does not know himself in the past and seeks desperately for ways through which the object, or a taste, miraculously may reveal to him that unknown part of himself. In fact Debenedetti observes:

---

[15] *Dialogues with Leucò*, translated by William Arrowsmith and D.S. Carne-Ross (Ann Arbor: The University of Michigan Press, 1965). Foreword.

[16] *Il romanzo italiano dal primo dopoguerra ad oggi*, notes on the lectures of Prof. Giacomo Debenedetti edited by Prof. A. Pinchera, Università degli Studi di Roma, academic year 1963-64, 22.

Here we do not find precisely a Proust who abstracts himself from reality and from the surrounding life in order to concentrate on *seeking* the essence of the roses. There is an immobile Proust, who exposes himself in order to be found by the meaning of those roses. (25)

In this case Proust would recognize an intentionality in the object, that the object must open itself, speak to us, recognize us "in the very moment in which it makes itself known to us, that the object becomes aware of that other than itself that we are intent upon watching it and exploring it" (26). In practice it is the object that acts on the individual. It is almost as if the object, having a consciousness, by projecting itself towards the individual, contributes to awaken the lethargic consciousness of the individual himself and to make it live.

In Pavese, instead, something different occurs. Consciousness doesn't exist outside the object, but in the observer — always. The miracle, if ever, does not occur through external, but internal factors — always. The sensory imagination that acts in Proust and which allows the object — by way of the olfactory illusion — to open itself and to speak to us, finds no place in Pavesian observation. In Pavese, man is always conscious of himself. It is not his senses which become uncoupled, but his reflexes. He lives in his reflexes. Thus the man-child, the dual image of life that Pavese traces so masterfully in the short story "La vigna" (The vineyard) does not nullify the consciousness of the adult, and at the same time creates that of the child reincarnated in the adult:

It is not even necessary to stop in front of the vineyard and to recognize the familiar and unheard of features. The moment of the encounter suffices and already the boy and the adult man have begun their dialogue which, rich in days, from the beginning does not change.[17]

---

[17] *Racconti*, 489.

They are two consciousnesses overlaid upon each other which co-exist in the subject, in him who has begun to observe. True, the object is the vineyard—but it has opened in a form unknown to Proust.

Pavese explains it in a note of his *Diary*, January 10, 1950:

> You have had the fruitful idea that destiny is myth, the savage (the emotion of La vigna) and that for this reason—once it has been explained—if destiny were to to remain as a concept in its archaic form, it would become superstition. Destiny is what is mythical in a whole existence, in a drama. It is what happens before one knows that it has happened. It is what looks like freedom but later reveals itself as dictated by the iron rules of a pre-established pattern. Destiny is the historian before he is understood in terms of his associations and of his necessity—freedom.[18]

The miracle which occurs, through internal, not external factors, is the fruit not only of the internal *emotion* of *watching*, but also of that all-pervading of substances—an almost mystical union of subject and object—which in the end allows the destruction of the I, the destruction of time, and so "to become that field, that sky, that woods."[19] To employ sartrean terminology, in Pavese the cosmic miracle, the destruction of time and of experience, would occur like in "La vigna" with the attainment of the perfect coupling between the *en soi* and the *pour soi*.

In a page entitled "Mal di mestiere," Pavese writes as follows:

> Sometimes if I approach this earth, I get an impetuous impact from it which carries me off like a river at flood-tide and it wants to submerge me. A voice, an odor suffice to seize me and throw me who knows where. I have become stone, humidity, dung, the sap of fruit, wind. All that remains to me of the human limit is the instinct to harden myself in words. But these are no longer

---

[18] *The Burning Brand*, 354.
[19] *La letteratura americana e altri saggi*, 317-318.

anything and I struggle like a tree or a beast who has already been a man and is now unable to express himself. I give up, fighting anew because I know that my nature is another, and each time I find a futile satiety at the bottom of this impetus. Every attempt to inflate the meaning- consciousness leads to this defeat. In short, it is a sin, like libertinism, like sadism and drunkenness. (317)

In a word Proust wants to save experiences. Since he is not satisfied with the present, he seeks a leap into the past. He is somewhat like Kierkegaard who distinguishes between an esthetic sphere of experiences and a religious sphere of experiences. Kierkegaard seeks his leap from the former to the latter. For him it is not experiences that must be saved, but the spirit, the soul. Pavese, instead, in his immobility enters into the destiny which accepts into itself—as myth—all experiences, those of the past and of the present, and those of the spirit. In short, Pavese is not a post-Christian like Proust and Kierkegaard.

But the Pavesian dimension of *immobility* extends even further. "Call me Ishmael,"[20] says the narrator of the story of the white whale. That self-presentation, that immediate declaration "Call me Ishmael" is an act of identification of the individual with the world. Behind Melville, in essence, the idealistic tradition still stands, namely that fixing of man in the universe by the philosophers because this universe is his true representation, his highest creation. Consider Lotze for whom the universe is friendly to man, being his loftiest representation, of man. And consider also Schopenhauer who finds in man the supreme will to movement, to action. Thus there is a creative will in the universe just as there is in man: "I don't know if I came from the hill or from the valley, from the woods or from a house with balconies. Who can say of what flesh I am made?"[21] Thus speaks the man without a name, the American or Anguilla, as he is known to our neighbors, who

---

[20] Herman Melville, *Moby Dick and the Whale* (London: Oxford University Press, 1958) 1.
[21] *La luna e i falò*, 385.

tells of what happens around him, and what happens to him in *La luna e i falò*. Ishmael has confidence in the world and therefore goes in search of experiences. He says: "I would sail about a little and see the watery part of the world."[22] The so-called American, instead, has already seen the world and now he does naught else but open himself to the phenomenological reality of others because he has already exhausted the reality of the objective world. He says:

> I have roamed the world enough to know that all fleshly bodies are good and are equivalent to each other, but this is the very reason why one grows weary and tries to establish roots, to make himself earth and homeland, so that his flesh may acquire worth and may last a little longer than an ordinary rotation of the seasons.[23]

Along with the compulsion to know by which he is driven, Ishmael wants to make himself known. No longer driven by this compulsion to know, the American does not even bother to make himself known, or to assert himself in the sight of others. The fact is that for Ishmael the world exists, and it is young. For the American the world cancels itself out, because it is too old. Ishmael is looking for an objective truth, or an objective reality which eventually will transcend itself and become symbol. The American has already stored up reality within himself. It is, nevertheless, a reality that is still devoid of intrinsic significance. Behind it lie anxiety and experience, work and seasons and exile. Eventually this reality will transcend itself, it will become myth when the American, once more in contact with "his" earth, feels the first intimations of the why of his return, in contact with "a warmth that I like," which has an odor peculiar to itself. In fact, he says: "I too am inside this odor … inside it there are so many vintages and hay-harvests and strippings of leaves, so many savors and so many longings that I no longer knew were inside of me" (400).

---

22 *Moby Dick*, 1.
23 *La luna e i falò*, 385.

The American knows (as does Nietzsche) that the universe does not bother about us, being wholly indifferent to human virtues and values. But in contrast to Nietzsche he does not say: nothing is true. And since nothing is true he does not say: everything is permissible. Nature is true and exists always, although it no longer exists as object but as a part of our reality.

In practice Ishmael begins where the American has ended in the matter of experiences. But the American begins where, eventually, even one of our contemporaries, Antoine Roquentin, would have to start out from. Instead we do not know whether Roquentin did write his book. At one time Sartre confessed that "I *was* Roquentin." But this is not enough. In a strange way, that is still nebulously romantic, Sartre projects himself on Flaubert: a Flaubert who is a disillusioned romantic. Sartre's shrewdness, however (which is part of his honesty), makes him use the verb in the past tense when he identifies himself with Roquentin. This is tantamount to saying that Roquentin's history, and therefore Sartre's, is the history of a non-being who struggles desperately in order to clarify himself and to become, in order to justify himself and to exist. Whether Sartre, the writer and philosopher, later realized his destiny as individual, his human destiny, merits a discussion that is no concern of ours here. What does concern us is the character Roquentin who left off where he should have begun. He is one who, although aware of the absurd, and now of his nausea, continues to live in the absurd. Sartre had hit the point dead-center by asserting that life begins on the other side of despair. But this is theory, whereas Roquentin is only the promise that the theory will become reality.

Pavese's American, on the other hand, is this reality. At the end of the book he is immobile. And this is why it is no longer important to identify him with a proper name. Roquentin, perhaps, will write the book and by so doing he will achieve self-realization. The American has achieved self-realization in the process of re-living a place, a world, a childhood. Now, at the end of the book, after having reached the peak of his maturity, of his essence, he finds himself strangely denuded. He will have to set out again. But this passage, which is very important for an interpretation of Pavese, merits further explanation.

3. THE MISUNDERSTANDING WITH THE EXISTENTIALISTS

The important, over-riding fact of this century is that Proust (and with him Joyce: we must never lose sight of the "epiphanies") inaugurates the new novel, and establishes a method for cognizing reality different from that of the naturalistic school. The whole structure of *A la recherché du temps perdu* gives the novel a two-fold quality: a level on which the narrator suffers, and the level on which the narrator has perspectives. Hence what is to be attained is to understand the experience in the moment in which one finds satisfaction (or happiness) in a recollection. By so doing one establishes the limits of the mind. The romantic, instead, wants the experiences of all things, of all sensations, immediately. Acceptance of the experience of memory, however, signifies acceptance of its limits. Practically, Proust begins where Rimbaud leaves off.

For his part Pavese begins where the existentialists ended. Roquentin will write his novel. Anguilla, in a certain sense, is "writing" it in the moment in which he relives himself in his Piedmontese native land. This is tantamount to saying that Pavese begins after Proust and after Sartre who began his *recherche* by asserting existence only. Roquentin sees himself as one *de trop*, in the moment in which he exists. He is a free and incomplete form without necessity, without an origin, and without a causality. He is a distant relative of Oblomov, a "superfluous man." His horror is to know that he exists without being able to project himself, neither in the past nor in the future, since past and future do not exist. Existence has no exit. But Sartre warns that every individual is free since he has the faculty of choice. He alone is responsible for his freedom. Therefore in order to justify his present he can accept the past and also the utopias of hope. Roquentin, in practice, arrives at the conclusion that in order to offer himself even a momentary sense of justification in the present, he must at least be capable of accepting that essential past which will assume some kind of form and some kind of clarity in the novel which he intends to write.

Hence Roquentin is now aware. And he leaves us with his awareness. It is an awareness that he is still—under certain aspects—a man prison, not wholly capable of living in his reality. Eventually he aims for action... on the other side of despair—in short to write the book. Anguilla, instead, is here with all his awareness—but without having closed the doors on fate. The myth occurs and reoccurs on the hill. The real occurs and reoccurs in human reality. It is the reoccurrence of this reality, which in Anguilla does not take the meaning of *engagement*, that gives a definitive dimension to Pavese's character.

Still the problem does not end here, and another perspective could be the following. By setting himself the aim of writing the novel, Roquentin, therefore, chooses. The choice implies an acceptance of the past. Perhaps Roquentin is already on the other side of despair. After the disintegration of the personality, after having completely annulled himself, he can begin the job of reconstructing himself from the beginning. He will always live with the awareness of nausea, and always in the frame of phenomenological reality, but at least the past will have an order, it will have a significance, because it is chosen and willed. And it is a past for which he alone, Antoine Roquentin, will be responsible. If his is a search for identity and justification, at least a hope, a possibility will remain to him. From this point of view it is logical to assert that Pavese begins where the existentialists leave off. The character who watches the vineyard or the corn field already has identity.

The French, in general, are in favor of action, they always want to change the course of history. And Sartre, in particular, is more bent upon solving problems rather than posing them. Like Voltaire, he is a moralist. He speaks of being "situated," insofar as situated means to have a particular position with respect to the object. This is the final problem of Roquentin and of the writer himself. For if the writer, as an existent, seeks to project himself always toward the future and remains, by definition, always free and situated, accepting the historicity of the particular moment, he is doing naught else but reformulating an individual and collective freedom.[24]

For Sartre the contrast between the existential and the social becomes the most urgent problem that must be solved. This is why he justifies situational literature, by putting the moral responsibility of the writer toward the audience, and at the same time asserts the autonomy of culture. Pavese does not deny this point of view, if he himself could write the following to a young unknown who had sent some manuscripts to read and examine: "I always try to write in such a way so that I can be understood by my grocer."[25] Nevertheless Pavese is not exactly "situated" in a historicist mode. True, he tried, because he intimately and sincerely admired the virtues of the humble, of peasants and of workers. But to brotherhood in action (Malraux), to the responsibility of one's calling (Saint-Exupery), to the consciousness of the absurd (Camus), to formulas which exalt human greatness, albeit desperately, Pavese can answer only that a man is a man, even when he is an enemy, as he does in *La casa in collina*.

In short Pavese's world is not a world to which one can apply the concept of freedom as a problem-solving mechanism, as a panacea. For Sartre existence precedes essence and history is a dialectic that proceeds on a voluntaristic basis. Pavese, instead, limits himself to the portrayal of the human condition. To be sure, he interprets it but he does not solve problems for the simple reason that he knows that there are no solutions. The sole and incontestable fact that man exists confers an essence, a destiny upon him. Everybody has a childhood, an adolescence, an old age, a solitude. In Pavese's works the individual as well as history follows a scheme which is repeated cyclically. But ultimately it is the very cycle of life that is repeated, that is revealed as an ontological progression with the advent of maturity, that is, when man rationally explains his myths.

---

[24] John-Paul Sartre, *Literature & Existentialism*, trans. B. Frechman (New York: The Citadel Press, 1962) 152.
[25] *Terra rossa terra nera*, 54.

Pavese is not an existentialist, even if some notes of his diary, and some of the characters of his novels, such as *Tra donne sole* and *Il diavolo sulle colline*, point up aspects of it. The existentialist problematic of the absurd, for example, poses itself in man during a specific phase of life, with the discovery of a dehumanized world. From this point of view Pavese's characters arrive at an awareness of the problem, but they do not confront it in order to resolve it. At times they simply accept suicide as a way out. But Pavese cannot be compared with the existentialists (nor with the neorealists) above all for the reason that the novels and the philosophy of the latter are marked by the absence of man's biological and physical completeness, that is to say the dimension of time, childhood in relation to maturity, etc. Now, also on the plane of style, if the existentialist or neorealist tries to convince, it is because they are induced to present ideas directly, whereas Pavese dramatizes even when his stories seem to be plotless. Pavese does not solve problems. Nevertheless it is also true that he effectively gets close to the reader, his "grocer," and in the process he brings into play not only the intellect (by virtue of the references to myths), but also the emotions, thereby requiring a more complete catharsis and a more intense participation.

4. THE MISUNDERSTANDING OF MATURITY

As has been stated, Pavese operates on different levels. While in many short stories he dwells on the portrayal of the character-landscape relation of the myth, in the novels he introduces another dimension. Anguilla, obviously, is a character of greater universality than those in the short stories. When he was a boy, he thought of leaving his village in order to seek an identity for himself which he believed he did not possess. In America, instead — and it happens to him as in a dizzy spell — he becomes aware of the fact that he possesses this identity within himself: "In the darkness, in that fragrance rising from the garden and the pine-trees, I understood that those stars were not mine."[26] The countryside, that is, or the stars,

---

[26] *La luna e i falò*, 395.

are found everywhere — like women — but in some part of the world there is a countryside that is unique, and it is "ours," and belongs to no other person: "Then I began to think that I could go back to the mountains again" (396). America is nausea, as the present is to Roquentin: "The bacon and eggs, the high wages, the oranges as big as watermelons, were nothing. They were like those crickets and those toads. Had it been worthwhile to come? Where could I still go? Shall I jump off the dock?" (395).

So Anguilla returns. His name is no longer a matter of importance to him. Now he knows. In the novel we have a clarification of his relation with the landscape, with its myths. Reality becomes eternal and immobile. When Nuto tells him about Santa's end, Anguilla becomes aware of time, of history. But the fact that all this happened while he was in America is important. The reality of childhood, his identity is removed from him with this revelation. Now even this countryside, "his" countryside, is no longer his. It is the reality of others that he receives now, that is given to him. Now, and only now, Anguilla no longer possesses anything. Precisely now, when he is an adult (for what other reason if not this, did Pavese place the utterances of King Lear, "Ripeness is all" as an epigraph to *La luna e i falò*), he becomes painfully conscious of the fact that he doesn't even possess a name — and Pavese, the man, realizes that he does not even possess a woman, a family, existence.

Will Anguilla at this point be able to accept his reality, transmitted into an historical fact? Will he ever have a constant identity? No. Nuto's revelation is merely the climax, a kind of final epiphany. It is a revelation which has been announced beforehand by other events — the recovered bodies, the political background, in short the whole atmosphere. Anguilla already expected the end even before Nuto talked to him about Santa. This is why he alludes to a new departure. After the cycle, life begins all over again. Just as there has been blood and death, destruction and misery in the countrysides of men desolated by the war, so will the grass of the fields grow again.

Pavese, with an awareness of the terrible suffering of the world and an extraordinary consciousness of himself and of things, has Corrado say, in *La casa in collina*:

> But I have looked on dead who are unknown to me, the dead of the Republic. It was seeing them that awakened me. If a stranger, a dying enemy has this effect, and one stops and is afraid to stride over his body, it means that even conquered, the enemy is still a human being, that having shed his blood, we must placate it, lend it a voice, justify whoever has split it. Looking at corpses is humiliating. They are not other people's concern; we cannot feel we have just chanced to be at the spot. We have the impression that the same fate which had stretched these bodies on the ground, nails us here to look at them, to fill our eyes with the sight of them. It is not fear, not common cowardice. It is humiliation. We learn through our eyes that it might well be ourselves in the place of these dead and it would be no different and that if we are alive, we owe it to this sullied corpse. Because every war is a civil war; every man who falls resembles the one who survives and calls him to account.[27]

And he closes the book as follows:

> I cannot believe that it can end. Now that I have seen what war, civil war is, I know that if it should finish one day, everybody will have to ask himself this question, "And what about those who have fallen? What do we do about them? Why are they dead?" I would not know how to answer. Not at present anyway. Nor does it seem to me that anyone else knows either. Perhaps only the dead know and only for them is the war really over. (131)

Corrado does not know this yet. Corrado has reached the end of the Vico cycle, the age of man. He is thoughtful about these dead, and he poses questions to himself. He will continue to go forward and to live because, perhaps, "only the dead knew and

---

[27] *La casa in collina*, Romanzi, vol. II, 130.

only for them is the war really over." But Anguilla knows it. He knows that after complete annihilation, in which there are no victors nor vanquished (consider Baracca: he killed Santa, believing justice was on his side and, in turn, he will be hung by others who believe that justice was on their side), the grass will grow again, the world will resume going round and round. Even he, now, is like one of these dead for whom the war is really over. The myth of the earth, of childhood, is also over with. This is why there will be a new departure for him.

According to some critics, Nuto's final revelation to Anguilla constitutes the attainment of maturity.[28] This is true. But for Anguilla this maturity also constitutes his failure. For these critics maturity signifies that the characters, after having abandoned the world of childhood, should now involve themselves into the moral world. Obviously, these critics have not understood that Pavese's novels are not *Bildungsromans*, novels of education. For Anguilla revelation, or the final vision, is at one and the same time a conquest and a defeat. For him this maturity is not a new principle, but the total end and the return, probably, of nausea.

Only Nuto, who is Anguilla's counterpart, is saved for the reason that he belongs precisely to this "moral" world of precarious justice, which is nevertheless a progressive, active, *engagè* world, even in illusion. In fact, Nuto will adopt Cinto and thereby acquire another son. Whereas Anguilla has nothing at all now. He is alone and deserted in the face of a deserted world.

Nuto, at a certain moment, by revealing Santa's end to Anguilla, had to (and perhaps wanted to) annihilate himself. His original reticence, and his modesty, and perhaps his nostalgia, at first sight indicate that the passage from one reality to another is impossible even for him. This is not at all the case. Instead, Nuto saves himself. Nuto continues to believe in the bonfires, whereas all that remains to Anguilla is to resume the journey... towards nothing-

---

[28] Franco Mollia, *Cesare Pavese. Saggio su tutte le opere* (Firenze: La Nuova Italia, 1963).

ness at that precise point where the cycle begins all over again, the principle of human history.

Let us hasten to the main point. If Pavese had stopped with the presentation of myth alone, the problem would be resolved. For myth is not alienation. If in a certain sense Pavese begins where the existentialists end, at the same time he ends where the latter begin; or better said, where Ishmael begins, Pavese's characters begin without an identity which they then find and then lose. By losing it they attain maturity and at the same time suicide. Childhood is the age of myth, of formation. Sartre's characters are adults who are in search of themselves. And they can seek themselves because they have lived and live in a context: the city, history. Instead, Pavese's works portray Vico's cyclical view of historical life: the age of the gods, the age of heroes, and the age of man. Obviously this cycle assumes other aspects in Pavese. In the *Dialoghi con Leucò*, the age immediately preceding that of the gods becomes the age of the Titans. It is this first phase, which is decisive "for a whole life" because this is the age of the birth of poetry, that is, of myth. The other two phases are represented in the progression from the countryside to the city, in the evolution from rural civilization to urban civilization. And the "I" of *Lavorare stanca* could very well be the archetype of modern man who finds himself divided and alienated between these two phases as for that matter Spengler's man suggests.[29]

It is hazardous, nevertheless, to give a definitive judgment on Pavese's work by basing oneself, as many critics have done, solely on the binomial countryside-city, by identifying it as the poles of the Pavesian world. We must also take the *Diary* into account, and clarify the relation which exists between this and Pavese's whole work. Otherwise we let Pavese slip into memorialism, and we run the risk of sentimentalizing his themes. The mechanism of memory is intimately connected with the creative act. But to assert

---

[29] Oswald Spengler, *The Decline of the West* (New York: AA. Knopf, 1926).

that Pavese repeats the major themes of Proust or of Joyce[30] signifies that one shuts himself out from the clarification of the Pavesian problem and creates confusion. Pavese's characters have never embarked on a search for lost time for the simple reason — as I have already noted — that the evocation of the past does not depend upon external contingencies. Instead, they have those remembrances that are valuable within them even if they are led to discover them as though for the first time. On February 12, 1942 Pavese noted in his *Diary* that the fundamental reason of much contemporary literature lay precisely in the return to childhood. It is for this reason that he inserts this motive in an archetypical vein and interprets it. His greatest purpose is to clarify myths and to justify their importance in the totality of life. But in works such as *La casa in collina, Tra donne sole* and *La luna e i falò* the concept of childhood transcends conventional symbology, and the infantile age does not represent innocence only.

If we compare the novels to the *Diary*, it will immediately be noticed that in the work there constantly exists an intellectual-artistic development, and, simultaneously, an existential-philosophical development in Pavese the man. Pavese does not fall either into complacencies or into sentimentalisms. He strives only to make human experiences manifest and to universalize them. True, the central core of his work rests in the ambivalence of the dualism countryside-city and man-landscape, in that countryside and city become personal myths and collective archetypes. But it is also true that Pavese never abstracts himself from the historistic exigencies of our time. Indeed, his novels reflect their linguistic inflections, events and anxieties. Pavese was so conscious of the fact that sketchy writing (bozzettismo) does not lead very

---

[30] Giorgio Pullini, *Il romanzo italiano del dopoguerra (1940-1960)* (Milan: Schwarz Editore, 1961). Pullini writes: "The theme of childhood as the ideal and lost age which is the hinge of the Proustian narrative and at least of Joyce's Dedalus, that is to say of the two most representative writers of the twentieth century avant-garde in Europe, not to disregard its beginnings in Leopardian 'illusion' and with the 'child' in Pascoli's poetry, is at the source of almost the whole of Pavese's work, and he has amply theorized about it in his critical writings" (12).

far that, in 1934, he could write: "The condition of every impulse of poetry, however lofty, is always a careful reference to ethical exigencies and naturally also to the practical demands of the ambience in which one lives."[31] And in 1949, shortly after the drafting of *La luna e i falò*, he notes in his *Diary*:

> You have completed the historical cycle of your times: *Carcere* (anti-Fascism behind bars); *Compagno* (anti-Fascism under cover); *Casa in collina* (resistance); *La luna e i falò* (post-resistance). Side issues—the war of '15-'18, the war in Libya. The saga is complete. Two young men (*Carcere* and *Compagno*); two forty-year olds (*Casa in collina* and *La luna e i falò*); two intellectuals (*Carcere* and *Casa in collina*).[32]

Pavese did not work on the basis of a rigid schematicism or cold a priori assertions. His thematic continuity is surprising. It is licit only to note that the totality of his art offers a constant elaboration and a continuous intellectual development that he lived as a search for truth. This is why Pavese never repeats himself but always adds something to the content. On the one hand his work presents a very precise historical reality, and on the other it dramatizes those realities which for Pavese constitute his human and intellectual concerns.

---

[31] *Poesie*, 129.
[32] *The Burning Brand*, 344-345.

Chapter II

THE CONCEPTION OF TIME

1. MYTH-SUPERSTITION

On October 28, 1935 Pavese made the following entry in his *Diary*: "poetry begins when a simpleton says of the sea: 'It looks like oil!'"[1] Immediately, however, he added that this discovery actually is not the most precise description of a flat calm. It is merely the pleasure of having perceived the similarity, the titillation provided by the establishment of a mysterious relation between the thing perceived and the idea of the thing, between the man who sees the object and his unconscious need to express it with a parallel, an image, a symbol. Pavese points out that this is how a typical poem begins, it is based on an idea. But then it is necessary to finish it. How? He says:

> Having started the poem, one must finish it, work up the idea with a wealth of associations and skillfully arrive at an assessment of its value.... But usually the writing stems from sentiment—the exact description of a flat calm—that occasionally foams with the discovery of relationships. The typical poem may possibly be remote from reality, consisting up to now (just as we can even live on microbes) of mere odds and ends of similarities (sentiment); constructive thought (logic); and associations caught at random (poetry). (32)

Nonetheless this wealth of associations or relations must be "allusive and all-pervading," wholly fused in the image. Otherwise the poem does not become flesh, it does not take on the blood of life and become history.

In another entry, October 10, 1935, Pavese writes:

---

[1] *The Burning Brand*, 31-32.

Why cannot I write about these red, moonlit cliffs? Because they reflect nothing of myself. The place gives me a vague uneasiness, nothing more, and that should never be sufficient justification for a poem. If these rocks were in Piedmont, though, I could very well absorb them into a flight of fancy and give them meaning. Which comes to the same thing as saying that the fundamental basis of poetry may be a subconscious awareness of the importance of those bonds of sympathy, those biological vagaries, that are already alive, in embryo, in the poet's imagination before the poem is begun. (27)

These two observations shed light not only on the orientation of the Pavesian poetics and the critical effort that has shaped it, but also on an aspect of the creative act. It is a weary pleonasm to assert that art is born of the relation between man and reality. But the dimensions, the intensity that this relation can assume reside exclusively in the personal sensibility (intelligence) of the artist. He is aware of this bond in his subconscious. Now the language of the unconscious is the image, the symbol. The unruffled sea that "looks like oil." The word is the language of the poet. Thus the awareness of the thing becomes poetry when the intuition of the thing becomes expression, when content, in short, becomes style. Which is to say when the poet succeeds in merging *mythos* and *logos*, image and word. It is well, therefore, to repeat that *mythos*, *epos* and *logos* represent the three stages of linguistic evolution: 1) language understood as a spontaneous representation of reality (intuition); 2) as a representation of events in time (narration); 3) as a form of rational inquiry (idea). These three phases constitute the creative process. The transformation now proceeds from an attitude towards reality which could be called the poet's "mythic vision." What is immediately striking in Pavese's poetry is precisely this mythic vision in communion between *man* and the *natural-ferine* world, a time "that gives us a glimpse of the community of interests between man and wild beasts" (158).

It is from this intuition that Pavese develops his theory of the equation between savagery and superstition. The *selvaggio* celebrates his most terrifying rites before an impassive nature which, in turn, is a collection of myths. What else is ritual if not the mythic repetition of an event that has occurred and that continues to preserve its uniqueness in the very act of repeating itself? The example of the myth which occurs and reoccurs in a ritual form is offered to us every day by the Mexican *fiesta*. One must be there, as spectator or actor, to bear witness to its sacral, hence tragic uniqueness because "the savage is not picturesque but tragic" (221), foretold, that is, as in Greek tragedy. The *fiesta* is the advent of the unusual. Time is annihilated, it no longer exists. Or it is transformed into a mythic past or total present. It makes use of sensations and of atmospheres. Space is the setting of the *fiesta*, which becomes a colorful and fantastic world, existing by itself. The persons who take part in it lose their own human and social characteristics and are transformed into living fancies.[2] Everything happens as in a dream, and death has never brushed so close. Everything attracts its opposite. The *fiesta*, inasmuch as it is a cosmic experience, is an experience of disorder which unites contradictory elements in itself, the selfsame ones that will engender a rebirth of life. It is "a return to a remote and undifferentiated state, prenatal or presocial. It is a return that is also a beginning, in accordance with the dialectic that is inherent in social processes."[3] Hence myth is symbolic language, like the dream which is the same for myth (at least in reference to Freud in respect to this last observation). Both function as channels of communication from ourselves to ourselves, and express deep-seated experiences, sentiments and ideas in the form which they at first had in the external world. Dream and myth are united, they have a visionary character. Obviously, however, the dream concerns the problems of the individual, whereas the myth—which implies religion and

---

[2] Ibid. See the note concerning Levy-Bruhl's *Mythologie primitive*, 60.
[3] Octavio Paz, *The Labyrinth of Solitude: Life and Thought in Mexico* (New York: The Grove Press, Inc., 1961) 52.

society — reveals the characteristics of the community and endows them with importance.

The journeys of Odysseus, of Jason and of Jonah, which are considered as myths, can differ from Ahab's journey which is also mythic.[4] But the truth is that there is always a particular adventure for every man, a particular setting which is delineated as the fancy of his secret life. This particular adventure, this particular setting will become myth (it already was), and therefore language. This language can be handed down, and it becomes poetry because myth explains it.

Pavese focuses his poetic attention on the myth-superstition ritual which always sits on the shoulders of the "*selvaggio*." And he explains that all such things (the most terrifying rites)

> are superstitious only if they strike us as unjust, forbidden by conscience, savage. Then savagery is overruled by conscience. As long as we believe in superstition, we are not superstitious. To be superstitious is essentially retrospective, in the realm of memory, an apt subject for poetry; like evil, which is always in the realm of past remorse.[5]

There is, however, a transition of common interest between primitiveness (superstition) and savagery (overruled by conscience). There is the primitive expression of the myth which, in turn, is the expression of the pre-rational ages of man.

As far as is known man had not yet developed any rational faculties in the pre-historical period. No distinction was made between feeling and volition. Man lived without self-questionings. He found himself in a world which he did not understand, but which for him was the only existent reality. It was an ordered reality. Thus the life of primitive man was lived in conformity with

---

[4] William York Tindall, *The Literary Symbol* (Bloomington: Indiana University Press, 1960) 176-178, where there is a discussion of *Myth in the Primitive Psychology* by Bronislaw Malinowski, *Language and Myth* by Ernst Cassirer and *The Forgotten Language* by Erich Fromm.
[5] *The Burning Brand*, 270.

those early laws of survival which he accepted unconsciously. Sometimes, however, something occurred in nature which did not repeat the order, and which man could not manage to assimilate. Earthquakes and thunderbolts were events of an ultra-real character beyond his comprehension. They were the expressions and emanations of some supernatural being or power. Gods or demons. Myth was born when man consecrated as sacred a locus in which he found refuge against the unknown evil. Thus he could hope. Man gave a name to these events. Hence the appearance of language coincides with the birth of myth. In fact *mythos* means word. Myths were not mythology or legend. They were reality. What had no name had no existence. Primitive man gave life to objects. By so doing he fulfilled a creative function. Persons with more experiences gave names to things unknown by others, and as a result they were considered magical. They were respected by the community for the very reason that they extended the frontiers of reality.

Primitive man did not possess analytical faculties. For him causality and other logical categories did not exist. It was only through myth that he learned to acquire knowledge and an awareness of reality. Symbology was the method with which he reorganized the world in his image. This is tantamount to saying that nature no longer existed in itself but in man and for man, by way of fantastic configurations. In other words nature forced man to create symbols which were naught else but the metaphorical representation of his experience of reality. The myth of Leda, violated by Zeus in the form of a swan, is the representation, not the logical description, of the conception that reality is conditioned, fertilized by spiritual, ultra-terrestial forces.

It has already been said that primitive man lived unconsciously, and that there was a mystic reciprocal penetration between subject and object. Now it is necessary to add that he not only lived in a pre-rational, pre-logical and pre-adult age, but also in the pre-individual age. The process of individuation had not yet begun. Probably the person as such did not even have (not yet) a logical name, but existed as a function of the community. Whatever had a tribal value also had individual value. For the individual's attitude towards life, his knowledge was the very same as that held by the tribe. The symbol represented individual and collective experiences. By way of the symbol the individual identified himself with a place, with a time and a society. The individual's life had a communal character. By way of the individual the objective unconscious, that is the psychic patrimony of the tribe, was handed down from generation to generation. Every man, in the depths of his being, is a primitive. Vestiges of communal experiences exist in the sub-stratum of the psyche, which Jung calls the collective unconscious. Later, this was to find expression in dreams, in legends, in religion and in art in the form of archtypes, i.e. images that repeat primordial solutions. The poet is a primitive who expresses his experiences by using the language of a civilization. Everybody has experiences. Everybody, therefore, has a relation with reality. One among all these is a poet because he feels the reciprocal reactions between man and object more intensely, more primitively.

Mythos also means mystery: the two words have the same etymological root. For the poet the world is a mystery, something sketched out only very vaguely which he discovers every time he writes a poem. Objects have an animistic and spiritual value above all. And this awareness, this "sub-conscious awareness" of which Pavese speaks in the aforementioned passage on the red, moonlit cliffs the poet must translate into intelligible phrases.

Pavese says of his poems that they were "an attempt to express a cluster of fantastic associations, of which one's own perception of reality consists, with a sufficient wholeness."[6] They are also an effort (and later an actualization) of man's pre-natal and pre-social transition, as exemplified in Vico's cyclical theory, of the primitive as opposed to the savage; the *rus* as opposed to the *ars*, of the "hick, the rustic, the boor, as opposed to the citizen."[7] The mythic unity of these stages of transition is indissoluble. And

---

[6] *Poesie*, 133.
[7] *The Burning Brand*, 275.

this is also the mythic unity on which Pavese's poetry is engendered and developed, assuming a substantiality of an unprecedented character.

2. CHARACTER AND LANDSCAPE

A first exploration of Pavese's poems leads to an observation that is also a revelation, namely that they are "felt," i.e. they have rhythm. Let us dwell for a moment on this two-fold insight, leaving a particular and detailed analysis for later. They are suffused with an ineffable feeling that transcends reason. Rhetoric is the most certain (and obvious) repetition of a solid, critical contact that has been established with expressed ideas. Here no rhetoric is perceptible. The rhythm is constant and reflects the development of a situation that is always concrete, as are its particular elements themselves. But the relation between object and subject, between character and landscape is ungraspable because it is seamlessly fused together. As has been said Pavese's concern was to suggest at first sight only an indistinct rhythm, an atmosphere which after all is naught else but a symbolic and primitive reality. These poems are primarily a series of landscapes at once governed and united by a primordial rhythmic background which creates and recreates the myth of existence. The character of the "poesia-racconto" strips himself of his rational individuality and becomes a very part (he is part) of reality. In "Il Dio-Caprone" (The God-goat), for example, the boy protagonist barely exists as a ratiocinating person. All we have are his impressions of the countryside. For him existence is nature. From this perspective the boy perceives with his instinct, like a primitive. Immediately the image is born. The countryside, for him, is "a country of green mysteries," a sensual landscape possessed by a spirit that also possesses the rustics ("… their faces are burnt, the color of earth"). The girls who make love are "in heat," they too act by instinct. Like the animals they too seem to be in the grip of the moon's influence. The God-goat is merely an evocation of the primitive. For his part, the boy sees the countryside shimmering in the summer-light. Summer means heat and harvest-time. This event is celebrated like the vintage and corn-cobbing, it is a ceremony of consecration or *fiesta*. In primitive societies it actually was a rite which was concluded with an unconscious release of every inhibition. Rite and magic persist in the countrysides now in the form of customs and beliefs. Customs and beliefs which Pavese, in an entry dated July 1, 1942 (referring to customs and beliefs of his native village of Santo Stefano Belbo) transcribes as follows:

When the moon is old:		When the moon is new:
	Sowing flowers They come	
Beautiful and With thick stems		Sickly and Slim and elegant
	Cutting down trees, they will be	
Healthy		Worm-eaten
	Except the pine tree which will be	
Worm-eaten		Healthy
	Washing the sheets with ashes will make them	
Clean and good		dirty – the ashes will filter through
	Pruning the vine and the buds will be	
Harmful		Fruitful

(226-227)

The moon is the static symbol of rites and of magic. Thus also the excitement of animals coincides with the moon's rising (which like a rite precisely accentuates the supernatural and the powerlessness of the will). The atmosphere, already frenetic becomes increasingly tense, oppressive:

And the bitches howl under the moon,
because they've heard the large goat who leaps

over the top of the hills, and sniffed the smell of blood.
Beasts stir in the stables.
Only the big and stronger dogs bite at the rope.
Some free themselves and run to follow the large goat
who sprays them with blood redder than fire,
intoxicating them.
Then, standing upright, they all dance,
baying at the moon.[8]

The large goat (who suggests the sorcerer of the tribe) performs the ceremony of anointment, he allows the other animals to participate in the rite. He is like a god. The rustics, for their part, work with their hoes under the moon. At the end of the harvest they dance and drink wine. The boy feels the sexuality of the countryside. Instead of expressing it with descriptions or concepts (qualities that come with adulthood), he defines it by the fantastical vision of the large goat (which for him has the feeling of absolute uniqueness) and by drawing the parallel with the rustics.

The mythic vision is established here by the connection of the events and by the objective movement of the sober style. But Pavese manages to establish the same dimension by virtue of a "tangle of fantastical associations,"[9] recounting situations that are often trite, as in "La cena triste" (The Sad Supper). This poem could be defined as a painting, a still-life. The male protagonist "has thoughts" and feels the surrounding countryside. He is sitting down to a meal in the countryside under a bower, with a woman. She embodies a season, a whole experience now past which remains alive in her: "The solid shoulders and the tanned cheeks again lock up the whole summer." At the end of the supper, only the tang of grape and of woman, of vintage and of life, remains in the air:

We are still, listening to and watching the sound
made by the water while passing the track of the moon.

---

8 *Poesie*, 14.
9 *Poesie edite e inedite*, 199.

This tarrying is the sweetest.
   The countryside that tarries,
still seems to be biting that cluster of grapes,
so alive is its mouth. The tang lingers
   Like the yellowish moonlight... (91-92)

The two persons are "watching" the sound of the water as if it were another person. The objects and abstract things around them become animated: "The chairs look at each other, deserted." "Neither the grapes nor the bread have moved." There is the implication that even the two persons are animated objects, mere presences in the vast rhythm of the countryside. They merge with that atmosphere of solitude and silence, losing themselves therein. It is night, perhaps autumn and there is no stir of life: "It's cold in the dawn, and the tight embrace of a body would be life." Even things "feel" it: "Tangs torment the famished shade." The being of the two persons mutually penetrates things. The woman and the water "tarry," the shade "does not even succeed in licking the dew already condensing on the cluster of grapes." There is a desire for contact that remains ungratified. The moon-beams seek the water and, perhaps, the man seeks the woman. Objects are persons and persons are objects. As in a painting by Giorgio Morandi objects and light are fused. In this poem persons, things and landscapes have a life, utterly unique in point of time and place.

Even in the progression in the poems from the countryside to the city, from life as instinct to life as order, the poet's transcendent vision creates and recreates the associations and cadences of time as a dimension of absolute uniqueness. In the characters who have moved to the city there is always a sovereign need for release which remains ungratified. The boy, in "Atavismo," sees a horse on a deserted street. The horse is bare, and absorbs all the warmth of the sun, as though the animal were in the countryside "bare and unrestrained," where the motionless plants "look." The boy too has a body but he must cover it, hide it under clothes. "If one has a body, it must be seen," and one must go out naked to "drown in the sun" (103-104). The characters, in short, would like to act in the city, where "it isn't done" as they do in the country-side where "it is done," because in the countryside life is in direct communication with objects. There one is a primitive, one has a body and one therefore is a boy. The city, instead, is a concept, practicality; it is another superstition but not memory. The coun-tryside, however, persists in those who have moved to the city. Sometimes an object, a light suffices to bring everything to life again. In "Il tempo passa" (Time Passes) the little old man must beg for alms whereas before he would go into the fields and gorge himself with fruits. Fruits in the fields belong to him who needs them, so true is it that they don't grow behind closed doors... Se-renely, the little old man used to look for the blackest vine and there he would "sit in the shade," without stirring, until he was full — as if the vine were the mother, the wet-nurse, which repeats the sacral function of existence. The gift is now substituted by the wine from the tavern which reminds him of the time of his free-dom in the fields. He gets drunk here and then the tavern-keeper kicks out the drunken oldster

> who sings and shouts,
> who wants a pumpkin
> and to stretch himself out under a vine. (95-96)

These are events that have been transferred to the memory and that, through some mysterious mechanism (the wine, the drunkenness which is the same as the orgy and the release of in-hibitions, though more artificial) return to be lived all over again. As in a dream, the little old man who sings and shouts, "re-feels," as it were, a point in time when, stretched out at his ease in a field, he was talking with a boy who was carrying a pumpkin.

The past is contemporaneous with the present in these con-frontations that spring up spontaneously. A story unfolds as if the characters were confessing and laying bare their lives. Pavese's mythic time is not nostalgia, neither is it the Proustian "time of the mind," i.e. involuntary memory. These characters never experi-ence the scene of the "madeleine dipped in tea." Nonetheless, for them, there is always an inner flux which brings those particular stratifications of the inner life to the surface in a vibrant and fresh form. But they are linked to the thrill of the unique feeling rather than to the remembrance of things past. For them, however, memory is a psychic kaleidoscope which is continually being re-shaped within grooves that were staked-out in the consciousness in a pre-rational age. Thus for Pavese the return of a "unique event" to the memory does not mean to isolate it in time and to contemplate it. Rather, it means to live it now, as if it were happening now for the first time. Only memory-images are tied to that "subjective life" of which William James speaks.[10] The very rhythm of Pavese's poems, seemingly tranquil but unbroken, which immediately remind us of prose narratives, conceals a rhythm which confirms the artist's objectification with the material being dealt with. If story-telling means progression in time, Pavese understands this as a psychic progression, that is to say as a relation between consciousness and reality, an "inner relation between things." The singular quality of these poems lies precisely in their thought, a series of fantastical relations that constitute a total reality, namely duration in the Bergsonian sense. This technique on occasion is reminiscent of a similarity with the "stream of consciousness." If, however, as Bergson admits,[11] the Lockean theory of the "association of ideas"[12] lies at the base of the stream of consciousness, here there is the dynamic factor of the "all-pervading" which is neither a fantastication of, nor a re-connection or a remembrance, of events and things, but a form of *cognition*. Now Proust, who also has something in common with Pavese, reconstructs experience on the basis of "momentary feelings." Despite the fact that he constructs his book not on mnemonic recalls from one experience or feeling to the other, "but on planes of con-

---

[10] William James, *The Principles of Psychology*, vol 1 (London: Macmillan. 1907) 239.

[11] Henri Bergson, *Matter and Memory*, translated by N.M. Paul and W.S. Palmer (London: G. Allen & Co, 1913) 220.

[12] John Locke, *An Essay Concerning Human Understanding*, Vol. 1, Bk. 2, Chapter "Of the Association Of Ideas," Oxford, M.DCCC.XCIV, 527-535.

ceptualism and mystical knowledge that reduce them to material for research."[13] Proust does not succeed in giving (or does not so wish) an absolute content to situations and people (themselves consequences of practical causes, as has been noted by Pavese himself [192]). Instead, Pavese's conception of time is the identification of the absolute between the "sacral" character of the first infantile identification of the unknown (that which occurred in an absolute sense in the boy's preconsciousness), and living or re-lived reality (which is the knowledge of experience).

Thus for Pavese story-telling is tantamount to the invention of a landscape, which is the story itself. A hill, a landscape, a myth are fixed symbols. They exist indefinitely, in an absolute state. Myth is also the desire to endow the particular with an absolute value. This signifies making the profane sacred. Thus a hill becomes "all" hills, a sea "all" seas, etc. This is precisely what took place in the mind of primitive man (or of the boy). Myth, says Pavese, "is a norm, the schema of an event that has occurred once for all time, and which derives its value from this absolute uniqueness which lifts it out of time and consecrates it as revelation."[14] With myth time comes to a stop and space is abolished. A whole existence is immobilized. Time is reduced to an image and to a "tang." What is felt once is felt again throughout the whole of life. Here is an example taken from the *Racconti*:

> It is as though I were talking with her, even though the conversation had taken place many years ago and even the words have been lost. For me that furtive look, which I have mentioned, suffices and suddenly the empty sky is peopled with hills and presences.[15]

The dramatization of the myth, the establishment of relations between myth and temporal things and especially between myth and people are the constituitive elements of the epic. In the poems

---

[13] *The Burning Brand*, 148.
[14] *La letteratura americana e altri saggi*, 300.
[15] *Racconti*, 363.

of *Lavorare stanca* the epic consists in reviving images of the past as over against the present. But this is not remembrance. Rather, it is a psychic process by means of which what occurred in the past invests the reality of the present. It is an evocation, not a re-evocation. It is enough for an old woman to lie down in the sun and to stretch her arms in order to effect the return of the "vibrant day in which the body also was young, more torrid than the sun."[16] "The flesh becomes remembrance," and the old woman gets drunk, inebriated, as though she felt her body rejuvenating. Her father and her husband, who also died old and worn out, live again. Past and present merge, becoming one. Thus also in "La puttana contadina" (The Peasant Whore) the woman wakes up in a room in the city. The smell of the bed, the dawn's hay-like color, make her re-live her adolescence and other awakenings in a stable in the countryside. A whole life elapses in the image, in this specific image.

Lavorare stanca is an epic, as has been said. Pavese defines the book as the

> adventure of the adolescent who, proud of his countryside, imagines the city to be similar. Instead in the city he finds solitude and seeks a remedy for it in sex and passion which serve only to de-racinate him and hurl him far from both the countryside and the city into an even more tragic solitude which is the end of adolescence. (141)

This is evident from the titles of the different sections of the book (*Forebears, Later, City in the Countryside, Maternity, Green Wood, Paternity*) in which the chronological progression remains implicit. There is no temporal development from poem to poem because Pavese is not "telling a story" about the physical evolution of a person in time. There are so many characters. What he registers is an attitude of the characters towards fixed symbols: hill, sea, city, countryside, etc. the interchangeable value which these symbols

---

[16] *Poesie*, 95.

have for the boy, the adult and the old man constitute the unity of the book. Pavese learned this lesson from Homer.

On February 17, 1936 Pavese wrote the following in his diary:

> It is good to go back to Homer. What is the unity of his poems? Each book has its own; unity of sentiment of attitude, whereby it is read harmoniously, as well as physically, as a whole. *Odyssey*, Book VIII: the pleasure of poetry, dancing, rivalry; song, the lighthearted golden myth; a vindication of the nobility of life, in an oasis of pleasure and idyllic tears. *Odyssey*, Book X: adventure, the succession of obstacles, human weeping, the growing callousness. *Iliad*, Book III: the beautiful woman, the war over her, and enervating love. And so on. Did Homer, or the man we call Homer, think of these definitions? I believe not, but it is a revealing thing that the book wherein all Greece comes to life is composed in this way, or which comes to the same thing, that it can be so interpreted.
>
> But let us be careful. The great fascination of the two poems lies in the material unity of their characters, which time after time flares up in a blaze of poetic fire. Which means that even from the first example of great poetry, written intentionality as such, we have this double play: a natural unfolding of events (which could be doubled or halved without adversely affecting the issue), and successive, fundamental poetic beams of light. The story and the poetry. The union of the two elements is merely a matter of aptitude, of skill.
>
> This opens up the problem of whether it may not be possible to recreate the miracle in separate poems, for the very reason that the mind, in all its manifestations, strives towards unity. To compose with inspiration, but with an underlying skill that merges the various fragments together to form a poem.[17]

In the poem-narrative of *Lavorare stanca* the miracle has happened in terms of *unity*, by means of epic, ideal links which tie one poem to another poem, bringing up and developing different themes through time.

---

[17] *The Burning Brand*, 43.

3. LANGUAGE = METAPHOR

The book's orientation appears from the time of the publication of "I mari del Sud" (South Seas). In the boy's eyes his cousin is "a giant dressed in white," a modern Ulysses returning to his native Ithaca (he recalls Anguilla, the "American" in *La luna e i falò*). For the boy the cousin represents a whole exotic world, of pearl-fishers and of extraordinary adventures in distant seas. He has been away from the village yet he has remained a simple man, rooted forever in the hills, the *langhe*. He is a legendary character, a whole childhood for the youth who now needs merely to go to the city to feel himself to be without roots. For now he has grown up and begins to feel the imperatives of life. He finds himself before "thoughts and dreams." Thus for the boy the cousin exists only as an invented reality.

If there is a "meaning" in *Lavorare stanca*, it is that contained in the last lines of "I mari del Sud" and in the poem "Mito."

> But when I tell him
> that he is among the happy few who have seen the dawn
> on the most beautiful islands of the earth,
> he smiles at the memory and replies that the sun
> was rising but the day was old for them.[18]

Life appears like an adventure to the boy. For the cousin life is experience, hard work. But in the poem "Mito" the "meaning" appears even more explicit. The protagonist notices that everything has changed since youth is over like summer. He no longer "feels" things as before. Before he seemed to be a young god, a being in contact with the spirit of things:

> Weariness now
> weighs on all the man's members,
> painlessly; the calm weariness of the dawn

---

[18] *Poesie*, 8.

which ushers in a day of rain. The dark beaches
know not the youth, for whom once it sufficed merely
to look at them. Nor does the sea re-live in the air
upon breathing. Resigned, the man's lips
fall back to smile before the earth. (117)

The youth is now alone. Even things are alien to him. He has lost his innocence. He is cut off from his Eden. Life is no longer an emotive, sensual-spiritual apprehension of things. Experience is concept and category. And it is also time. He feels the weariness which is the day-to-day weariness of life. To work with weariness (*lavorare stanca*) means to live. It is only when the awareness that man is mortal sets in that there comes the realization that life is not a dream, when existence is accepted with all its burdens and sufferings, that maturity succeeds adolescence, and the young god becomes a man. By the gesture of his suicide it appears that Pavese, in one stroke, might have wanted to wipe out the existential view glimpsed in this poem and restore himself to the origins of innocence, and thus become once more the boy, the young god, and no longer be a grown man. But myth is also destiny.

For the reason that the mythic vision is an intuition, a mystical participation in reality, these poems cannot be reduced to an idea and to a formulation. If this happens it is only because the poet has explained to himself the "meaning" of his intuition. He has tried, that is, to transform a sentiment, something unconscious, into something completely conscious. For primitive man to transform a feeling into a word, to give a name to an object, was tantamount to living them. Language was the myth itself because nothing existed if he — primitive man — did not give it a reality, a representation. Language was experience. The word co-existed with the image of god or demon. By way of language primitive man transformed a subjective emotion into something of an objective character. Thus reality was at once personal and impersonal, an inner world and an outer world. It is different for modern man. Language is something completely objective. By way of language modern-day man does not feel but contemplates reality. Which is to say he is separated, alienated from it. The concept precedes the image. Man thinks in words which represent images. By way of the concept man can think of things which he has not even seen. Instead, primitive man did not think. He expressed himself instinctively in words which at the same time were feeling and experience. He spoke only of things that he could perceive. Concepts lend themselves to relations and implications. They are an inducement to expansion. They are system. Myth is coalition. It is something that happens in a time, in a place and in a peculiar way. What the poet feels is similarly unique, and essential. This is the lesson of *Lavorare stanca*.

The words with which the poet expresses himself are connotative. They represent something indistinct, but it exists for a person, in a situation. And reality, the "meaning" of the poem, it is what is felt while reading it. The greater part of Pavese's poetry makes no sense if it is read literally. Pavese expresses himself by way of an invented jargon which is metaphor. It is only with metaphor, however, that the immediacy of perception can be retained, and form (style) becomes the medium between *mythos* and *logos*. Metaphor is endowing material things with immaterial relations. The originality of the poet consists in discovering new relations among things (*mythos*), and in giving a new meaning to language (*logos*), and in the invention of new metaphors. Now in Pavese's poems the language is pruned of all those rhetorical and quotidian growths. It retains its pristine meaning, which is precisely slang. But in this slang the metaphors are wholly new and imbued with feeling. Two examples follow:

> A tender moon and hoar-frost on the fields in
> the dawn, murder the wheat. (20)

> You are but a cloud of the most gentleness,
> white, entangled one night among the ancient
> branches. (31)

At a certain point some of these comparisons no longer seem even to be metaphors, and they acquire a direct value by virtue of their simplicity:

> Dawn squats on the black hill
> and cats doze on the rooftops. (59)

Thus the epic unity of *Lavorare stanca* is also given by the linguistic unity which consists of the repetition of adjectives, nouns, expressions, and of correspondences in punctuation and of images converging on a common and single progressive unfolding of all the poems. Even the characters are compared with situations that are nearly similar.

In a page of his diary (October 14, 1936) Pavese writes:

> ...it remains true that only what we think actually exists (our style, our time = the object of our knowledge) is worth writing about. If we are aiming at pointing out a new way of seeing things, and, therefore, a new reality, it is evident that our style must be accepted as part of the *truth,* making its influences felt beyond the printed page.[19]

Which implies the Pavesian principle of *cognition*. At this point it is obvious to assert that in *Lavorare stanca* (the singular, i.e. the most unique book of the whole of modern literature) there exists a unified, firm construction, not only of an intuitive but also of a logical character.

---

[19] *The Burning Brand,* 125.

Chapter III

THE CYCLICAL DEVELOPMENT

1. PROBLEMS OF FORM

Pavese divided *Lavorare stanca* into six separate sections. These sections are: *Antenati* (Forebears), *Dopo* (Later), *Città in compagna* (City in the Countryside), *Maternità* (Maternity), *Legna verde* (Green Wood) and *Paternità* (Paternity). It is always a poem that provides the title for each section. But this does not indicate that the poems which offer a concept to the different sections are the more interesting. Often, they have the sole function of marking time, to hollow out a track and to create a cycle.

The poems of the first group concern the world of childhood, an inherited time and condition. The town and the countryside are in the frame of this time and of this condition. The most important poem is "I mari del Sud." The section *Dopo* tells of the discovery of woman and sex. *Città in compagna* presents the world of adults seen through the eyes of an adolescent. *Maternità* is the universe of woman. *Legna verde* is political agitation, internment, revolt. *Paternità* is the man who has failed paternity; he is the alienated man, the solitary, man as matter and end.

As has already been pointed out in the previous chapter, Pavese tried to explain the thematic unity of *Lavorare stanca* to himself. Is it a *canzoniere* or a collection of different, autonomous and separate poems? But, as has already been said, if in *Lavorare stanca* there is no direct logical development from poem to poem because each one remains an independent entity in the completeness of the poem, the book is unified in character because the poems are tied to unifying themes which enclose them all in pre-fixed schemes. In this sense *Lavorare stanca* is an epic, and its movement, its internal flux is constituted by the dramatization of the journey countryside-city, which is the corollary childhood-maturity, and of the alienation of the past.

This cyclical development offered to us by Pavese, however, does not simplify the analysis of seventy-five different poems. In order to expound adequately the thematic note we would have to study at least fifty of them, a task that would require a separate book. Therefore, in our discussion of the content of *Lavorare stanca*, we shall first analyze the general structures and then, for each section, one or more of the more representative poems.

Pavese invented two terms to describe the poems of *Lavorare stanca*. The first is *poesia-racconto* (poem-narrative), and it indicates the concentration of events and objects in a narrative rhythm stripped of any kind of subjectivity. In "I mari del Sud," which opens the series of these objective poems, everything is scrupulously externalized. The body of the cousin, the hills, the houses, the sky etc. are treated in terms perceptible to the senses, but nothing is left to the imagination. It seems a painting of the fifteenth century in which the whole of external reality is borne on a foreground rich in reliefs, details and minutiae, and whose contours are precise.

The visual annotations are many and varied, as if the eye of the observer were a movie camera:

> . . .In the shadow of the late twilight
> my cousin is a giant dressed in white
> who moves calmly, tanned in the face,
> taciturn.
>
> . . . .
>
> My cousin has a sharply-etched face.
>
> . . . .
>
> And he walks along the slope
> with the meditative look that I saw, as a child,
> customarily worn by slightly tired peasants.[1]

---

[1] *Poesie edite e inedite*, 11-12.

The story has an intermittent flow, subdued, which gradually widens into broader ramifications of a Homeric character, and the two characters assume a constantly greater relief. The cousin is fixed in time and space:

> . . . he does not speak Italian,
> but slowly uses the dialect, which the stones
> of the very hill, is so rough
> that twenty years of different idioms and seas,
> have not scratched it. (11)

The feelings are also externalized, indeed one can say they are painted. Not even the psychological treatment, that is to say, authorizes leaving something unsaid, a reference to a non-explored profundity. By making his cousin act and speak, and by telling about him in both the past and present, Pavese makes a stage-character out of him, delineated in all the dimensions. Moreover the atmosphere of late twilight that envelopes the two characters, which is subdued and solitary, is insistently described with the repetition of the word "silence," and others still such as "taciturn," "shade," "calmly." The ample and paused verses such as:

> We were walking one evening (*pause*)
> on the flank of a hill (*pause*) in
> silence (*pause*)

create a slow rhythm of monody which is in harmony with the protagonist as well as with the twilight.

The initial poems of *Lavorare stanca* more or less have the same objective development of "I mari del Sud." The poet seeks to dissolve himself in the flow of an external reality, and takes care that he himself, with his weight, does not intervene between things and words which alone must fix the terms of the meaning that is intended. "Pensieri di Deola" (Deola Thinking), for example, consists solely of fragments of thoughts, all externalized. But this poetry also constitutes the limits of the *poesia-racconto* because it stiffens almost into a mechanism. In "I mari del Sud" we feel beyond the naturalistic narration—a more intimate bond between poet and subject, even if it is not so apparent at a first reading. Things, events, persons, in fact, betray the emotional participation of the poet. In "Pensieri di Deola" it is the events, the happenings that create reality and not the poet's sensibility which is wholly absent here. This is an important poem from the viewpoint of realism. But the inhuman detachment of the poet from creation, this purely cerebral myth of Flaubertian objectivity leaves us intellectualized, cold, non-involved and therefore absent.

The construction of realism, imposed on himself by a first attempt at a reconciliation with life on the poet's part, soon, however, succumbs to a subjective vein. Pavese feels that the image, the metaphor and the symbol have become indispensable to him. The latter, however, cropped up involuntarily from depths that realism had merely covered over. One day Pavese noticed that, while he was writing "Paesaggio I" (Landscape I), he was inventing a "fantastic relation" between character and landscape, between the hermit, the hills, the vegetation etc. Reality, therefore, is no longer the observed object but the totality of those "fantastic relations" in which the object is found inserted in the work by the consciousness which perceives it.

In "Paesaggio IV" (Landscape IV), which Pavese cites as an example of the new poetics, reality is perceived by the mind which filters it, attenuating its real contours:

> The woman who swims
> without breaking the water sees only the green
> of her short horizon. Between the sky and the plants
> extends this water and through it glides the woman
> without body. Clouds are suspended in the sky
> as though motionless. The smoke hangs in mid-air. (87)

Here it is the woman who sees the reality around her, in an aura of mysterious lightness and static silence which is naught else but a personal sensation. The lightness of the woman in the water is imagined by the men on the bank who feel the heaviness of their bodies on the grass.

> There is grass beneath the chill of the water. Suspended
> The woman passes through; but we crush it,
> the green grass, with our bodies. The length of the water
> there is no other weight. We alone feel the earth. (87)

Convinced of the inadequacy of speech with respect to all that beyond the rational and prosiness, and persuaded that things as they are are not entirely explainable, Pavese takes recourse to images to adumbrate realities that are too profound for reason:

> We think, lying
> on the bank, of that darker and fresher green
> that submerged her body. Then, one of us
> plunges in the water and crosses, uncovering his shoulders
> in foamy strokes, the motionless green. (87)

Here Pavese, through the images of the color green, of water, of chill, is weaving a web of "fantastic relations" between the woman, the water and the men. In the water that covers over the woman's body, enveloping her entirely as in a warm and immobile embrace, Pavese suggests a relation of intimacy, of a mysterious silence, which the man tries to break with violence.

Nevertheless Pavese was not completely satisfied with the new poetics. The *imagine-racconto* (poem story) could transform itself into a play of images, into useless "rarefied atmospheres" (202). Pavese, in a word, succeeded in dominating the reality of the poems, but he was still uncertain of the new orientation. Stylistically more refined, his poems became more interesting and more effective. But he had not yet found the perfect technique, the medium to which to entrust his ideas.

Up to here the fundamental esthetic problem was to find a theory of expression. Art signifies courage, faith in oneself, which is imparted only by experience. Pavese was still a young man and he did not succeed in imparting his convictions. Pavese seems to have found this faith, this sureness in creating in the poems written after 1934 and which he did not include in the first edition of *Lavorare stanca* (January 1936). Poems like "Mito" (Myth), "Semplicità" (Simplicity), "Paternità" (Paternity), "Lo steddazzu" (Morning Star) "Estate" (Summer), "Il Paradiso sui tetti" (Paradise on the Roofs), "La voce" (The Voice), "Mattino" (Morning) e "Notturno" (Nocturne) are among the most beautiful in the collection.

"Lo steddazzu" (in the Calabrian dialect it means morning star), which is one of the last poems of *Lavorare stanca*, can serve as an illustration of an achieved maturity. A man, alone, waits for the dawn before the sea. Alone, he lights a fire at which he warns himself. Now Pavese wishes to establish a particular relation between the man and the universe, no longer a fantastical relation between character and landscape.

> There is nothing more bitter than the dawn of a day
> in which nothing will happen. There is nothing more bitter
> than uselessness....... (202)

Here narrative, image and feeling coincide. It is symbolic poetry, therefore. The image, the pale green star, the rhythm of the language present a feeling of futility and solitude, and an utter anguish, symbolized by the star that falls among the mountains and by phrases such as "there is nothing more bitter" and "the slowness of the hour."

"Lo steddazzu" and the other poems that have been mentioned constitute the peak of a first poetic phase. The second phase is incorporated in the Pavesian conception of myth.

In "A propos of certain poems not yet written," Pavese not only reaffirms what he had learned from *Lavorare stanca* but also foretells his future as a poet:

But it will not be a question of *narrating images,* an empty formula as we have seen, because nothing can distinguish the words that evoke an image from those which evoke an object. It will be a question of describing — whether directly or imaginatively does not matter — a reality that is not naturalistic but symbolical. In these poems the events will come to pass — if they will come to pass — not because reality wishes it so but because the mind so decides. (204)

2. FOREBEARS

Pavese's characters belong to a particular breed. Workers, prostitutes, adolescents — they are all more or less "outsiders," or anyway people who live on the margin of society. The ambience of the poems, save for some exceptions, is the city — namely Turin — or the countryside, the Langhe region. The characters are merged with a place, inseparable from Santo Stefano and from the hills, like the cousin of "I mari del Sud." For this reason images and details are derived directly from nature and from the street. Although they always attempt to achieve a universal character, the poems of *Lavorare stanca* are rooted in a definable cultural reality. "I mari del Sud" is one of the clearest examples of universality within the limits of a particular ambience.

In order to define a man he must be put in relation with some other things. The writer needs a point of departure in order to carry out what is his most important function, namely to be an interpreter of the human condition. Or, as Pavese would have put it, of fate. Pavese knew this — and this is proved by his particular interest in American literature and in a new Piedmontese literature, and in addition by the conviction that art must correspond to the cultural requirements of one's own environment. Thus for Pavese the point of departure was the theme countryside-city and the symbols of Santo Stefano and of the Langhe, with all their implications. The development of the two key symbols of countryside and city, the *essere in natura* (being in nature) = childhood, and the *essere in se stesso* (being in self) = maturity, implies a conception of time.

In *Lavorare stanca* the countryside represents the vital source, the necessary component of the protagonist. Thus in the section *Antenati* we find the poet's entire past, and the countryside becomes a mythic patrimony, an immutable symbol in which past and present are fused. Dominique Fernandez notes ten principal and fundamental images in Pavese's poems — street and hill — and the spatial emphasis of images derived from nature. After quoting several references and allusions to hills, Fernandez says: "Each one of these lines (which present the hill as the dominant image) ... is a means of placing before his eyes the country, the fields, the hills, of fixing them as points of reference throughout the entire poem."[2] The street, instead, leads away from the hills in the direction of the city. And this street is always peopled with drunks, prostitutes, rootless drifters, who by being constantly on the move help to form the spatial perspective.

Lavorare stanca is a search for the roots of existence. The hills and Santo Stefano not only make a lost time re-appear but, as symbols, they clarify and determine the present. The "being in self," the childhood state of grace cannot be lived over again. Man is alienated from that past which persists only as a myth of a Golden Age, a lost Eden despite the efforts made to recover it. This is why Pavese's characters have the characteristics of *Homo ludens* (Man the Player) because they try to transport themselves to the age in which things are not so real, permanent, terrible or logical as they seem to be.

That the poetry of *Lavorare stanca* is a poetry of myths is obvious since the appearance of "I mari del Sud." But Pavese became aware of it later, probably towards 1935, when he wrote one of his best known poems: "Mito." Less elaborated than "La casa" (The House) and "La notte" (The Night) it very clearly presents the concept of myth as seen through the young god who has become a man, with the deathly smile of the man who has understood.

For Pavese the transition from the mythic age to that of mechanization occurs with the separation from the countryside and with the entry into the age of adulthood, the age of duties.

---

[2] Dominique Fernandez, *Il romanzo italiano*, translated by Franca Lerici (Milan: Lerici editore, 1960) 123.

Let us try to make a rapid examination here at the different sections of *Lavorare stanca.* In the first section, entitled *Antenati*, the world is pre-history and fantasy. In the poem which gives the section its title, Pavese talks about his ancestors who are "solid men, masters of themselves." It is a breed of taciturn men, without mistaken ambitions. They are so vigilant and conscious that they ignore women, who serve only the purpose of procreations.

> And the women don't count in the family.
> That is, here the women stay in the house
> And bring us into the world and say nothing
> And count nothing and we don't remember them
> Into our blood each woman infuses something new
> But each destroys herself in the effort and we,
> thus renewed, are the only ones to endure.[3]

This attitude on Pavese's part, which can seem too harsh, too differentiated, has, however, an internal logic. There are no sentimental relations in primitive life which, instead, in more civilized ages are accepted as the natural order of things. The fact that Pavese himself suffered from an unendurable incommunicability as regards woman does not attest to a personal "whim." I do not glimpse any animosity in this attitude, nor a personal and distorted view of woman. Pavese, instead, is only the victim of the stubbornness and the somber gloom of his ancestors. In the modern world he himself - at least under this aspect - is an ancestor. Only with him this incommunicability is dramatized, it becomes a duel and a shout because Pavese — as regards culture and sensibility - has one foot where the world ends and the other where it begins.

Pavese's ancestors, or better said, our ancestors — were men who were always wrapped in their thoughts, full of "vices," "whims," "horrors" but "never shadows and nobody."

Because work alone is not enough for me and mine;

---

[3] *Poesie edite e inedite,* 23.

> We know how to break our backs, but the greatest dream
> of my fathers was always to do nothing cleverly.
> We were born to roam about on these hills
> without women, and to hold our hands behind our backs. (24)

The vagrant countryman, the young god who lives in direct communication with nature are, as we have seen, the archetype of *Homo ludens*, already presented in "I mari del Sud." The cousin will build a garage for himself with the "gasoline pump."

> Then he put a mechanic there to take in the money
> And he wandered in the hills, smoking.
> Meanwhile he had married in the village. He took a girl
> slender and fair like the foreigners
> that no doubt he had met one day in the world.
> But still he went out alone. (12)

In the "Dio-Caprone" Pavese introduces the figure of the *selvaggio* in a collage of violent sexual images. These seem exaggerated and artificial, but nonetheless they effectively define the dimension of irrational primitiveness. The first stanza is composed of allusions to the sexual organs and to copulation:

> But nobody knows if the snake has passed through
> the grass. (50)

The Goat God, grandiose in his violence, represents the awesome forces of the unconscious and of the ancestral past. The goat is sex and blood, the forces of nature.

Together with "Luna d'agosto," "Il Dio Caprone" represents a mythic world which was suggested to Pavese by his readings from *The Golden Bough*. Frazer traced the origins of certain peasant customs back to myths and tribal rites. At a certain moment Pavese writes in his diary:

In 1933 what did you find in this book? That the vineyards, the wheat, the harvest, the husking had been dramas and to speak of them with words was to touch profound meanings, in which the blood, the animals, the eternal past, the unconscious were excited. The beast which fled through the field was a spirit—you blended the ancestral and the infantile, your memories of country mysteries and tremors took on a unique and bottomless meaning.[4]

With the help of anthropology Pavese traces peasant customs back to myths and tribal rites. But insead of describing them in a descriptive or conceptual form, he creates the fantastic vision of the Goat God and his parallel with the rustics. A vision, an imagination and a parallel of which only a boy is capable.

Another theme of this poetry is that of the danger of abandoning oneself to instinct:

> Because when a beast does not know how to work,
> And keeps himself only for studdings he likes to destroy.[5]

For Pavese work signifies order as opposed to chaos. His art is an attempt to clarify and order his personality which he felt tended towards hedonism.

Another representative poem of this group is "Luna d'agosto." It explores death in terms of the mythic aura.

> And the moon rises. The husband is stretched out
> in a field, with his skull deft by the sun
> -- a wife can't drag a corpse
> like a sack. The moon rises, throwing a bit of shadow
> beneath the twisted branches. The woman in the shadow
> lifts a terrified glance to the huge face of blood
> that coagulates and floods every fold of the hills. (116)

---

[4] *The Burning Brand*, 296.
[5] *Poesie edite e inedite*, 51.

Here the image of the husband fuses with that of the moon which rises with its bloody face. The effect is a transposition of the acts and events of poetry from their temporal confines to a prehistoric, i.e. to a mythic world.

The poem which concludes the group of *Antenati*, "La notte," clarifies the others preceding it:

> But the windy night, the limpid night
> that memory only grazes lightly, is remote;
> it is a memory. A stunned calm endures,
> this also of leaves and of nothing. Nothing remains,
> of that time beyond memory, except a vague remembrance. (153)

The events contained in this poem are not fixed in time in order to constitute the mythic base of Pavese's personality. An act, a gesture, assume significance because they transcend time itself. It is the child of a long time ago who from his window looked out on

> the night on the hills;
> fresh and black, and was astonished to find them amassed
> vague and limpid immobility. Among the leaves
> that rustled in the dark the hills appeared
> where everything of the day, the slopes
> and the plants and the vines, was distinct and dead
> and life was another, of wind, of sky
> of leaves and of nothing.
> Sometimes it returns
> in the immobile calm of the day,
> that distant wonder. (153)

3. LATER

If the poems of *Antenati* can be said to represent the mythic age, the poems of *Dopo* can be said to mark the demythification that the individual undergoes in time: it constitutes a process toward the rationality of the urban world.

In the first poem of the section, the predominant images are the hills, i.e. the Langhe, which are the spatial scheme of the myth. These poems also contain images of woman in relation to the growing solitude of the poet in the discovery of sex and sophistication in the world of the city. From now on the progression of events is temporal, no longer mythical in character.

According to Davide Lajolo, Pavese's first love experience was a painful one. The woman never wanted to accept him as more than a friend. Yet she succeeded in upsetting his life for several disastrous years. In his poems, where she is often referred to as the "woman of the hoarse voice," she becomes the symbol of the poet's solitude, of his failure in the communication with the other, and therefore with history.

This symbol is immediately defined in the first poem of the section, "Incontro" (Encounter):

> I met her, one night, a clearer spot
> beneath the ambiguous stars, in the summer mist.
> In the air was the odor of these hills
> profounder than the shadow, and suddenly came forth,
> as though from these hills, a clearer voice
> at the same time harsh, a voice of times now lost. (29)

The voice that comes from the hills is identified with nature because it has the vastness of the past. But the poet cannot understand it because he does not understand mythic reality, now lost:

> I created her from the depths of all things
> to me most dear, and I can't understand her. (29)

In practice it is the very symbol of life. The poet re-awakens to his Unconscious and it reveals his solitude to him. This solitude is highlighted in the poem "Mania di solitudine." In darkness the poet is at peace and in harmony with nature surrounding him.

The theme of this harmony is the mystical interpenetration of nature, which he saw as the origin, the raw material that is in us, the lymph that nurtures us:

> A gulp of drink and my body savours the life
> of plants and rivers, and it feels detached
> from everything. (52)

In "Mattino" the poet sees a woman's face behind a window half-open on the sea: a face that seems to merge with the waters. The sea, which repeatedly appears in Pavese's work, suggests the futility of living and an existential solitude. In 1945 when Pavese was working on the poem "La terra e la morte" (Earth and Death) and was about to begin the *Dialoghi con Leucò*, he wrote this sentence in a very important paragraph of the diary: "Aphrodite came from the sea."[6] The goddess of love derives her divinity from the sea which signifies silence and omnipresence, the lack of a concrete and definite horizon. Now all of Pavese's women are in one way or another associated with waters and their silence. The woman-goddess who renews in him the most intense sensations and the deepest experiences, thereby becomes the symbol of nature's emptiness. She remains an ungraspable symbol like the evanescent sea:

> No memory exists on this face.
> No word exists to contain it
> or unite it with the past. Yesterday,
> it vanished from the small window as
> it will vanish in an instant, without sadness
> or human words, against the spread of the sea.[7]

In "Estate" the image of the sea is repeated twice, always in order to describe the light that surrounds the woman. In "Not-

---

[6] *The Burning Brand*, 283.
[7] *Poesie edite e inedite*, 160.

turno" the woman's mouth "has the crease of a sweet hollow among the distant coasts" (163). These and other passages, like the following one, give the woman a mythical dimension, but now the myths live again only intellectually in the poet.

> But you live elsewhere.
> Your tender blood was created elsewhere.
> The words you utter have no counterpart
> in the rugged sadness of this sky.
> You are but a sweet cloud, white
> entangled one night among the ancient branches. (163)

In "Agonia" (Agony) the little girl becomes a woman, mistress of herself, in search of colors and life. Although the woman is myth, and therefore a symbol for the poet, she lives a life without myths, free of the poet's past. This explains why the women in Pavese's writings are often prostitutes or exist without any precise definition. They are always free:

> One arrives at Torino by night
> and at once on the streets sees the artful women
> dressed for the eyes, that walk alone.
> There each works for the clothes she wears,
> but adapts them to every light. There are colors
> for morning, colors for going out on the avenues,
> for pleasures of the night. The women wait
> and feel themselves alone know life to its depths.
> They are free. They deny nothing. (117)

They are city creatures and they destroy myths and illusions. Thus the boy of "Terre bruciate" (Burnt Lands) listens to the youth talk about Turin and he too dreams of going to the city one day. What will happen in the city is suggested by "Due sigarette" (Two Cigarettes). In this poem a man meets a prostitute on the street and goes with her to her room to make love: "Every night is a liberation" (44). But it is an absurd act, devoid of meaning, because the two always remain outside each other. Their consciousnesses do not meet, they remain tied to the anonymity of the city.

The other poems of *Dopo* belong to two groups: poems that have the same characteristics of "Notturno," "Mattino" etc., and naturalistic poems like "Pensieri di Deola." Of the first group the most interesting are "Donne appassionate" (Passionate Women) and "Dopo."

The dominant image of "Donne appassionate" is a threatening sea which seems to swallow anyone who enters it. The girls on the beach are enveloped in a silent anxiety which is represented by the foreign woman who disappeared one night when she was swimming in the nude in that sea. In "Dopo" there seems to be a mystic relationship between the woman and the landscape. The first verse expresses the union between the sexual act and the mythical reality of nature:

The hill is extended, impregnated in silence by the rain. (85)

For the poet the act is rendered mythic by the eternal presence of the hill, but the woman is not aware of the hill and her love encounter is wholly exhausted in the present. Once more the woman comes to represent the materialism of the city where life loses the profundity of the past:

She does not see the naked hill
dozing in the dampness: she goes out in the street
and those who bump against her don't know. (85)

This poem is the point of arrival of the boy of *Antenati*; the mythical age is now lost. There is a complete break between the past and the present:

towards evening
the hill is covered by patches of fog
the window gathers in even their breath. The street
is deserted at this hour; the solitary hill
has a life remote in its darker body. (85)

61

Sylistically this poem is important because of the felicitous expressive balance that Pavese had arrived at. The realism of the first poems, inapplicable in a description of states of mind such as these, is substituted by an expression which describes by means of indistinct rhythms and of atmospheres. It is a poem that is to be "felt" rather than read because it contains an ineffable quality which transcends reason. They are the "fantastic relations" between the man and the hill, the woman and the rain, which are made even more impalpable by the memories which absorb and fuse everything into a solitude of landscape.

4. *CITTÀ IN CAMPAGNA* AND *MATERNITÀ*

The group of poems *Città in campagna* portrays life in terms of order and duties. It is the adult age in which, after the experience of sex, man is confronted with work and the other responsibilities of community life. But an ungratified, deep desire and nostalgia for the pre-rational age always remains in individuals. This nostalgia is the attempt to re-create oneself and to revivify oneself in a return to the Eden of before the fall, thereby cancelling out the whole historical contribution of good and evil, of the just and unjust, of truth and falsity. These are attempts, however, which remain incomplete, frustrated and for this reason the contrast between the two aspects of life perseveres in the individual.

The first aspect, that of present-day life, is exemplified in "Disciplina" (Discipline). Here is a view of mankind which wears itself out in work, which at times would like to "lift up its head," but instead lowers it, defeated. In "Indisciplina" (Indiscipline) the drunkard refuses to submit to the rational. Things once more appear unreal to him: "The drunkard sees neither houses, nor sky, but he knows them" (76). Thereby, he arrives at a happy state of instinctual immediacy:

> Walking peacefully he would even enter the sea
> and, vanished, he would walk on the same way at the bottom.
> (77)

The boy in "Atavismo" (Atavism) sees a horse on the deserted street. The horse is bare and soaking up all the warmth of the sun, heedless of the trees and thickets that are "watching" him. The boy too has a body but he must hide it, cover it with clothes, because by living in a mythless city, our nude body is estranged from us. Nor can one go about without clothes in the city or in the countryside because there nature does not tolerate the human body: "One could do so in the countryside, if overhead there were not the depth of the sky which terrifies and disheartens" (103). One might go about without any clothes in the countryside, however, only on the condition that one did not feel lost therein. This theme which recurs in *Il diavolo sulle colline* and in *La casa in collina*, is one of the leitmotifs of Pavese's work. For Pavese, for whom mind is the only cognitive form, the body is an external reality, like so many others, against which consciousness collides.

The boy (a primitive) perceives instinctively. His impulse is to act like the horse until the rationality of the city blots out this impulse. In adults even an object, a memory is enough to bring myth back to life.

In *Città in campagna* life is understood as seriousness in work, as necessity, that is, as a repression of instincts which are everything for the adolescent. Life is "ancient civilization" and it is symbolized by the father who frustrates the boy's impulse to catch flies and "to make a big jump" (58).

The poem *Lavorare stanca*, which provides the title of the collection, expresses the solitude which creeps into the ordinary man—the one who does not get drunk—at the end of adolescence:

> Crossing a street to escape from home
> is only for boys, but this man who wanders
> the streets all day is no longer a boy
> and doesn't escape from home. (99)

A boy is allowed to run away from home, the symbol of "ancient civilization," but for adult man, the flight is only from him-

self, through drunkenness. In this poem the man, alone in his solitude, is bereft of any illusion of happiness and of the countryside.
This man walks the streets and sweats and labors and yet in the
streets there is no life and loneliness is always with us:

> Is it worth the trouble to be alone, to be always more alone?
> When one wanders, the streets and the squares
> are empty. One must stop a woman
> and speak to her and convince her to live together.
> Otherwise, one speaks to himself. (99)

The woman would be able to resolve or alleviate solitude, to
constitute a point of reference. But the man roams the streets with
the desire of an encounter that we already know is impossible.

On a broader plane, the relationship with a woman signifies
communication with the world. And here we feel Pavese's anxiety
to establish a contact with external reality which, however, is
made impossible for him because of his congenital incapacity.

If, however, the poems of *Città in compagna* are easier to describe, those in the section *Maternità* are the most difficult. The latter have much in common with the poems in *Dopo*, and several
could very well be inserted in that section without radically alter-
ing the structure of *Lavorare stanca*. In this group of poems we find
different figures of women and not the exaltation of "one" woman. But these are merely minor differences and the fact remains
that *Maternità* is more of an addendum to *Dopo* than it is a new
section in itself.

In poems like "Piaceri notturni" (Nocturnal Pleasures) and "La
vecchia ubriaca" (The Drunk Old Woman) the true subject is the
secret body of woman. The reality that woman encloses within
herself is still nature:

> We shall return tonight to the woman who sleeps,
> To search her body with frozen fingers,
> and a heat will stir our blood, a heat of the earth
> blackened by moisture: a breath of life.

She too was warmed by the sun and now finds
in her nakedness a sweeter life,
that fades in the day, and recalls the earth. (71)

Woman is life, she brings forgetfulness of the icy night. On the streets the wind envelopes man in a cold casing, where the smells of the earth and of the surrounding objects no longer establish a contact with him. Woman, instead, is salvation, she is earth and life. And there is trust in her, things that wipe out the exile.

. . . . the warmth of her body
is the same as the blood which murmurs in us. (71)

In "Una Stagione" (A Season) maternity and sex are represented without sentimentality naturalistically. But here the universal symbol of fertility is not understood as joy, but as impoverishment. Maternity is negative already in the woman because it exhausts her and destroys the body "which now is worn out by too many children" (48). And in the end the children also are destined to loneliness which even sex cannot fill:

Above all he likes, since he has engendered
on that body, to leave it to wilt and to return to himself. (49)

The woman's maternity angers the man who merely seeks to gratify himself in the sexual act. The girl, accommodatingly, hides her maturity in order to enjoy the act together with the man. She knows that she must not make him mad with the sight of her "deformed belly" (49).

In "Un ricordo" (A Memory), a poem marked by a biographical tone, the woman remains far away. She is an ungraspable figure whom neither time nor persons can ever touch:

There is no man who manages to leave a mark
on her. Whatever has been dissolves in a dream,
as though vanished in a morning, and only she remains. (129)

She is a symbol of nothingness — even though past and present are enclosed in her silence. But it is also the symbol of the impossibility of communication through love inasmuch as the latter never succeeds in being an absolute mystic interpenetration of consciousnesses.

A need of the absolute, therefore, is destined to failure because love is exhausted in a brutal collision — the sexual act, with external reality — woman.

La voce expresses the poet's state of mind after the failure: his sorrow over the loss of the woman with the hoarse voice is now attenuated by time, purged from the memory. Now it is a muffled anxiety, in the silence of his room and of his interior solitude:

> Each day is the same.
> And the voice is the same, not breaking the silence,
> Harsh and ever the same in the immobility
> of memory. (150)

The feelings are suspended, but:

> If the voice were to sound, even the brief throb
> of that silence which endures would become pain.
> The gesture of the futile pain would return,
> striking everything in the roar of time. (150)

This poem provides an insight into Pavese's mind. For him the miracle of art repeats itself; by moving from one level of life, it transcends and dominates its violent motions. This is a cathartic function that is always stressed in Pavese's work because in few other cases have life and art been so indissolubly united. To the measure that Pavese discovered in himself the motives of his anxiety, these composed themselves into artistic forms until they triumphed completely over the misery of his life, in *La luna e i falò*.

5. *LEGNA VERDE* AND *PATERNITÀ*

Lavorare stanca has a secret structure. As has already been said, even though order and arrangement were imposed on the book after the poems had already been written, there is nevertheless a definite development among the first four groups and the last two, *Legna verde* and *Paternità*. It could be said that up to *Legna verde* the background of the poems is a past from which the man-protagonist is now separated. A past in which existence and nature, subject and object, were one and the same thing. For the boy of "Il Dio Caprone" the landscape is wholly alive: it is the reflection of his "being" that he sees in objects. And this animated, mythic world is really lived by him. Alienation sets in when the adolescent begins to enter into the world of "ancient civilization" and to "perceive" objects. The past, then, persists in the myth but renders the man-protagonist ever more conscious of his alienation. The woman-goddess also represents this myth. Sex, in "Pensieri di Deola" and "Due sigarette," is an act deliberated by two living objects, and therefore it is an abstract and impersonal concept. It is mechanical. On the contrary, the relation between the woman-goddess and the man always retains an emotional and psychic charge: the woman becomes sex. At the same time his silence is that of the past. Therefore, in order not to undergo disappointments that coagulate the feelings, in order not to be separated from the woman, the man of "Incontro" transforms her into essential myth.

In these two last sections of *Lavorare stanca* the alienation from the past is viewed in terms of the "ancient civilization." There is political activity and social struggle in *Legna verde*, whereas *Paternità* is marked by resignation in a sterile present.

Pavese viewed political activity as an allegiance to the present and to the myths of history. Man is his destiny also in a political sense because he is forced to choose, to give himself to an order and to a morality. Pavese tried the political path just as he tried the road of communication through the woman. Pavese wanted to dig roots for himself. But these roots seemed to him too ephemeral, insecure and irrational. His political allegiance was an allegiance to the work of his companions, and constituted his effort at reconciliation with historical reality. Pavese contributed to the commitments of the present as a man and as a writer. But these commitments rebelled against him. They were a new and even more bitter disappointment. The fact is that when Pavese writes about solitude and about the myth he is translating personal sensibilities. Even his theories of myth and of art, after all, are inspiration and feeling rather than intellectualism. His political works, instead, are much less felt, and the least successful in terms of art for the simple reason that they deal with and elaborate abstract ideas which do not involve the individual Pavese. Save for *La luna e i falò* and *La casa in collina*, Pavese's political commitment dies in indeterminateness and doubt. His morality never ends in propaganda, "Fumatori di carta" (Smokers of Paper), which is probably the most suggestive of the "political" poems, contains allusions to the fascists of the aftermath of the First World War. Pavese criticizes above all the lack of organization, and the trust in words rather than in actions. The workers are portrayed in the exhausted musicians who try to play a dance. The bandleader — the first draft of Nuto of *La luna e i falò* — arrives in Turin in order to look for work and a better life, but all he finds is misery, social injustices, and "raucous women, drunks, lost scarecrows, staggering" (31):

> He had come to Torino
> one winter, among the factory lights and smokey scum,
> and he knew the meaning of work. He accepted work
> as a hard destiny of man. But if all men
> accepted it and there were justice in the world. (31)

Pavese tries to express the desperation of the working classes through the vicissitudes of the protagonist, the clarinet-player, the description of Fascist Turin and the image of the peasant musicians. Pavese also expresses the idea of where this desperation will eventually lead. Because there are companions all around.

Every house has families of them. The fascist and unjust city is completely encircled by them.
Moreover:

> The face of the earth
> was all covered with them. They felt in themselves
> enough desperation to conquer the world. (31)

Under this aspect "Fumatori di carta" is a poem of perfect revolt. Few writers of this century manage, as does Pavese, to evoke an entire scene and an entire world in a few lines. But the final shout, a kind of invitation to action, with its violence of a proletarian manifesto, almost blots out the rhythmic, lucid, nervous beauty of the central verses:

> Suddenly he shouted
> that it wasn't destiny if the world suffered
> if the light of the sun brought forth curses:
> it was man, guilty. (31)

The shout does not subside in the last three verses which Pavese wrote in italics. Nevertheless the determination to revolt broadens into a desire for concrete action, and the verses, furious and external as they may be, are effective, despite their apparent fury.

"Legna verde" is perhaps less striking than "Fumatori di carta" and the other poems of the section. But it is better structured, more intense, and suggests uncertainties and thoughts that concern more the man who leaves prison than that of the group or that of the man of the political group, and in terms of him. This man leaves prison and looks at the hills that surround him. For a moment he undergoes the charm of that earth because he feels its innate, unmistakeable warmth. But he must resume political activity, probably face new injustices, vexations, desperation and prison. And this is a harsh and pitiless reality which is almost blotted out in the face of the countryside. He thinks, for a moment, that his political comrades or city-fold do not know the land the way he does:

> The companions don't live in the hills;
> they were born in the city where, in place of grass
> there are the tram tracks. Sometimes even he forgets. (81)

Occasionally this countryman also forgets that the hill is different from a tram track. But he is an adult who has chosen to stay with those who are in prison. The prison is the reality of the moment, the countryside is an insurmountable nostalgia:

> But the smell of the land that reaches the city
> no longer recalls the peasants. It is a long caress
> that causes the eyes to close and one to think
> of the companions in prison, the long prison which awaits. (82)

"Legna verde" summarizes an impossible condition: the antithesis between a personal interpretation of reality and the concept of reality which society represents. This is a dualism that reappears with even greater insistence both in the diary and in the novels. On the one hand Pavese knew that he could not abandon either the city or his friends. He abandoned them once, in 1943-45, and thereafter he was tormented by the thought that he had betrayed them and had thereby limited his destiny as man. *La casa in collina*, for example, is a novel inspired by a feeling of guilt. At the same time this novel best explains the reason for this guilt, and transcends it. At a certain point man recognizes himself in man, in that dead man who could be me, you, the others, one of the living, and in that awesome death he glimpses the infinite vanity of his existence. The war continues, therefore, and we accept it as men. This is the reality. But it is a reality bereft of love.

The poems of *Paternità* close *Lavorare stanca* and complete the cycle. These are the poems of man alone, of the uprooted man who is sterile without any more myths and virtues. It is nausea and maturity, it is old age and regret, it is suicide as the end of the adventure, and it is destiny.

These poems are so many finished paintings. In "L'istinto" (Instinct), the old man watches two dogs in coitus on the street, and recalls the times of his youth. In "Paternità" and "Lo steddazzu" we have the man alone in front of the useless sea. (In *Tra donne sole* Momina says: "It looks like a sewer. You can spit in it."). In "Mito" the young god becomes aware of the passing of time and of his weariness and, resigned, he tries to "smile before the earth" (127). Practically, the boy of "Antenati" is replaced by the alienated man who does not succeed in creating a family for himself, who has never participated in the world (and if he has done so, it was only to fail), and who is destined to disappear forever. Thus man's sterile adventure concludes with death, the absolute and supreme negation. At bottom the family, love, duty etc. help man to forget his exile. Freud is right when he speaks of the separation from the maternal womb. But Pavese's characters are even denied illusions. In the Pavesian conception only death destroys separation, annihilates the prison. This death, which in the western world is permeated with fears and trembling, assumes in Pavese almost the appearance of the Hindu nirvana, the supreme overcoming of anxiety and of desires. This philosophy, this stoicism is contained in "Paradiso sui tetti" (Paradise on the Rooftops). Death is peace and quiet, it is supreme harmony:

> It will be a day of tranquility, of cold light
> like the sun that is born and dies, and the glass
> will shut the filthy air from the sky. (157)

Thus the "futile gestures," the painful morning risings, the solitary and desperate roaming through the deserted streets of the city ceases. Remembrances, thoughts are lost in the shadows of the room. Emaciated faces and distant voices no longer disturb sleep:

A shadow with flesh will repose on the supine face.
The memories will be the clots of shadow
concealed thus like consumed embers
in the hearth. The memory will be the flame
that even yesterday consumed in the eyes now closed. (157)

If the woman-goddess represents the myth of the earth, death represents the return to a universal silence and a status of pure harmony.

The window will suffice to dress each thing
in a peaceful glimmer, almost a light. (157)

Thus concludes the cycle of *Lavorare stanca*, which is the very cycle of life. If the cycle of life begins with the myth of the fore-bears and the identification with the hill, the village, the earth. And if the woman-goddess is the world itself, voraciousness and passion, transcendence and transparence, death is the definitive return to the earth and to origins. This universal and archetypical cycle is based on myths which sooner or later have appeared in every culture. Pavese has merely re-expressed them, giving them new and actual forms. Therefore the poetry of *Lavorare stanca* is the poetry of man, and for this man it could again become an oral poetry.

Chapter IV

AB INITIO

1. RELATION WITH THE HERMETICS

In *A proposito di certe poesie non ancora scritte* Pavese says that "only critical awareness brings a poetic cycle to an end."[1] In this sense that which had been the poetry of modernism, that is to say the poetry of the '20s, already in 1936 represented a period that had come to a close. A closed period which — at best — allowed only variations on its main themes.

The greatest living poets of the time — Pound, Eliot, Valèry — had already formulated their experiences and now they merely amplified them. For their part the young poets were taking other directions. In England the Oxford group was decisively in favor of a poetry of social significance. In Italy, the advent of Quasimodo registered the first indications of a poetry that was galvanized and reinforced by the war and not, as was held by many critics, transformed by it. Although W. H. Auden and his friends, Quasimodo included, tried to give new contents to poetry, they nevertheless wrote in the modernistic hermetic idiom. In every case, the critics were conscious of the new orientation, albeit not exactly convinced.

Modern poetry achieved recognition when the critics perceived that it not only responded to the questions and urgencies of the time, but that it also represented the end phase of an evolution that had begun with romanticism. In this sense *Lavorare stanca* was and remains a novelty. It can not be set within the frame of the cultural background. The hesitations of the critics in judging the book are to be attributed precisely to this fact. To cite an example, let us recall that in 1936 nobody, or almost nobody, took note of

---

[1] *Poesie*, 140.

Lavorare stanca, while the general attention was drawn to a study by Francesco Flora in which he deluded himself that he was announcing a new phase, the "hermetic" phase of Italian poetry. And when Pavese was discovered in the confusion of the immediate post-war period, another perspective loomed on the horizon and it brought other exigencies in its train. The poetry of *Lavorare stanca* was grouped together with the poetry of social significance and of commitment, with which it did share actual similarities. But it did not have a common pre-history, nor even a common orientation.

Definitively the difficulties that the critic has in approaching Pavesian poetry are above all to be attributed to the fact that Pavese did not participate in the experiments of his contemporaries, nor did he seem coinvolved in their vicissitudes. The poetics of Italian hermeticism evolved within the terms established by Ungaretti and by Montale. Composition is Ungaretti's main preoccupation, and as such his poetry is autonomous, it obeys a rhythm, a syntax, a sound peculiar to it. Content and form draw increasingly closer to each other to the point of interpenetration. The words are counted, they do not crowd the page, but are wrested from silence almost painfully, and with all their meaning. Avoiding adjectives, arbitrariness, Ungaretti retains the virginal and conceptual value of the word which, isolated in the space of the page, becomes a hieroglyphic, an ideogram. In this poetry, harsh, bitter, real sounds are rarely found; just as rare are onomatopoeic metaphors which spray color and emotion, and forcibly intrude on the reader. The word has a sound because it has weight and a violence at the moment it reaches the reader. But Ungaretti's poems lack sonorousness. They suggest contemplation rather than sensation, a lament rather than a strident shout. The dimension of this poetry is the order of silence, a reality that presents itself as eternal, immutable and irreversible like a melody, a dimension that surpasses life and which at the same time contains its reflections. Ungaretti's encounters — his reality — are evening and morning, empty spaces, islands outside time. This contemplation by Ungaretti is virility in contrast to the symbolists who represent a contemplated reality.

Montale constitutes the other pole of Italian modernistic poetry, and it has nothing in common with Ungaretti. If behind the latter there are French cultural experiences, both the *Calligrammes* of Apollinaire and the echo of Mallarmè, Montale has a plasticity of verse and visual qualities which bring him close to the Imagists. If Eliot can describe with a new taste the dawns of an English slum in contrast to the idyllic images of the Victorians, Montale's poetry becomes thuds, whirlpool, noise, matter that beats against matter, rolling rafters, flotsam and jetsam among the algae. The word resumes its imitative and onomatopoeic function, while the detail becomes minute and the desolation is graphic. The glance, as though it were the eye of a camera, falls here and there, restless, and then comes to a halt on the ego. The object is Montale's obsession and in contact with it the poet receives a profound impact, a metaphysical anxiety. But Montale's object does not rest upon a benevolent nature, nor does it reflect a cosmic order. He is very far from the *pathetic fallacy* of the romantics. Montale's nature is sterile and decomposed, it is made of "slime" and of "moulds," and discloses the horror of an immobility without end. Montale lives in a de-humanized present, where only the ego and reality exist. Hence his frantic rummaging in space, in the cavities of his memory in order to bring a relic of the past to the surface, becomes an anxiety-ridden search for time, for roots. Montale's anguish is the anguish of the poet who feels himself to be incarnate, to be a body. It is the anguish of man who is prey to a historical recurrence that does not justify being. It is that *osso di seppia* (cuttlefish bone) without a causality, buffeted and worn out to the point of agony by the eternal waves.

Pavese's orientation, instead, rejects modernism and also rejects the poetic experiences of the past. His purpose is "to begin again at the beginning."[2] Dissatisfied with his youthful attempts, he tried to turn to the origins of poetry. On the other hand his

---

[2] *Poesie*, 129.

translations of American novels, putting him in touch with a young literature, confirmed his convictions. When Massimo Mila, in his preface to *Lavorare stanca* notes that a genre of folklorist story-telling in dialect still exists in Piedmont, which is a Celtic substratum, an epic vein which is not found in the southern regions, he simply indicates that Pavese already had a regionalistic tradition in his bones.

The first poems, which are the fruit of this search, are descriptive and naturalistic. Pavese does not waste words, but the construction remains linear, simple. The hermetic poet, on the contrary, tries to present an emotion directly, to objectify. Hence the importance of structure, of language which intensifies expression.

In the poem-narratives emotion is presented indirectly by the events that have been dramatized. Therefore the emphasis is not on the plastic-evocative value of the individual word but on the development of the narration. In other words, while the hermetics reconstruct an emotion, Pavese also invents a reality. Both the "I" who speaks, for example, and the cousin of "I mari del Sud" are presented by Pavese objectively, as characters. If the cousin is indirectly the subject of the second or third stanza, in the fourth the boy, the "I," speaks of himself. In the poem the words are precise and concrete but not denotative. In practice the phrases "on the side of a hill," "late twilight" do not specify or photograph. Instead the ambiences and atmospheres are perceived. The "I," the protagonist does not disjoin the attribute of the thing from the thing itself because he assimilates the things in their substance. When Montale in the verse says "era il rivo strozzato che gorgoglia" (it was the strangled brook that gurgles)[3] he attributes to the brook functions that do not belong to it, but by so doing he tries to reproduce something of an objective character glimpsed in an emotion: the dried-out brook. Pavese, on the other hand, does not have recourse to emotion and presents things objectively and universally as though it were not he who is describing them, as though things presented themselves naturally, by themselves.

---

[3] Eugenio Montale, *Ossi di seppia* (Milan: Mondadori, 1963) 107.

Pavese had assimilated the culture of his time but he rejected hermetic poetry because, based as it was on the concept image-language, it remained a subjective, lyrical form and therefore too often a gratuitous expression. Now Pavese's preoccupation is not a question of genre, but one having much deeper roots. We must bear in mind that the hermetic poet reduces himself to a relativistic, nauseous and contingent reality with its search for objective reality. For both Ungaretti and Montale the anguish of living derives from a lack of form. Their historicism is caused by an attitude towards reality that does not change, that cannot change, whereas Pavese's reality is a whole cosmos: essences and archetypes. The object, therefore, does not become an end in itself but is in relation with the man who gives it life. If Pavese never goes in for minute description, and instead makes use of substantives, it is because the object represents an essence. The man who returns to the countryside, who looks at the hill or the vineyard, does not become a boy but is a boy. He has no need of memory because he contains the object and the object contains him: because he can look at himself, mirror himself, recognize himself. This is also the reason why the characters of Lavorare stanca never descend into themselves, that is, they are not introspective.

2. RELATION WITH THE HERO

Let us recapitulate. The section Antenati is the prologue of Lavorare stanca. The myth is presented and the protagonist defined. In the poem "Forebears" he says: "I found companions finding myself."[4]

What he means to say is that he found himself in the myths but that he also found the others: the myth has universal value. The protagonist lives the fundamental traumas, the core experiences. His fate has already been marked in childhood because all the contingencies of future life have filtered into the myth. The myth transforms the quotidian, history, into legend, and gives a form to the future.

---

[4] Poesie, 9.

The section *Dopo* contains, *in nuce*, all the rest of *Lavorare stanca*. It begins with the poem "Incontro" and it is singular because the adventures of the adolescent and of the adult will always be fugitive encounters in the street, in the journey that leads far away from the country. Nevertheless the problem of the protagonist is not the country because he is never entirely cut off from it. Rather it is the city because here he does not feel in harmony with himself. He does not succeed in possessing it and therefore *belonging* because he will never be able to raise the city to the level of myth. Now he is a grown man conscious of his actions, who investigates and analyzes. The city has no mysteries, and mystery is the precondition of myth. It has no mysteries because man builds it and understands it. For the boy who runs away from home, the street is a mystery because he does not know where it leads. In the city, however, everything is explained because life is an eternal present, a prison. The countryman who comes to the city suffers the anguish of being identified, recognized. It is an anguish that is different from that of Sartre's characters or from the "I" of Montale who are citizens, people without a fate. They are in the grip of the real, of the object because they live in a de-mythified reality.

Lavorare stanca speaks of a journey, as do all the epics. The hero at times descends into the Avernus, into the kingdom of the dead, before concluding his adventures. It is a journey into the unconscious, for this after all is what the caverns, the sea etc. represent. The adventure comes to an end only when the hero returns to the world. He returns, that is to say, when the spiritual is in harmony with the real, when the unconscious and the conscious manage to maintain proper proportions, when the personality achieves full integration. Now in the descriptions of the protagonist of *Lavorare stanca* the hills are almost always enveloped in darkness, or submerged in the moonlight. They could represent his unconscious. The impossibility of renewing the myth of the country in the city represents the impossibility of establishing a normal relation between the conscious and the unconscious. The result is not a complete personality, but a sundered one. This is why the hero in the epic of *Lavorare stanca* never obtains the state of grace as instead happens in the ancient epic when the hero, after overcoming all obstacles, happily concludes the cycle of his experiences: Ulysses by finding Ithaca, Aeneas his fatherland, Dante by arriving in the sight of God. The cousin did not find the exotic world of the southern seas, peopled with islands and whales, and he returns home with the meditative air of tired peasants. The adolescent leaves the hills in search of something new and violent, as though he wanted to overcome his personal fate, and instead loses himself in the very search to find himself. At bottom he is part of the modern epic. His transcendence is in recurrence, because for Pavese life signifies precisely recurrence, ritual; the fundamental encounters repeat themselves.

The difference between Pavese and his contemporaries is that the latter used the mythic past (consider Eliot) as a simile in that, for them, to believe in history transformed into legend would have been equivalent to a rejection of their poetics. Instead, Pavese with the help of myth, dramatizes the experiences of his contemporaries, and encompasses them within himself. Hence his poetry is not limited in time but embraces the whole of human history.

3. RELATION WITH WHITMAN

In conclusion: for the critic schooled along hermetic-modernistic lines, Pavese based his poetics on a premise which cannot be accepted. Those critics who, in tracing Pavese's poetic evolution, look for the neorealistic key and the "American" key in him, are also wrong. Meanwhile Whitman's influence on Pavese's poetry is taken for granted. The technical problem, the long verses of the poem-narratives are approached with the inevitable allusion to the *Leaves of Grass*. Pavese himself had foreseen the terms of the parallel, but he let it be noted that he was lacking "in both the breadth, and the temperament" (5) to make use of them.

In some cases, the comparison could even hold:

I CELEBRATE myself, and sing myself,
And what I assume you shall assume,

For every atom belonging to me as good belongs to you.[5]

Failing to fetch me at first keep encouraged,
Missing me one place search another,
I stop somewhere waiting for you. (76)

And Pavese:

Ma anche questa è passata; non sono più solo
e, se non so rispondere, so farne a meno.
Ho trovato compagni trovando me stesso.[6]
(But even this has passed; I am no longer alone.
And, if I cannot respond, I know how to do without it.
I have found companions finding myself).

The lines are of similar length, and always contain a sentence. But obviously the rhythm changes. The first quotation which is the opening of the *Song of Myself,* prepares for the crescendo and introduces the biblical tone of the verses that follow. And in the second quotation we still hear the oratorical echo, we remain with the final emphasis which is precisely that. In contrast there are more pauses in Pavese's poems; the narration develops slowly, with a staid, placid rhythm.

The difference, however, is not only rhythmical but ethical. Whitman wants to assert himself and others. He recognizes himself in others, in the objects that surround him, for the reason that every man is a microcosm, an entity that encloses a whole universe. The long lists are the definition of *myself,* which is a formulation that could become endless. At the end, after the ecstasy of identification, the "I" loses itself in brotherhood becoming universality. It loses identity, that is, but paradoxically it still retains individuality, like a leaf of grass. In the *Song of Myself,* Whitman be-

---

[5] Walt Whitman, *Leaves of Grass and Selected Prose* (New York: The Modern Library, College Edition, Random House 1950) 23.
[6] *Poesie,* 9.

gins precisely with the "I" which is defined, amplified in time and space and then represented as the very personification of the universe and of the macrocosm.

The poet is a man, like all the rest, an average man who, however, manages to glimpse, almost to perceive the order of the world. He is a *voyant*:

> The greatest poet hardly knows pettiness or triviality.
> If he breathes into anything that was before thought
> small it dilates with the grandeur and life of the
> universe. He is a seer… he is individual. . . he is
> complete in himself. . . the other are as good as he,
> only he sees and they do not.[7]

He is a mystic who succeeds in reconciling extremes, in rediscovering harmony in the reality of facts, or science:

> When the full-grown poet came,
> Out spake pleased Nature (the round impassive globe, with
> all its shows of day and night,) saying, *He is mine*:
> But out spake too the Soul of man, proud, jealous and
> unreconciled, *Nay, he is mine alone*:
> - Then the full-grown poet stood between the two,
> and took each by the hand;
> And today and ever so stands, as blender, uniter, tightly
> holding hands,
> Which he will never release until he reconciles the two,
> And wholly and joyously blends them. (423)

He is a prophet who while exalting the present looks to the future, who while glorifying the body glorifies the soul. Thus the journey across America not only represents the discovery of the *common man*, of the democratic man, or even that of a great nation, but is above all the discovery of a new spirituality. Once he has

---

[7] Walt Whitman, *Leaves of Grass and Selected Prose*, 445.

arrived at a kind of mystical collaboration with the world, the poet puts himself in touch with God.

> And I know that the spirit of God is the brother of my own. (27)

> I see something of God each hour of the twenty four, and each
> moment then,
> In the faces of men and women I see God. (73)

> Do you see O my brothers and sisters?
> It is not chaos or death — it is form, union, plan —
> it is eternal life — it is Happiness. (74)

These in brief, are the principal Whimanian themes. And one might note in passing that the poetry of several American contemporaries continues on this track. The so called "beats," for example, render more tangible what in *Leaves of Grass* was still contemplation, to which they add social protest. Consider these lines from Alan Ginsberg:

> America I've given you all and now I am nothing.[8]

> I want people to bow as they see me and say he is gifted
> with poetry, he has seen the presence of the Creator.
> And the Creator gave me a shot of his presence to gratify
> my wish, so as not to cheat me of my yearning for him. (27)

In *Lavorare stanca*, instead, Pavese constructs, invents a reality. Both the poems and the book have an end that is determined by the narration. *Leaves of Grass* is also a *canzoniere*, but the development is not so explicit as in Pavese's collection. If the leaves of grass represent the poetry, once the expression of the poet — in the *Song of Myself* is defined — the order no longer becomes important.

---

[8] Alan Ginsberg, *Howl and Other Poems* (San Francisco: City Lights Bookstore, 1963) 31.

As in fact happens in the listings, an image could precede another without changing the meaning or the effect of the whole.

Leaves of Grass is a book which necessarily remained unfinished for the reason that the encounter with an inexhaustible reality has no end. For example, if every thing, every object contains a macrocosm but is also complete in itself, in order to know the universal the "I" must individuate every particular. In fact it seems that in order to repeat his experience Whitman must accumulate example after example. In his poems we find not a qualitative organic development, but only a quantitative organic progression. Whitman avoids the symbol, the concentrated expression in order to remain spontaneous. This is in contrast to Pavese who purposes to present, but not to select or interpret, reality. Mysticism allows Whitman to glimpse an order by accepting diversity. For Pavese, instead, the order does not exist in itself but is unconsciously contributed by man through myth.

More recently some young critics have tried to bring Pavese more closely to Italian poetry, but still skipping over the hermetics. Beguiled by certain allusions which Massimo Mila, in his introduction to *Lavorare stanca*, makes to a certain Piedmontese dialect poetry and to Costantino Nigra, these critics have been persuaded to add a minor Piedmontese poet to the scene, Guido Gozzano, who is, however, the greatest among the *crepuscolari* poets. Thereby their intention was not to transform Pavese into a crepuscular poet, but once more to try to find some antecedents, some ancestors for him. In order to explain this enormous equivocation certain facts must be pointed out. Gozzano was reacting to the sensualism and the romanticism of the D'Annunzians. He redimensions, so to speak, their effusions with the view of the prosaic almost colorless life. But the twilight poets have a place in Italian literature above all for the reason that they introduced a new language, stripped, miniscule, and prepared the way for the futurists. Now Pavese also was reacting against a poetics, against the hermetic "word."

Having noted the parallel the critics girded themselves to find Gozzanian influences in the poetry of *Lavorare stanca*. They paused to dwell above all on the language and the narrative technique adopted by the poets.

The difference between the crepuscular poets and Pavese should seem obvious. Here is Gozzano:

> M'era più dolce starmene in cucina
> tra le stoviglie a vividi colori;
> tu tacevi, tacevo, Signorina;
> godevo quel silenzio e quegli odori
> tanto tanto per me consolatori,
> di basilico d'aglio di cedrina...[9]
> (It was nicer to stay in the kitchen,
> among the bright-colored crockery;
> you were silent, I was silent, *Signorina*;
> I enjoyed the silence, and those smells
> of basil, garlic, and lemon-scented verbena,
> so comforting to me.)

Pavese:

> Stupefatto del mondo mi giunse un'età
> che tiravo dei pugni nell'aria e piangevo da solo.
> Ascoltare i discorsi d'uomini e donne
> non sapendo rispondere e poca allegria.[10]
> (Stupefied by the world I arrived at an age,
> where I beat my fists against the air and cried alone.
> To listen to the utterances of men and women
> not knowing how to answer and little happiness).

Gozzano describes trite non-"poetic" situations with a simple language non-literary and non-rhetorical. The tone is lightly ironical, the inflection is provincial rather than urban. Pavese instead,

---

[9] *Lirica del Novecento*, edited by Luciano Anceschi and Sergio Antonielli (Florence: Vallecchi Ed., 1963) 14-28.
[10] *Poesie*, 9.

starts out from the origins, adopting a jargon directly derived from spoken speech. In the above quotation he adopts syntax, rhythm, expressions in dialect, just as writers had done in America and Sicilian regionalists in Italy. Whereas Gozzano made a more realistic version of the ideals of his time, Pavese situated his poems in an ambience where culture did not exist at all.

We come, finally, to the technical narrative. In "La signorina Felicita" (Miss Felicity), the "I" who tells the story represents the poet. In Pavese's poems events are dramatized. Even the "I" becomes an autonomous person, a spectator presented objectively.

The comparison either with *Leaves of Grass* or with "La signorina Felicita" is an erroneous and unfruitful one especially if one begins with the image-narrative. The reason for this is simple: neither Whitman, nor Gozzano construct a reality. They express themselves in lyric forms essentially. *Lavorare stanca*, instead, must be compared with dramatic forms, like the epic and the theatre, with works, i.e. with characters who act in the frame of an invented reality. Homer and the Elizabethans.[11]

---

[11] In note 51 of his essay, "Myth and De-Mythification of Pavese's Art," Rimanelli makes reference to his unpublished book and to subsequent works on Pavese that promote similar ideas and that reaffirm the Piedmontese writer's importance in the contemporary Italian literary landscape: "This essay constitutes a part of a book of mine called *Pavese's Journey*, written in 1965, yet never published. Armanda Guiducci's book [*Il mito Pavese*] proves that certain ideas of mine about Pavese's art are still of some usefulness. I'm glad, however, that books like Professor Heiney's *Three Italian Novelists*, which deals at great length with Pavese's life and art; and Professor Biasin's very recent *The Smile of the Gods* [Cornell University Press, 1968], which is a serious study of Cesare Pavese's works, came to the fore in recent months to reaffirm, once again, the compelling importance of one of the most difficult, yet dearest, Italian contemporary writers" (39).

PART TWO

PROSE
(1938 - 1950)

Chapter V

THE EARLY NOVELS

1. TRANSITION

There is a similarity of development and theme between Pavese's writings in prose and his poetry. In *Lavorare stanca* the epic-narrative language constitutes an integral part of the mythic representation. Now Pavese uses calculated words which suggest a reality. Obviously here it is no longer a question of the concentrated and metaphorical language of the poems because "raccontare è come ballare" (story-telling is like dancing),[1] and prose-writing above all signifies the clear and direct development of ideas. Pavese, however, attempted the new genre, prose, above all in order to renew his fundamental theme and to situate it in larger range of interests. The first short stories were a reaction to the subjectivism of the last poems.

This establishes the fact that he did not leap into the new experience with closed eyes. On the contrary, he came to it through deliberation and through considerations related to his *mestiere* (craft). For Pavese, writing was a craft (Eliot also calls it a *métier*). And this craft requires meditation and self-analysis. Already in 1934, in fact, he had noticed that the poems poured out from him almost already formed, because of the mechanical character with which he employed the expressive means which, now, had been reduced to awareness. He realized that if, on the one hand, his images had become increasingly more complicated, on the other he could no longer avoid falling into virtuoso feats that displeased him. The years 1935-1936 marked a turning-point in his whole life. It is significant that he began to write the *Diario* precisely in this period. The youthful optimism vanished. Pavese fell back upon

---

[1] *La letteratura americana e altri saggi*, 325.

himself and now he tried to objectify his emotions. The crisis that he underwent first during his political banishment and later in Turin, led him to an esthetic and moral reconsideration which compelled him to renew his poetics. He convinced himself that the *imagine-racconto,* after all, is not fully justified whereas with a straight short story "you can express the absurd, ingenuous, mythical outpourings that cunningly interpret reality."[2]

In 1940 he realized that *Lavorare stanca* perhaps possessed an organic unity. His judgment was positive, but now the transition between poetry and prose had already taken place by way of his short stories. In fact his first story-telling experiments took place between 1936, the year of the crisis, and 1938, the year in which he wrote *Il carcere* (The Political Prisoner). It was in 1936, however, that he noted in his *Diario*:

> There is not only a similarity but an actual parallel between a life given over to the voluptuousness and the writing of little isolated poems, one every so often, with nothing to link them together. It becomes a habit to live by fits and starts, without development and without principles. The lesson is this: to build in art; or build in life, lavish sensuousness from art, as from life; exist tragically. (35)

By way of this analysis, in short, Pavese becomes aware that he had not shaken off all his hedonism. Pessimistically, he concludes that poetry has already declined into an otiose and empty literary game. Thereupon the short stories begin to come to birth in him as experimentations with a new style. They are important because they lead to the novels and to his maturity as a narrator of the subsequent decade. The posthumous collections in the volume *Notte di festa* were never published by Pavese because his attitude toward them was marked by an extreme critical schizophrenia, so to speak. Nevertheless in them he experimented with characters and situations that later were to find a justification in the works

---

[2] *The Burning Brand,* 81.

that were to follow. "Terra d'esilio" (Land of Exile), for example, the "Intruso" (The Intruder), "Viaggio di nozze" (Wedding Journey) and "Suicidi" (Suicides) already contain the kernel of typically Pavesian themes: solitude, political banishment, incommunicability. But the short stories are primarily the first steps to *Il carcere*, *Paesi tuoi*, *La bella estate* and *La spiaggia* which form the quartet of the early novels and include the period that goes from 1935 to 1941.

2. *IL CARCERE*

The style of these first novels is naturalistic, and the characters move in precise, carefully detailed atmospheres, in which they are defined not by way of a psychological development but through confrontations with situations deliberately invented by the author. Many critics saw in these novels the influence of certain American writers, and Pavese himself with his essay "Ieri e oggi" (Yesterday and Today)[3] explains what the discovery of American culture meant to him: liberation, in other words, from the spiritual stasis in which fascist art blissfully wallowed. This art was a retreat to old formulas and theses, whereas its American counterpart strained for a definition of man in his relation to nature. Nevertheless Pavese absorbed the American lesson in order to give it a development that was entirely personal. For example, he does not employ the interior monologue to explain the motivations of his characters, but their relationship to events and environments. If these novels are lacking in plot and organic structure in the classic sense (for which the critics reproached him) it is because the nineteenth century art of the *Bildungsroman* was replaced by essayistic notations and by symbol. It is not the meaning of man in his ideological, political and economic aspect that interests Pavese but man *sub specie aeternitatis*, a dimension, that defines him in the totality of being.

The novel *Il carcere*, written in 1938 and published eleven years later together with *La casa in collina* in the volume *Prima che il gallo*

---

[3] *La letteratura americana e altri saggi*, 193.

canti (Before the Cock Crows), misled many critics. In England it was published under the title *The Political Prisoner*. But it is not a political novel, nor one of social protest against a regime. It contains only one allusion to politics: "Here's your gain then! Excuse me engineer, but you were a damn fool. One doesn't discuss with the government."[4] Instead, it is a novel of solitude, as are for that matter *La bella estate* and *La spiaggia*. Politics is not the problem of the political exile Stefano. The atmosphere of political banishment is evoked again only by the occasional visits of the police inspector and later by the anarchist who is separated from the rest of the prisoners in another part of the village.

The novel revolves around the different meaning that solitude and incommunicability have for the engineer from northern Italy, confined as a political prisoner in the south. After being released from prison, Stefano in the beginning is almost happy to be interned in that unknown town: at least he can stay in the open air and he is allowed to move around. Even if the town is small and nothing very much ever happens in it, at least he can meet people and chat with them. In fact by visiting the tavern, he can actually have contacts with people. People are the same in all the world. But all this is illusory. He is restless because the town is not his, it does not belong to him. At first his solitude is of a physical character which, little by little, becomes metaphysical. This town is nothing more than another prison. In fact the surrounding hills suggest three iron walls to him, and the fourth is formed by the "useless sea." Moreover, living with the idea that he could be transferred to a different town from one moment to the other, and even be returned to prison, he never unpacks his suitcase. He is in a state of alert and, in practice, the prison is within him. His restlessness gives a pungent feeling to his solitude but the latter, before all else, is caused by the lack of real bonds with the landscape which appears to him like "a den of sordid people" (13). The sea, finally, which is the fourth wall of the cell, acts as a catharsis within him. Thus he goes swimming in it, alone, as if to liberate him-

---

4 *Romanzi*, vol. 1, 24.

self from a burden. The burden of being a stranger in the environment and in life, of having no relationships with the world.

The awareness of his solitude - that jail from which he cannot manage to escape which is one's own "I" is given to him by Elena a woman from another town, the landlady's daughter, with whom he gets involved. She is older than him, and married to a soldier from whom she is separated. But Elena does not bring Stefano into a meaningful relationship with the town, with the world from which he is separated, but at best another solitude. And the two solitudes, in the fleeting, wordless intercourses in the morning never become reality, i.e. freedom. Stefano responds evasively to the woman's tenderness, telling her that he is "a savage type" (36). And this because the woman does not incarnate passion, or imagination, but passivity. Concia, instead, the feral little servant girl whom he had seen "roam around in town—by herself—with a springing and restrained step almost like an impertinent dance" (14), represents a symbol, an ideal for him. She forms part of the "grey and hostile" (14) ambience of the town, but she represents the most primitive and sensual part of this town - her color is red not gray - this is why she stirs his blood and this is why, with his reveries, he identifies her with the scarlet geraniums of the window-sill of the house and with the clay water-jars which give the water a taste of earth. The thought of Concia annihilates, at moments, his solitude, i.e. the present. This woman is another personification of the "selvaggio," only now the savage is elusive and unreachable. Stefano is a city-man, not a countryman. Further, his fault is that he cannot assimilate. Nevertheless even when Stefano found out that Concia was a "she-goat, ready for all he-goats" (31) and that she had had a daughter from an old man and that the boys ran after her, his imagination does not surrender. It does not surrender because the present is torment, or indifference, or responsibility, but not mystery. Elena, with less tenderness, with her body and with her desire to find escape in love, instead, is entirely in the present and this may explain why Stefano would always like to put on the light when he must make love with her.

For the political exile the obsession with the present is transformed into a necessity to isolate it, hence to liberate oneself from it after having understood it. By so doing he establishes a bond with the past. But which bond? Memory is set in motion, one day, when he returns from a visit to Giannino's parents, when he recalls the villas of his childhood in association with the objects in the room and the walls. Here, however, remembrance does not function as in Proust. Pavese does not try to reimmerse himself in the past in order to escape the present which for Proust is illness and for Pavese banishment to a town in Southern Italy. Pavese tries simply to isolate the past in order to be able to isolate the present, in short, in order to be able to achieve a continuity through which objective reality could be abolished. Political banishment, therefore, has an ambivalent meaning. Stefano is a stranger in town, but he cannot leave it without the permission of the police inspector. On the other hand, he suffers, because he is unable to choose and to keep custody over his solitude which would constitute a means for achieving self-mastery. Confinement is a kind of real jail also for the reason that he is not free to be alone. Note the observation: "The door was open. This also recalled the cell: whoever put in an appearance could come in and talk to him. Elena, the goatherd, the water-boy and Giannino could walk in like so many jailers" (57).

One of the key themes of this book is the absence of charity towards others for the sake of gratifying selfish individualism. Lorenzo Mondo acutely observes that Stefano's desire for Concia is nothing else but the denial of charity with respect to Giannino, the anarchist, and to Elena.[5] For at the end of his exile, Stefano will bring his jail with him, even if he has had a presentiment that Giannino would have lived with him as a remembrance, "provisional and pathetic like all remembrances."[6] In fact the entrance of Giannino in the novel, like that of the anarchist, as well as the epi-

---

[5] Lorenzo Mondo, *Cesare Pavese*, 46.
[6] *Romanzi*, 36.

sodes connected with them, are directives leading to this conclusion.

Giannino is a native of the town and he is supposed to get married in order to please his parents, but he feels like an exile in this town. Hence he allows himself escapades in the city, and one day he is arrested for rape of a minor. Stefano and Giannino used to see each other every day. Yet when Stefano learns about his arrest, he feels no emotion, or compassion, also because the other knew about his relation with Elena. Thus Stefano rationalizes that with Giannino "vanishes the last obstacle to solitude in the truest sense" (67). But after a brief period of disorientation he becomes aware of the fact that maybe the physical suffering of being in a cell is much more real and more human than his own suffering. Now that Giannino is gone he feels closer to him, now that he no longer determines his coming and goings, now that he is no longer a kind of jailer.

The same situation is repeated more or less with respect to the anarchist. Stefano receives his note but does nothing to meet him, even though "he would like to give him the comfort of feeling that he is not abandoned" (89). He does not meet him because both Giannino and the anarchist—insofar as they are separated from him—are memory's points of reference which alleviate solitude without destroying it. And the episode with the prostitute whom the men in the tavern import into the village is another confirmation of Stefano's solitary schizophrenia, not a proof of his charity or understanding. He pays her, in fact, and then doesn't touch her. This brings him to the rationalization that "a triple suffices in order to be alone: abstinence" (88). This signifies that solitude is nothing else but distance, detachment. And it is precisely of this type of solitude that Stefano is most guilty, because in this sense solitude is negation, refusal, another form of betrayal toward man the comrade.

Certain pages of the diary, written before the novels, lead to the supposition that Pavese was in search of a more open and humble contact with the world, that is to say of a more spontaneous love in the context of human solidarity. He writes: "Only charity is respectable. Christ and Dostoievsky."[7] By interpreting *Il carcere*, i.e. by using the diary as a corollary, as has been done, critics may have accidentally stumbled upon the truth. But by so doing they also stumbled upon moralism, and moralism is another limitation. Actually, even more simply, it could be said that with *Il carcere* Pavese went beyond limitations and presented a universal problem: exile purely and simply symbolizes life.

Beyond this the story follows the naturalistic vein as has already been pointed out, in the sense that Stefano poses and solves problems. But caution is quite in order here. Here Pavese makes some strange leaps. Stylistically he employs unusual sentences, while the adjectives, as he uses them, give a new sense to the words. Here are some examples: "Motionless street," "Giannino of the good pipe," "ante-lucem walk," "deadened countryside," "useless petticoat." In practice, Pavese is transporting the *fantastic relation* of the poems to the prose. If in the poems and in the prose he transforms the landscape into myth, and at the same time inserts the character into an order of things, into a cosmos of hills, vineyards etc., here the *fantastic relation* is already a story, the external and internal reality of man. The use of these cadences belongs to classicism. In fact, the epithets in the *Iliad* almost always have the same function. When Homer says, "Hector of the shining helmet," or "Achilles, tamer of horses," he not only describes but places the character in a relation to a series of values. Now Pavese employs the simile of comparison not so much for the rhetorical meaning that it can suggest, as for the purpose of conferring a more intimate meaning upon it, "of constituitive parts of a totalitarian fantastic reality, whose meaning would consist in their relation."[8]

3. *PAESI TUOI*

Il carcere is a book dealing with uprootedness, subjectivity and inner confusion. It still lives in the spellbound atmosphere of the poem "Mito" when "we awaken one morning and the summer is

---

[7] *The Burning Brand*, 94.
[8] *Poesie*, 134.

dead, and in the eyes splenders still riot as yesterday,"[9] when, as in "Lo steddazzu," "the slowness of the hour is merciless to one who no longer waits for something" (134). For Pavese *Il carcere* constitutes an experience which must be brought to a close. He knows that he must get fresh strength, and the only valid way to do this is to return to the myths of his native earth, in order to live the "drama of a man in his own environment."[10] Thus was born *Paesi tuoi*, which is a singular, violent novel, suffused with sensuality, remade almost according to the exact measure of "Dio-caprone."

Here even the plot, albeit simple, is more adventurous, that is to say cluttered with events. Pavese, as a writer who tells the stories of other people, vanishes and he introduces the narrator, Berto, a Turin mechanic who works in the countryside for the family of a man named Talino, whom he met in prison and who is half-mad. The book opens with the pair just at the moment of their release from jail. Talino proposes to Berto that he come along with him to Monticello. But Berto, who knows Talino to be a sly and cunning fellow, tells him to wait for him at the station while he takes a quick look around the town. In fact Berto has no intention at all to come back. But the city fills him with disgust. He goes to see his best friend. Instead of finding the friend, who is in prison, he finds his mistress. He makes love with her, after which he once again roams the streets of this city which has nothing to offer him. He goes back to the station and Talino is still there, waiting for him. They leave for the countryside together. Berto, however, quickly realizes that the work which Talino has offered him is only a cover-up for something else. Actually Talino needs a witness who could protect him from his father's wrath. Talino had been sent to jail for having set fire to the cow-shed of a neighbor. Even in this case Berto is to function as a screen.

Although everybody expects the neighbor to revenge himself, nothing happens. Finally Berto realizes that Gisella, with whom

---

[9] *Poesie edite e inedite*, 127.
[10] *The Burning Brand*, 158.

he makes love, has had incestuous relations with her brother. The physical sign of Talino's violence is a scar which the girl carries on her belly. The story reaches its tragic climax when, one morning, Gisella refuses to give the water-bucket to her brother saying that if he drank from it he would pollute the water for the others. Talino, gripped by a sudden fury, slashes her throat with the hay-fork. Gisella dies and Talino runs away. The women do not seem very concerned or sorry about this sudden and violent death. Indeed, the father had a presentiment of it, and now that the inevitable has occurred, it is already accepted as a matter of fact. Even the *carabinieri* do not bother to pursue Talino, and when the latter returns he is seen going off with his father towards the stubble-field. Berto plans to return to the city.

When this novel was first published, much criticism was expended on it, and many — especially the fascists — saw in Pavese's stylistic orientation a refusal of the Italian literary tradition in favor of current American writing. But for the critic Emilio Cecchi the book constituted a new and vital voice.[11] What concerns us here, however, is not the evaluation of an old polemic, but to establish a continuity between Pavese's early novels and his poems. It is a continuity of genre, of course, not of content. Under certain aspects, especially in this book, there is the rendering in prose of certain poems. Pavese plays with the atmospheres, while the character consciously or unconsciously exists in a state of interpenetration with the spirit of nature itself and of the landscape. If in "Dio-Caprone" the boy visits the countryside in the summertime, and immerses himself in that landscape, perceiving its tremors and its drama, Berto is no different than the boy, although he is an adult. The earth has the color of "burnt faces"[12] in "Dio-Caprone," and the rustics seemed to be one with the earth. In *Paesi tuoi* the feet of the sisters seem "clods of earth"[13] and the bonfires of the poem, that grass fire, are the same ones that Berto sees in

---

[11] Emilio Cecchi, in *La nuova antologia.* Florence (March, 1942).
[12] *Poesie*, 13.
[13] *Romanzi*, vol. I., 140.

the distance. For the boy of the poem "the countryside is a land of green mysteries,"[14] but sensual. It is likewise so for Berto who calls the hills "breasts" and to whom the smell of hay, which is the very smell of the countryside in the summer, recalls the smell of woman.

Berto and Talino immerse themselves in the countryside in a period of full solstice, in the month of June which is harvest and threshing time, a time therefore of intense heat. In the poem the bitches howl under the moon because they have heard the he-goat who stomps and leaps on the crest of the hills. Here the animals "sense" that Talino has returned and, in the evening, the bitches begin to bay, biting their ropes.[15] Talino, then, "locked with his eyes in such a way that he too looked like a he-goat" (136). The sultry, sensual atmosphere is intensified by the moon which has power over the animals and which seems to exert an influence even over Talino. There was a moon on the night that he set fire to the barn, before he was sentenced to prison. In "Dio-Caprone" the bitches in heat go alone at night behind the woods and the he-goat runs to find them. "But as soon as the moon rises, he draws himself erect and disembowels them."[16] A few nights before Talino "disembowels" Gisella with the hay-fork, a she-goat broke loose and ran towards the stubble-field, in the canebrake. When she was found, she no longer had any milk. It had been sucked out of her by a grass-snake. Berto makes love with Gisella on this very spot. Thus Pavese in the story repeats the parallel between men and beasts which he had already established in the poem. And if in this case Talino is the he-goat, he lives by instinct, like the beasts.

It is no accident that Pavese places Gisella's murder at the climax of the threshing season. Reaping and the whole harvest are a rite. Gisella's murder is like the consecration of the rite. As is known, goats are sacrificed during the harvest in certain primitive

---

14 *Poesie edite e inedite*, 50.
15 *Romanzi*, vol. I, 118.
16 *Poesie edite e inedite*, 50.

societies.[17] The she-goat lost in the stubble-field where she is drained of her milk by the grass-snake on the very spot where Gisella makes love with Berto, is an extension of Gisella's spirit. Gisella, moreover, is also identified with trees. At first the identification is with an apple-tree, and Berto, after eating its fruit, says they have a "sour" taste.[18] Later, she is identified with a fig-tree that no longer yields fruit. Talino knows about the affair between Gisella and Berto, and now, for him, his sister is sterile, like the she-goat.

Other parallels can be found. Gisella is a sensual girl. Her blood wets the wheat, as though it should fertilize, fructify the earth. For Talino, therefore, her death has a two-fold value: it is a sacrifice—unconscious and at the same time communal—and a vendetta—conscious and personal. The last lines of "Dio-Caprone" sound like a commentary on *Paesi tuoi*:

> Because, when a beast doesn't know work
> And keeps himself only for studding, he likes to destroy.[19]

In practice Pavese, with this book, wished to exhaust the nightmare, the oppression, and the magic spell of his countryside. It was an experience that pressed on his blood. The symbols that he employed, although still in a manner that was crude from a literary point of view were to serve him as a framework to the novels and poems of the future. To cite only a fortuitous example, consider the poems of *La terra e la morte* where the symbol becomes metaphor ("... you are like the voices/ of the earth—the splash of the bucket in the well, / the song of the fire, / the fall of an apple [168]). Consider, also, the cremation of Santa in *La luna e i falò* , which is also a symbol but no longer in relation to the landscape as occurs with the symbols of *Paesi tuoi* but which are to be

---

[17] J.G. Frazer, *The Golden Bough*, abridged edition (London: Macmillan, 1960) 564.
[18] *Romanzi*, vol.1, 125.
[19] *Poesie edite e inedite*, 51.

interpreted, perhaps, as the end of a landowning class, offered in the last bonfire as an act of propitiation to a new generation.

4. *LA BELLA ESTATE*

La bella estate is already a new genre because in it Pavese faces the drama of life or its entities in terms of the daily life. Perhaps it is Pavese's most pessimistic book. Now, however, the theme of solitude is posed in relation to the problem of maturity. The characters are not intellectualized, they express their humanity with the most direct and bare frankness. Ginia comes towards us with spontaneity and goodness. Her end, with the end of summer, suggests human tenderness.

This Turin girl works in an atelier; she is care-free and trustful. She is not simple-minded but she believes in others and believes in herself. She and her friends are always roaming about and their youth is prolonged and care-free as though it were permanent summer. She has faith in the future, but she guards over her hopes in secret. She lives with a brother and takes care of the house. She even manages to enjoy some brief moments of solitude. During these moments she indulges in day dreaming, open-eyed, and begins to differentiate herself from her companions. She is not different from them, but perhaps she understands more than they do. At least, that's what she believes. But one day when she learns that their friend Rosa has a lover, this knowledge shakes her and annoys her. She who still lives in a state of trepidation and of virginal expectancy on the way to becoming a woman, in practice, has not yet had an encounter with adult life. She becomes a friend of Amelia, an artist's model, out of an unconfessed desire to break with adolescence. Amelia introduces her to Guido. But the new world which she entered disorients her. Nudity terrorizes her. To pose for a painter signifies to submit to scrutiny and hence no longer to be herself, to lose her identity. In short, to become an object. And "even Amelia by shaming herself in that way became another."[20] In the beginning she betrays the same modesty with

---

[20] *Romanzi*, vol. I, 203.

regard to nudity even with Guido, whose lover she becomes. She does not want to be observed. Then she overcomes her shyness and "now that she and Guido had seen themselves nude, everything looked different to her" (253). Nevertheless the most difficult trial that she must undergo occurs when Guido hires a model in order to paint nudes. In order not to lose him she agrees to pose on condition that no stranger is to see her. Instead, Rodriguez emerges from behind a curtain. Ginia dresses and runs away. Now she realizes that the others were making fun of her, pulling her leg. Her naïve attempt which was to represent entry into the adult world, a rite of initiation, is transformed into a sacrifice. Now Ginia knows that she is truly alone, but she also knows that she cannot turn back. Maturity is cynicism and corruption. One day she learns that Amelia has contracted syphilis… from another woman. And when Amelia kisses her on the mouth, almost casually, Ginia is afraid that she too is infected. Later, after the end of the affair with Guido, Ginia is ready to accept everything, even Amelia. In fact she abandons herself to her. The novel ends thus: "Let's go where you please… You lead me" (263).

The novel had opened on a happy note: "At that time it was always a feast. It was enough to leave the house and to cross the street, in order to become like lunatics, and everything was so beautiful, especially at night, when coming back, dead tired we believed still that something might happen" (187). And the novel ends, precisely because everything has happened. Ginia is presented as one who accepts life and dreams of life. She hopes to enjoy unforgettable hours with Guido. Instead Guido, Amelia, Rodriguez, adult life, in short, have no dreams. And innocence is not preserved where sex, or love, becomes vice. Amelia, for example, has something animal-like and libidinous in her that goes against nature. She is even worse than Guido. Later, when she is roaming about the city all alone, amid the mud and the snow, the fragrance of the summer nights overwhelms her. She would like to be in a virginal state all over again. "The seasons are always there," she says (262). But she must immediately withdraw into herself. "I'm old, that's what it is. All the beautiful things are over with" (263).

Maturity, however, signifies acceptance. So, resigned, she accepts everything that has happened and all that which will happen. In short she has become an adult.

La bella estate is a novel about the city, and in the city nobody is saved. Only Guido, perhaps, has something in himself which gives him strength and renews him. "I only feel good when I'm on the crest of a hill," he says (236). If for Ginia maturity is the beginning of a sterile existence, for Guido to paint "a woman stretched and with breasts in the sun" (256), symbolizing the painting of a hill always means retaining a contact with his sacred world, even if only illusorily. But the irony is that he, too, is alone.

This novel is the last one that Pavese wrote in the third person. He was to return to the subject of the city, and more or less with the same themes, with *Tra donne sole*. Yet *La bella estate* is a dense, fluent story. The language is clear and evocative. The didactic description is limited, and the narration hinges on the dialogue. Pavese had taken a great stride forward from the times in which he wrote *Il carcere*. Here the characters already move in a climate that smacks of the theatre. And Pavese now specifically set his sights on the novel as theatre.

5. *LA SPIAGGIA*

Pavese is very severe in his judgment of *La spiaggia* which is the last of his early novels. For him the experience of writing it had been a valid one only because it constituted "a frank search for a style."[21] Yet *La spiaggia* is important not only for its style but because, in embryo, it contains all the themes of his early fictions (city-countryside, solitude etc.), and certain others which he was to develop later (adolescence, return).

The story is static. Indeed it could be defined as a series of conversations by the sea. The chief protagonist of the novel is the sea-shore because it symbolizes a way of life, a state of mind, the

---

[21] *La letteratura americana e altri saggi*, 248.

monotonous coming and going of the bathing season and the repeated efforts to overcome boredom. The human protagonists are Doro and Clelia, husband and wife; the narrator who is a 30-year old professor, a friend of Doro; young Berti. Berti is always sad and desperately enamored of Clelia. Another character is the vain and entertaining Guido, who is a friend both of Doro and Clelia.

Life on the beach is insipid. Yet it conceals a tension, an anxiety. The constant flux of the sea, its vacuous rhythm, and the vacuousness that it gives to the futile gestures and the many words of the characters, has a secret voice for each of the characters. The restlessness of the sea reveals and explains their own restlessness. The narrator, for example, feels a physical discomfort in being on the beach. Here, on the beach he is unusually nervous and even overly self-conscious. He says: "One speaks with a strange caution when one is semi-nude: words don't have the same ring, and sometimes one keeps silent and it seems as though the silence, by itself, discloses ambiguous words."[22] And Clelia, who at home frequently repeats that she is bored, near the sea can feel herself surprisingly alone, or better, as part of the landscape, merged with it. The narrator observes that Clelia had an ecstatic way of enjoying the sun - stretched out on the rock, of merging with the rock and of flattening herself against it, facing the sky (287). Doro, instead, goes to the beach above all for those stupid pictures that he painted, to no avail (308). He paints from nature but—this is an interesting detail—he does it for distractions sake, he is not really involved. Doro is transplanted in his wife's milieu in Genoa, and he goes to Turin in order to look up his professor friend, the narrator, with whom he takes a trip to the places of their childhood, the Langhe, since he is still obsessed with the idea of returning there. In their student-days they had discovered the hills by roaming through them and now, as adults, they try to recreate that vanished time. They wander through the fields for a whole night, drunk and singing, and in the morning they leave for the Riviera where Doro has a villa. The narrator knows that his friend is rest-

---

[22] *Romanzi*, vol. I, 287.

less. He attributes the cause to domestic tensions. But after questioning the pair, separately, he discovers nothing abnormal in their relation. Clelia tells him: "We can't make peace because we've never quarreled" (282). The narrative proceeds without any jolts and events of any deep significance. Guido tries to paint, the narrator and Clelia lie in the sun on the beach. At night they go dancing. At a certain moment, the narrator meets a former student and introduces him to his friends. But this youth is overly sensitive and peevish. He ends up by falling in love with Clelia and, one night, he behaves foolishly. The book ends with Clelia pregnant. She and Doro cut short their vacation and return to the city.

What is important in this book is not only the style, as has been said, but the themes that are glimpsed and the almost casual study of the characters.

The sea, for example, is an indispensible factor in order to define Clelia. Even when she is swimming in the sea by herself, Clelia is no longer alone, she is assimilated by the sea. Solitude, if ever, is others company. For example, she and her husband have nothing to say to each other. And Doro's problem is that, even though he is not unhappy, he has nothing to say to her. They are two sensibilities that do not meet. The sea which is a myth for Clelia, on the other hand, bores Doro. The hills of his childhood are a myth for Doro. In fact he tries to explain their meaning for him to his wife, but Clelia merely wants to sleep. If, as Guido observes, the sea represents Clelia's infidelity to all of them (288), the hill, the fear of growing old and of losing his hearing, the deep nostalgia to change his status, that is, to become a boy once more and to be only a painter if he could, almost make a defeated person of Doro, one who hides a subtle sorrow behind the mask of one who has arrived and is self-sufficient. At first sight paternity presents itself to Doro as a conquest of his wife: he brings her back to the city to wrest her away from the sea. For Clelia, instead, maternity constitutes a loss: in fact, this will be the last summer she enjoys as a girl. Thereafter returning to the sea will be something different. The myth is over, and in the last analysis the child will not even solve Doro's problem, his need for communication and to live intensely. Clelia was never his lover in a complete sense and, now having become a mother, she will certainly no longer be. Before leaving he says to the narrator: "Clelia is already resigned... She makes me furious when she's resigned" (323).

The other characters, the narrator, Guido, and Berti, are counterparts to Clelia and Doro. Berti is the most intense of the three. He is the adolescent on the threshold of manhood, who looks at the adult world with arrogance and therefore with naivete. The figure of the narrator must also be considered. His problem is not dissimilar from Doro's. He returns to the town of his childhood with his friend not because he feels such a need within himself, but just to please Doro. Even when he gets drunk, he does not let himself go. The narrator also, like Doro, lives a de-mythified life. At bottom the two, even though they were together and re-evoking their childhood, did not empathically recognize each other. The sea-shore, a point of fact, had a voice for all the characters of the novel — if we exclude Guido — who perhaps does not hear it.

From the point of view of technique Pavese tried to transform biography into a novel. The narration is objective, but the "I" who narrates already knows the events that are destined to happen. The important fact is that the narrator does not limit himself to observing the others, he too is a character.

6. CONCLUSION

Pavese wrote these four novels between 1938 and 1941. They are marked by a unity of themes which we will later find, formulated with greater precision, in all the other works. An interval of five years falls between *La spiaggia* and *Il compagno* during which Pavese no longer wrote novels, concentrating, instead, on the short stories of *Feria d'agosto* and in the *Dialoghi con Leucò*.

In practice Pavese, with these four novels, had aimed to exhaust in prose all the motifs already contained in *Lavorare stanca*. The man of "Lo steddazzu" who slowly lights his pipe and prepares to live another monotonous day is Stefano of *Il carcere*, the end of adolescence. The sea is the dimension boredom and the present, which is dismay and separation. Separation as in *La spiaggia*, and the conflict of the characters between an immanent world and a mythic world, rationality and objectivity and fantasy and childhood. Nostalgia is a dominant theme. But nostalgia comes only to him who has already lived. In *La bella estate*, for example, there comes the day when Ginia poses nude for the painter. In *Paesi tuoi*, on the other hand, it is Berto who discovers the countryside. The city-countryside theme, however, is a constant one in these novels. They are studies and variations on the poems. For example, *La bella estate* recalls "Due sigarette" as well as "Pensieri di Deola." Before the novels of his maturity, Pavese had need of a third phase that might serve as a counterpoint, not to the thematic line, but to the rhythm and the expressive manner, in his poems as well as his prose. Thus *Feria d'agosto* was born as an essay and as a clarification of themes and *Dialoghi con Leucò* as a rhythmic and intellectual rendering of these themes. Pavese had come face to face with destiny.

Chapter VI

THE WORLD OF MYTH

1. THE TERROR OF HISTORY

Elsewhere it has already been pointed out how a continuity of thematic development exists in Pavese's work. It suggests a constant process of maturation and intellectual realization, but it also gives moments of an intense dramatic character to its development.

Both the poetry of *Lavorare stanca* and the prose of the early novels find their complete fusion of themes and structures in the works that Pavese wrote in the three years 1947-50. But it was the third phase of the Pavesian journey — that of the war and of the years of Serralunga, characterized by the contemplation of the past and by a religious meditation which borders on mysticism — which gives his work its definitive stamp. In short, the years from 1941 to 1946 are extremely important because they allowed the writer to re-evaluate his concept of myth and to make it more precise, as well as to give a new vigor to literary speculations and propositions which already seemed solved and exhausted. *Feria d'agosto* and the *Dialoghi con Leucò*, which are works of this period, do not constitute a new transition of genres and of forms. Nevertheless they are books that are very different from the preceding short stories. Their novelty lies in their uniqueness.

After 1947 the annotations in Pavese's *Diary* assume an existential tone and above all concern Pavese's personal tragedy. In fact, the polemical impulses are ever less frequent as are also those broad discussions which always reveal the thrill of discovery and the writer's emotion. Too busy with the novels and with the act of living itself, Pavese does not willingly theorize. In short the seclusion in Serralunga was a period of incubation, of charging psychical energies which were to find fulfilled expression in the novels, articles, publishing activity etc. of the post-war period. In these years, however, the essential presuppostitions of his poetics were set forth as well as definite themes like the *selvaggio* and *destino*.

The war acted upon Pavese like a catalyst. After the short novel *La spiaggia* his writing became much more minute and subjective. The city, which still exists as a social context in *La bella estate* and *La spiaggia*, rapidly degenerates into chaos as the war moves forward. It loses that temporality which is the characteristic that it has in *Lavorare stanca* as well as in the four early novels. Desperation and death now fill the boredom and the emptiness of the city's limits. On July 10, 1940 Pavese jotted the following in his *Diary*: "This war has produced perhaps the richest crop of treacheries that has ever been born; which indicates a revolutionary climate—a climate, that is, where the initial state of things is gradually changing and the general standard of discernment is beginning to differ from the views of this or that group."[1] It is the terror of history. Pavese after all can choose only his fate as man alone, which later he says is an "art," and he classifies himself among the weak, the contemplative, the humble, the sentimental, the victims, the impassioned, the ingenuous. When, in 1944, he transcribes in the *Diary*, a passage from *The Spirit of Liturgy* by Romano Guardini, the annotation was meant only as a re-confirmation of his meditations of Serralunga, and that is that "in the general sphere of our life definite priority should be given to *being* rather than to *acting*" (259). His ontological view, therefore, both on the plane of spiritual life and of art becomes antithetic to the Christian-Catholic and to the Crocean-historicist conception of Italian literature. Because of the impossibility of establishing an empirical contact with external reality, Pavese accepts archaic spirituality and becomes a primitive.

At this point the book that could best explain Pavese's antihistorical conception is undoubtedly Mircea Eliade's *Le Mythe de l'éternel retour*, published in France by Gallimard in 1949. The letters that he exchanged in that same year with the Sicilian professor Giuseppe Cocchiara reveal that he would have wished to see

---

[1] *The Burning Brand*, 185.

the book translated and published by Einaudi because "it seems most opportune to me amid our rampant historicism."[2] Eliade does nothing else but describe with the thought of a specialist all that which had already been realized in narrative form and lived by Pavese. Eliade underlines that the primary difference between the man of archaic and traditional societies and the man of modern societies, lies in the fact that the former feels himself indissolubly linked to the cosmos and to cosmic cycles, whereas the second insists that he is connected only with history. For archaic man the objects of the external world and human actions do not have an autonomous and intrinsic value. Objects and human actions acquire value, i.e. they become real because they participate in a reality that transcends them.[3] Among so many stones one in some way becomes "sacred," hence immediately saturated with "essence," because it constitutes an hierophany. It resists the notion of time. Its reality lies in its perenniality. In the same way the significance of human actions does not lie in their purely physical aspect, but in their property of repeating a primordial act, a mythical example. Thus the act of eating repeats a eucharistic marriage, and a collective orgy recalls mythical prototypes. In short, for archaic man what is being done has already been done before. His life is a ceaseless repetition of gestures initiated by others. It is from this tendency to be paradigmatic that primitive man derives the feeling that he is real, that is to say in possession of the fullness of his being, to the measure in which he ceases to be himself in order to imitate and repeat the gestures of another. Thus one could say that this primitive ontology has a Platonic structure, and in this case Plato could be regarded as the greatest philosopher of the archaic mentality.

As I have already pointed out in the second chapter of this book, discussing the conception of time and language in Pavese's poetry, an abolition of profane time, of history understood as be-

---

[2] Davide Lajolo, *Il vizio assurdo*, 326.
[3] Mircea Eliade, *Cosmos and History: The Myth of the Eternal Return*, trans. by Willard R. Trask (New York: Harper Torchbooks, 1959) 4.

coming, is implicit in the tendency of archaic man to be archetypical. The person who reproduces the mythic act feels himself
transported to the mythic epoch in which its revelation occurred.
Eliade points out that archaic man endures history with difficulty,
and he makes an effort to abolish it periodically with cyclical returns. In the last analysis his rites conceal, in their depths, the will
to strip value from time and reveal his metaphysical thirst for "being" and the "static." In the Christian tradition, for example, time
is no longer cyclical but it has a linear dimension. A straight line
traces mankind's course from Original Sin to the universal Resur-
rection. Time is "real," that is valid in this moment, because from
the act of Redemption onwards the whole flow of history acquires
a unique value and significance insofar as it is re-connected with
an event of unique character: the Incarnation. Christ died for the
sins of men only once, once and for all time. It is not an event that
is repeatable. Therefore the destiny of mankind and the destiny of
every individual evolve in a concrete and irreplaceable sequence
of time, namely that of history and of life (143).[4] Nevertheless in
contemporary thought itself there is noticeable a constant tendency to return to cyclical theories. In political economy there is a
tendency to rehabilitate the notions of cycle, fluctuation periodic
oscillation. Nietzsche revived the myth of eternal recurrence in
philosophy. Spengler and Toynbee, in their philosophies of history, are concerned with the problem of periodicity. In addition, a
great re-flowering of "mythographic" literature has been in process for two decades now, especially among Anglo-Saxon and
Germanic peoples (146).[5] All this signifies that attempts are still
being made to give a trans-historical explanation to historical
events, for which reason we again find ourselves in pre-Hegelian

---

[4] For the development of this concept Eliade quotes also Henri-Charles Puech,
"La Gnose et le temps," *Eranos-Jahrbuch*, XX (Zurich, 1951) 70 and, also by Henri-
Charles Puech, "Temps, histoire et mythe dans le christianisme des premiers
siecles" in *Proceedings of the VIIth Congress for History of Religion* (Amsterdam,
1951) 33-52.
[5] See also A. Rey, *Le retour eternel et la philosophie de la physique* (Paris, 1927); Arnold J. Toynbee, *A Study of History*, III (London, 1934).

positions, in short we are back to Vico. The validity of historicist solutions from Hegel to Croce, from Marx to existentialism, through which a value is conferred upon the historical event in itself and for itself, is again brought into question.

Historicism, after all, remains the philosophy of our century. This is a position accepted by the majority of our thinkers who define man as a "historical being." Nevertheless not a few artists of our time have produced works permeated with nostalgia for the myth of the eternal return (consider Thomas Mann) and in the last analysis for the abolition of time (Faulkner: *Absalom! Absalom!*). They belong to the band of "Mythopeics," whom Thomas Mann described as living a life "between question marks." But they are also the most modern in the Jungian sense, in the sense, namely that by refusing the compromise with historical conditions they have given the possibility of projecting themselves beyond history. This is their besetting sin, but also their modernity.[6]

Now the charge that Pavese is a decadent stems from his anti-historicity.[7] Alberto Moravia's condemnation of Pavese is proper only from the point of view of Moravia, from that of a writer rooted in the historicist position. But it does not touch Pavese because, as we have seen, he is rooted in the other philosophical position. The two writers do not meet because they do not speak the same language. The terror of history is *hic et nunc*. Only one possibility is left to modern man, that of choosing how to be, which is his freedom, and his responsibility. Pavese went towards his destiny with full consciousness.

2. *FERIA D'AGOSTO*

If in his stories written before the war, Pavese experimented above all with the third person (born of his need to objectify), and paid much more attention to the development of events and the organic progression of the narration, now he submerges himself completely into the first person (born of his need to subjectify),

---

[6] C. G. Jung, *Modern Man in Search of a Soul* (New York: Harvest Books, 1960) 198.
[7] Alberto Moravia, *L'uomo come fine*, 70.

which is also a meditative withdrawal into himself and a synthesis. That measure of inwardness and of concentration, for example, that ecstasy of remembrance which in *Feria d'agosto* transforms even the most apparently theoretical and discursive pages into a fantastic tale, into an event narrated by way of intellectual forms and passages, are completely lacking in the stories written between 1938 and 1941. Now Pavese aims to write without having to use a character for the purpose of investigating effects, but for the construction of a totality, of an idea, of a meaning. The reality that is recounted here will be the same even if it must be drawn from pre-Homeric myths. It is also for this reason, then, in addition to the most superficial stylistic correspondences — such as the lyricism of the remembrance and that tone either harsh or subdued — that the *Dialoghi con Leucò* bear a direct connection with the stories of *Feria d'agosto* which constitute a prelude to mythological evocations.

The prose-style of these stories lies between straight narration and poetic disquisition. *Feria d'agosto* could be defined as a book of commentaries even because it is thematically richer than all Pavese's other books. Both the stories and the passages in poetic prose deal with the formation, the discovery and re-evocation of the mythic world of childhood. But more than all else they are a series of encounters between the "I" and the myth, the past and childhood, in which just as many destinies are alluded to but not elaborated. The characters find themselves as whole beings, they undergo their epiphanies only when they are brought face to face with events, that are essential for them: the vineyard, the sea, the corn-field, the thing lived, etc. These are elements that alienate them from quotidian contingencies and give them a moment of intense, total, cosmogonic beatitude. In this beatitude dwells the significance of the words spoken by the man who pauses at the edge of the corn-field: "That field owes me nothing, because I can do otherwise than remaining silent and letting it enter into my being. And the field and the dried stalks little by little graze me and come to a halt in my heart. No words are exchanged between us. The words were uttered many years ago."[8]

Here the "I" is not concerned with describing the details of his field, but he sees it and assimilates it into himself as a substance. It represents a sacred place, a live and perennial presence that has shaped the days of the protagonist and which very probably remains his true reason for being, his strength and his reality. The revelation of the corn-field or that of the vineyard—which is truly beautiful also from a poetic point of view—allow the "I" to root itself in a fixed point, to possess an absolute reality, to find "its" world, that is to say to live in an authentic sense and therefore to acquire an orientation outside the chaos of homogeneity and relativity, of the profane, neutral, geometric world. The animistic attributes that the protagonist confers upon the field contribute, moreover, to its identification as a "unique place," that is, sacred. Authentic existence, therefore, the whole of a life, is a moment of identification. Man again talks with the gods.

In another story, "Fine d'agosto" (End of August) Pavese gives an even greater prominence to this theme, by adding the relation with another person to the relation with the object. Of his mistress the "I" of the story says: "Sometimes we play at conjuring up mystery among ourselves, and at intuiting that each one is a stranger for the other, and thus escape from monotony. But now I could no longer forgive her for being a woman, one who transforms the remote taste of the wind into the taste of flesh" (330).

As in the section *Dopo* the woman tries to uproot the "I" from her past, her childhood. On the other hand, the Pavesian man would like to make of this woman a living and perennial entity, of flesh and matter, like a field or a hill. These themes are amplified and dramatized in *Dialoghi con Leucò*. Born, as has been said, at the same time as the prose-writings and stories of *Feria d'agosto*, it is not a vicious immersion in Hellenic mythology but the reactivization of ancient myth in terms of modern man, in his loss of Eden and of his thirst to recapture it. Modern neo-primitives such

---

[8] *Racconti*, 362.

as Eliot, Yeats and Joyce employed the classic myth as a device, an historic-fantastic prolongation beyond the borders of the temporal sphere which, nevertheless, does not abolish it. Pavese, instead, revives that myth as a saga—and this constitutes quite a difference.

Let us try to orient ourselves. The hill, the vineyard, the cornfield, in short myth, becomes a norm in *Feria d'agosto*, a psychic schema with which man knows his world and through which, always unconsciously, he filters and interprets reality and experience. That which has happened, happens again, the events of childhood repeat themselves until the rupture takes place through the encounter with the homogeneity, of the adult world. It is precisely these events, absorbed by emotion or by memory when the world of the boy was still in *statu nascendi*, which in general lines fix in advance a great part of life. After becoming emotive references they come to represent all human knowledge, all that which is given to man to know through the senses. Mythology, now, is nothing else but the dramatization of myths. It corresponds to rite, or better, to life changed into fate.

It is already the end of Eden for the post-Homeric world. Aristophanes' satires and the realism of Euripedes are irrefutable examples. But for the true primitive, legends and fables have no symbolic value. They are in no sense inventions or products of the imagination. On the contrary they are chronicles, events, lived life, true stories handed down from father to son which attest to the existence of a paradise, a mode of being different from and superior to the present.

The characters of these fables embody a heroic period of history, but they come together with myths that have a collective importance even for posterity. This explains why the mythological story is nothing else but a series of myths interconnected with human action, on which a model, a pattern is imposed with etiological functions, very probably meant to illustrate the beginning of things. It is the eternal present of the mythic event that renders possible the enduring character of non-sacred historic events. Now the primitive is conscious of re-activating or reproducing paradigmatic acts which gods or heroes carried out *il illo tempore*. If the fables that are recited always begin with the phrase "once upon a time," no less do the Gospels use precisely *il illo tempore*. This explains, to cite an example, that in the legends Chimera and Pegasus are myths which when placed in relation with the adventures of Bellerophon become an integral part of a new myth. Now, Pavese, by utilizing the obsolete forms of our cultural heritage — which are part of the Collective Unconscious in Jung's words because the patterns in their variations have an absolute value -, and by adding thereto his own concepts he changes them and saturates them with a new problem context. Just as the Athenian tragedians, each in a different way, dealt with the Theban saga, so does Pavese interpret the ancient myths with his personal license, re-inventing Greek mythology.

His dialogues are nothing else but short stories which are suffused with the breath of irony or marked by a terse, subdued and sad lyricism, according to the situation. By using the language of symbolic words which subtly interpret reality, Pavese now dispenses with didactic descriptions as well as the discursive linkages peculiar to the short story. Yet the dialogues are short stories. The very figures of the characters reduce the individual dialogues into narrative material.

Once having established this, the relation that exists between the *Dialoghi* and the works of the three year period from 1947-50, should not escape us at least with respect to technique. In the novels Pavese inserts the myth, which in the course of a life of an existence, implies a specific ontological position with respect to the object. The return of the characters to the scenario of childhood — Anguilla, Clelia, etc. — represents a phase of the pattern of a contemporary mythology. Naturally there is much more in the novels: the ambience, for example, and the historical characterization. But for the protagonist, the only character of the journey who remains in point of fact, the only irreplaceable "event" of the narration, the process is always the same. We find this rhythm, albeit on a naturalistic level, even in *Il compagno*, Pavese's longest novel. The cycle closes with the return to Turin, which had been the point of departure, and Pablo's education is completed. The dramatic formulation, then, which adds different dimensions to the story, will become another postulate for Pavese. On January 14, 1944, in fact, he made the following entry in the *Diary*: "Dialogue, *conversation*, is our natural custom. We prefer to avoid long, informative accounts of events (narration), or, rather, we change even these into conversation by putting them into the first person and coloring them according to the personality of the speaker. In short, what we look for in a narrative is *drama*, not scenic effect."[9]

3. *DIALOGHI CON LEUCÒ*

Structurally *Dialoghi con Leucò* has much in common with *Lavorare stanca* to the extent that in the latter every poem is directly inserted into the plot, whereas in the former book every individual dialogue is a variation, or almost, a variation on the fundamental theme. It is easier naturally to glimpse a development in the collection of poems by virtue of the I-protagonist, whereas in the dialogues the causal narrative linkages are lacking — or seem to be. Nevertheless a certain formal structure becomes visible by analyzing the most representative of the dramatized encounters.

The dialogue which opens the book, "The Cloud," is important if only because it prepares the themes that are to be developed — that of the savage and destiny, mortals and immortals, natural and super-natural. It could even serve as a prologue. *Nephele*, the cloud, in fact, announces to Ixion the beginning of a new era in the history of the world: the advent of the Olympians who after having defeated the ancient Cthonic deities now decree a law "which didn't exist before."[10] They are so powerful that they can take everything from man, even his last possibility of escape, death as a free choice, by petrifying him with a gesture. "They will turn you into a kind of shade, a shade that wants to live but never dies." Relations with the gods are a sin, a prohibited event which

---

[9] *The Burning Brand*, 254.
[10] *Dialogues with Leucò*, trans. By William Arrowsmith and D. S. Carne-Ross (Ann Arbor: University of Michigan, 1965) 3.

always ends in disaster. But despite the warnings Ixion perseveres in looking for the cloud who, in reality, is the mistress of the oaks and of the mountain crests, that is the consort of Jove. Ixion will be punished for his boldness.

But every man seeks his god, and the encounters always take place in nature, on the mountain. Thus, in these dialogues, nature appears to us under two perspectives – it depends upon how we see it, whether through the eyes of mortals or of immortals. Men, for example, conceive nature in terms of blood and sex, that is, of violence, savagery. They live in time and in seasons, prisoners of time and seasons. The gods, on the other hand, who live outside of time and who know nothing of the passion that devours mortals, consider nature as a nothing, a void, where nothing really happens. Their world is static, that of mortals is cyclical. Virbius, in "The Lake" (103) resuscitated by Diana and carried off to Italy on the Alban Hills – now he too an immortal – to perpetuate the cult of the virgin-goddess, laments over his new condition. There, where he is now, it seems to him that he is "a shadow among the shadows of the trees," and the silence is inhuman while he, in order really to live, needs to draw to himself "a warm and fraternal blood" and thereby have "a voice and a fate." Even if he lives with the names of Virbius, he is always in the land of the dead and "he doesn't even know if he exists" because he does not recognize himself in the places, i.e. in the contingency of time and space. In short, he would still like to be the other "I," Hippolytus, he who will overcome the roebuck and the she-wolf, thus as Diana saw him, and "slash its throat and plunge his hands into its blood." Now, instead, life and nature have become memory for Virbius.

The dialogue teaches that men always struggle between the two opposites of essence and existence, of destiny and freedom. Man is worth little without the other. If certain characters of the dialogues climb the mountain in order to pursue their dreams and hopes, others walk along roads, traverse seas, go to their ruin almost without having a sustaining will of their own any more.

They live out, in short, the events assigned to them by a superhuman will which is a law.[11]

Men try to create a form for themselves for a certain period of their life. But when they realize that they have always acted according to a rule, of never having been able to make free disposition of themselves, they surrender to despair. On the other hand, the words of Odysseus (when Circe foretells his journey into Avernus and the vicissitudes that await him) could be the lament of Meleager whose life is decided by a fire-brand and of so many other characters of these dialogues. Circe speaks with Leucothea: "That day when he wept in my bed it wasn't because he was afraid, but because the last journey was imposed on him by fate, it was something he knew in advance. Then why trouble to make the journey in that case he asked me as he buckled on his sword walking down to the sea" (113).

Nature is adventure, dream, slaughter, the fate of men. And man walks through nature and violates it in order to identify himself with it and no longer be alone. Nature is the mother, the grotto, the haven and the faith. In "The Guest" we find the identification of the fertility of the earth with the rite of the shedding of blood. The apparent paradox, the irrational is that the gods by themselves are the *spirit of nature*, while mortals create the "selvaggio" in their anxiety to humanize nature. In the last analysis, the dialogue between man and god is nothing else, on a symbolical level, than the dialogue between man and nature. In a little essay entitled "La selva" Pavese wrote:

The wildness that interests us is not nature, the sea, the forest but the unforeseen in the hearts of our companions — men. It is wildness which through a simple effort of attention can become deliberate will. In the city, woman practices a ferocity towards us of which every uncultivated countryside is only a symbol... The savage invents words, he toils to clarify himself in words

---

[11] The gods are not fixed symbols. But in their ambiguity they serve to weave together the various levels of the narrated reality.

which then separate within him and ravage him. In the beginning there is only nature: the city is a landscape, there are cliffs, heights, sky, sudden patches of ground, woman is a wild animal, a flesh, an embrace. Then it becomes words, the natural was only a symbol, we know true wildness; and it behooves us to howl.[12]

Here the meaning is extended to include all the silences that the individual man must meet. When they become words, that is events, the mystery that lay behind them begins to torment man, and they themselves become the symbol of that which Pavese calls "the torbid, frightful pullulating human forest." Woman can become all nature in the act of the man who seeks to penetrate and possess its mystery, the silence that separates them. This is the key for "La belva," in which Endymion can see Artemis only in dreams: in order to meet her he must no longer wake up.

Man always emerges annihilated, reduced to a mere presence following his encounters with the gods. But this dialogue is clarified also by a note of the *Diary*: "The Gods, for you, are the *others*, individuals who are self-sufficient, supreme, seen from the outside."[13] Artemis is woman, the goddess, the *other* who remains inscrutable, impenetrable, and with whom man cannot do without. She is the wild beast who takes away consciousness. But even in the process of destroying himself Endymion, the eternal dreamer, must meet her. Artemis is now his myth. And perhaps he knows, at bottom, that any woman whatsoever who truly is important to a man is nothing else but the crystallization of his feelings. By seeking her, Endymion seeks conjunction with himself. Hence the anxiety for possession, even if in the end it is Artemis who possesses him. This is the source of the Pavesian conception that the sexual act is inevitably a savage struggle, something forbidden like homicide, like an act that calls for blood-letting. This is the reason, in the dialogues as well as in the stories, that despair creeps into man when the bond with the other, nature, is inter-

---

[12] *La letteratura americana e altri saggi,* 31.
[13] *The Burning Brand,* 284.

rupted or reveals itself to be illusory. The unconscious assumes mastery over the conscious and the irrational occurs. A harsh, bitter existential core persists in the human — divine dualism. In truth the gods do not exist: they are static essences. But for men who always try to approach them and to possess them they could always represent the objectification of the "I" (the reduction in *en-soi*) to be counterposed to and reconjoined with freedom (the *pour-soi*). It is a sufficiently significant fact that Endymion should want to sleep and at the same time remain awake. Hence the perfect union with the other, with the secret immutable *en-soi* of a person becomes impossible. Sappho, in another dialogue, expresses herself even more clearly with the metaphor of the reef and the foam of the sea.[14]

Diana is still the woman-goddess of *Lavorare stanca*. She has no name, and yet she possesses all the names. Even the city-countryside theme recurs in these dialogues. If Olympia is the city of silence, the abstract, the poet's roots (or better, his incurable nostalgia) lie in the age of the Titans. He tries to reduce the city and the woman-goddess in terms of the real, the savage vainly trying to wrest them from their immutability. It is a struggle for life, not for death. Diana warns Endymion that he must never wake up because the day on which he will be completely awake - the day on which he will realize that he can no longer dream of her in terrestrial and celestial terms and will become aware of how alone he is and of how everything in the universe is empty and without meaning — then he will also know that life is not worth the living. "It's enough to know," wrote Pavese in that famous passage in "La selva," "what the end of the day and tomorrow and the future would be if all the symbols were to disappear, if mystery were to vanish, if we were not alone at night. We would be more dead than the dead."[15] Man would die if he did not find himself before the mystery of the symbols that he has invented to

---

14 *Dialogues with Leucò*, 41.
15 *La letteratura americana e altri saggi*, 322.

explain the world. And "if it were possible to destroy the symbols, all the symbols, we would only destroy ourselves" (323).

The parallel with *Lavorare stanca* is valid, as has been said, because beneath the mythological tale at the base of every dialogue there is implicit a cosmology that corresponds to the typical Pavesian world, to the hieratic landscape of hills and vineyards. At bottom even in the dialogues the life of a man follows a schema which, connected by means of evocations and correspondences to natural cycles and collective events, reveals itself as a mirror in which the whole of reality is reflected. For Pavese the focal point of every life is the transition from adolescence to maturity, which occurs when man becomes aware of fate. It is precisely in the unexpected moment in which awareness strikes upon man with the force of a revelation that the *via crucis*, the tragic character of existence begins. In this sense the dialogues, in which the protagonist is Oedipus, are especially important. In the first "The Blind," Oedipus is still the happy tyrant of Thebes. But there is no escaping the sympathetic but ironical tone with which Pavese elaborates his story. After having narrated how he was punished with sexual transmutation for having disturbed the two snakes, Tiresias says: "Have you ever asked yourself, Oedipus, why the unhappy go blind as they grow old?"[16] For the blind person things are essences that never change. They are all the same. Intelligence does not decide, does not externalize emotions by adding attributes to nature. The oracle knows that its encounter, its moment of truth, was inevitable. For him all is fate: even human life is work, an object. But, ironically, Tiresias sees where the mind and experience of Oedipus, the *real* blind man, do not yet penetrate. The other dialogue, "The Road," could correspond to the second tragedy of the triad of Sophocles. After having left Thebes, Oedipus roams through the countrysides as if he were still in search of the last, most complete revelation. He holds that the gods have inveighed against him with a special demonism and that the fate of others is in some way different, and therefore he rebels. But the reply of his

---

[16] *Dialogues with Leucò*, 18.

interlocutor becomes even more eloquent if we consider that he is but a beggar: "I'm about to say that even your desire to escape fate is perhaps fate itself" (62). From the darkness of the maternal womb to the blindness of old age, the arc of life reechoes the ancient law: every flux, every thing returns to the primal state.

In *Dialoghi con Leucò*, as in Pavese's subsequent works, fate is presented on a personal level and on a universal level. All live in rhythm—birth, life, death—from which there is no escape. But everybody sooner or later discovers his deficiencies, his flaws, his problems, in short a destiny that is peculiarly his which confers a particular essence upon him and which reveals itself to be just as inevitable. For Bellerophon in "The Chimera" and for Jason in "The Argonauts," all life is contained in a gesture, in the heroic act of their youth. But, aware of time, of flesh, all that remains to them is regret and the futile curses against the gods and fate. In "Sea Foam," Sappho says of fate: "I don't accept it. I *am* my fate. Nobody accepts his fate" (43). To which Britomart, a sea nymph, replies: "Nobody except us. We who know how to smile."

The gods differ from mortals principally because they know that every gesture or action is nothing else but assertions of fate. They smile ironically and that's enough. It is their destiny, and they know it. On the other hand the life of man rarely appears as a fate to this man. He knows only that one day he will die, and nevertheless every day seems different to him and the future always makes him promises. This man is Odysseus, who in the words of Circe, "never looked on the endless cycle of days as destiny, he ran towards his death knowing what it was, and enriched the earth with words and actions" (113). However, Pavese made this remark in his *Diary*: "In the *dialoghetti*, mortals sigh for divine attributes and the gods for human qualities. The multiplicity of gods does not affect the issue. The work is a conversation between divinity and humanity."[17] At times man envies the Olympian detachment of the gods, and their sureness in knowing their destiny. The difference is that the gods have no blood, whereas man is

---

[17] *The Burning Brand*, 298.

guided, suffocated, resuscitated by his blood. But men have at least one attribute of the gods, memory, as Circe reveals. And memories, words and names, are the true contact that man establishes with fate and immortality. Hesiod in "The Muses" climbs the mountain to talk with Mmemosyme the muse of memory. Hesiod, who is a prisoner of time who measures mortal life by way of facts and events in a progression that ends only with death, views life as a futile thing, without meaning and without purpose. But before Mmemosyne he knows that he can transcend time because "in your voice and in your names is the past, every season I remember."[18] The return to the past imposes the discovery of a mythic fixity, which is another word for fate. The past is always fixed, it exists outside time, and does not change. Through contemplation of the past, man can identify himself with an external form. The anxiety of discovery, of the unknown and the unexpected has been eliminated. Mmemosyne is this past, without a name and yet having so many names: "You are like a mother whose name is lost in the past." It is a voice, and therefore a symbol. What is the symbol? "It is an object, an attribute, an event which a unique value, an absolute, has wrested from naturalistic causality and isolated it in the midst of reality."[19] In short the symbol is the past, the swamp of blood. Whereas the present, even if it contains great moments, does not constitute a life. At bottom the return to their native-towns by the characters of Pavese's novels is Hesiod's climb up the mountain. "I feel a weariness for things and works that a drunkard feels. Then I stop work and climb up here on the mountain."[20] It is the peak of a psychic rhythm which evolves at the same time as the natural cycle of life, and it is consciousness.

Cosmology is still more evident in these dialogues on a general plane. Remembering how the Cloud revealed to Ixion the beginning of a new era, it should no longer be difficult to intuit the

---

[18] *Dialogues with Leucò*, 160.
[19] *La letteratura americana e altri saggi*, 301.
[20] *Dialogues with Leucò*, 35.

significance of these constant allusions even to a distant past, on the part of the gods. There was a time when Kronos and the Titans reigned—when life was not yet differentiated, when men and gods lived alongside each other. Chiron, the wise centaur describes it: "In those days wild beast and swamp brought gods and me together. We were mountain and horse, plant and cloud and running water, we were everything then, everything on earth. Who could die in those days? What was bestial then, if the beast in us was like the god?" (35). Primordial chaos represents the childhood of the world. Even if man invents things through a word, a fable handed down to him, even if he is always emotionally stirred where he has already been emotionally stirred, (he does not live the objects in themselves but the signs, the concepts of the objects), he is happy in his childhood precisely because imagination, intelligence and reality have not yet been separated. The age of adulthood having arrived, having discovered their own individuality the characters of the dialogue—men, monsters and gods—live only for themselves. They are no longer nature: they live in the world. If men could be identified with the "I" of the novels and the gods with the others, the centaurs, who know they are monsters and hold themselves apart, the hybrids and the savages would be those who live with an awareness of the missing conjunction, with a full consciousness of fate. Oedipus as well as the other characters are deformed. In the dialogues man remains the dreamer, the adolescent who upon arriving at maturity for the first time knows the pain of the flesh. He becomes a savage physically as well as psychologically. Men and gods are also a variation of the dualism countryman-city-man, as has already been seen. Olympus represents the city and the plain represents the countryside. The monsters, therefore, recall characters like the protagonist of *Lavorare stanca,* such as Anguilla of *La luna e i falò*—people doomed to a solitude that is also metaphysical, to living suspended between two modes of being.[21]

---

[21] The key for the *Dialoghi* is found in *The Burning Brand*, 301: "The monstrous and golden era of Titans was the age of indifferentiated men-monster-gods. You

By way of polyvalent symbols Pavese aimed dramatically to portray the moment when man, who believed himself to be an absolute entity suddenly discovers that he is a relative one. But even without suggesting ways out, facile and illusory hopes, he does not let himself be overcome by an immoral pessimism. Orpheus, in "L'inconsolabile," is a resignation of a wholly different kind which calls to mind the smile of Camus' *Sisyphus*. Whoever believes that Pavese is a nihilist should note the way in which he has refashioned the myth. Returning from the Avernus with Eurydice behind him, Orpheus turns around not in a moment of distraction but because he has willed it. Telling about his adventure he explains the problem: "When I wept I was no longer looking for her, but for myself. For a fate, if you like, I was listening to myself."[22] "In life a man does everything. Believes everything. He even believes that his own blood runs in the veins of others. Or that what has been can be undone. He believes his ecstasy can scatter fate. I know all this and it is nothing" (74). Orpheus knows now that he is separated from himself. But even if he will later be torn to pieces by the Bacchantes, because he has revealed the mystery of existence, he tries to live.

With the dialogues, Pavese goes beyond the novels and the poems. While the cloud, Nephele, announces the beginning of the Olympic age, Mmemosyne foretells another. The cycle closes, therefore, in the last dialogues. Man's education can be considered as completed. In fact—and this is important—if Ixion belonged to an epoch that was still heroic, indeed in many aspects golden, Hesiod is the precursor of the tragedians and of the humanists. But the title of the dialogue that precedes the "Flood" is sufficiently clear. When, on the summit of the mountain, Mmemosyne asserts that the shepherd-poet knows immortal life, it is practically tantamount to saying that man has his justification even in solitude. He has experienced his encounters, and even explaining the myths, the memories—now become stone—remain, and nobody

---

have always considered reality as a titanic idea, or rather as a human-divine chaos (monstrous), which is the perennial form of life."

[22] *Dialogues with Leucò*, 73.

can undo them. Even though the gods do not suffer from the corruption and decay of the body, they are at bottom more sad and futile than man because they must acquiesce to the instant, the present which repeats itself eternally. Lajolo comments that "the sadness of the gods was deeper than that of mortals precisely because suicide was not granted to them, they being eternal."[23] They lack the temporal dimension. Hence if for Proust only the artist succeeds in saving himself, by rummaging through his memory, and by letting himself be guided by his sensations, by bringing to the surface some flotsam of memory in a privileged moment, thereby fixing his existence in the work of art, for Pavese man, any man, can also live in defeat.

The conclusion is that *Dialoghi con Leucò* must be regarded as a novel even if there are no linkages from one chapter to another, and even if it is set on so many levels, at bottom it narrates a human event. The fact that, with respect to the works of maturity, this book is lacking in social orientation in the most obvious sense of historicity, it has induced some critics to judge it as little more than a literary exercise. But in the dialogue "The Vineyard" the rustic cunningly tries to beseech the gods by calling them masters. In "The Guest," Heracles, a titan, a monster, tames the superstitious wild game of Lityerses. In short, whereas the ancients in their mythologies dealt with incredible events as though they were real, in these dialogues Pavese interprets real events as if they were incredible. The problem-complex, therefore, is modern. It could be added that Pavese tries to mythify the present without recourse to an adventurous plot, that is, without inserting it in a past reality, in a continuity that is also cultural. Aside from the style which is always pure, rhythmic, gushing forth like an open vein, many dialogues — for example "The Lady of Beasts," "The Blind" — are pages of lofty poetry, which means above all modernity. Moreover even the mythological fiction is something novel and original in the literary production of our time. *Dialoghi con Leucò* remains the most significant book of the postwar period in Europe.

---

[23] Davide Lajolo, *Il vizio assurdo*, 318.

Chapter VII

THE NOVELS OF MATURITY

1. THE POLITICAL COMMITMENT

Pavese's social-political relation to the men, the literature and the history of his time has already been elucidated in the introductory first chapter of this book. Raised in the anti-fascist and liberal cultural ambience of the Turin of Piero Gobetti, Augusto Monti, Leone Ginzburg and Franco Antonicelli, Pavese could not avoid having a social consciousness. Only, in contrast to his intellectual friends, he was not a man of action. He did not succeed in releasing the yearning for human brotherhood into active political participation. He paid the penalty of political banishment more because of his associations than for any other reason. And although it is not the case here to insist upon guilt complexes—for not having engaged himself in the partisan struggle, according to Lajolo—even his membership in the Communist Party, in the postwar period, was not dictated by a sudden interest in politics but by a deeper sense of humanity. Indeed, one could add, by a metaphysical necessity.

For that matter the struggle for social justice is the dominant theme of contemporary Italian literature. The theme of the offended world, the offense perpetrated against man is to be found in Vittorini, Bernari, Silone, Jovine, Levi, Berto, Rigoni-Stern, Moravia, Scotellaro, Del Buono, Pratolini, Calvino, Bassani, Ugo Moretti, Cassola, Montesanto, Alvaro and others. For centuries Italy has had to endure enormous historic pressures, and this history has revealed itself as a continuous terror. Like the Baltic countries, the Balkans or the colonial territories, Italy is a nation marked by "historic fatality" on the one hand, and on the other by an ancestral poverty, social injustice and a Catholicism that is often sterile and abusive. Marxism came to insert itself into Italy's culture more as a popular form of the return to man than as a party ideology, and as a defense against the terror of history and a way out of despair. The Italian intellectuals, who clamored for membership in the Communist Party in the fervor of the postwar period, had been prepared to receive Marx in one way or another because they had gone through both Croce's *storicismo* and Gentile's *attualismo*. All of them knew very well that Hegel, despite his tenacious defense of the Prussian constitution with the assertion that what *is* must remain in the manner *in which it is*, really wanted to save the Universal Spirit in history, the freedom of man. But the pathetic thing of the Hegelian dialectic lies in the fact that it remains an abstraction. That is to say, it does not know how to point out the paths for the redemption of all these injustices, massacres, concentration camps, and unheard of sufferings with which universal history is saturated. Marx, on the other hand, is much more accessible because he is much more consistent than Hegel, and imbued by a much deeper religious-social spirit. He returned Hegelian philosophy to earth insofar as he sees in historical events a concatenation, a structure, and consequently a finality. Marx proposes "salvation," by the elimination of crime precisely in history. Moreover, he "re-confirms on a strictly human plane, the value of the primitive myth of the golden age, with the difference that he places the golden age at the end of history instead of also placing it at the beginning."[1]

Pavese's return to man inserts itself into the context of these postulates, and in that general anxiety with respect to the regeneration of the "offended world" which was characteristic of the immediate Italian postwar period. The article published in the newspaper *L'Unità* of Turin, on May 20, 1945, precisely under the title "Return to Man" better clarifies Pavese's state of mind at that time. He writes:

Now we know in what sense it behooves us to work. The scattered allusions that we gathered in the dark years from the voice

---

[1] Mircea Eliade, *Cosmos and History: the Myth of the Eternal Return*, 149.

of a friend, from something we read, from some joy or from some sorrow, have now composed themselves into a clear speech and into a certain promise. And the speech is this, that we will not go towards the people, because we are already people and all the rest is non-existent. We will go, if ever, towards man. Because this is the obstacle, the crust that must be broken: the solitude of man—ours and that of others.[2]

At that time, however, while the memory of fascism was still fresh and pungent and while awaiting an imminent electoral lining up of political forces, at times the responsibilities of the writer towards readers risked becoming an all too obvious responsibility towards a party. In a certain book of mine which was brutally frank and which is not worth the trouble to recall, not even for the many woes that it caused me, I noted:

> The artist who does not have his own moral security, his own intimate balance, is an easy prey to flatteries. It will depend on the fact that the Italian, by nature, pays little attention to his selfishness. Selfishness is personality, is defense, whereas generous impulses, especially when they are directed towards a social collectivity, are lost in the collectivity of intentions, wane in the structures. Thus at the end of the war it happened that the Italian writer found himself engaged or 'encaged,' and a prisoner of thematics, without deeply sensing it or being aware of it. After the change in the political climate, and now that he had greater freedom of action and of inspiration, he set to work generously trying to "have art enter life."[3]

---

[2] *La letteratura americana e altri saggi*, 218.

[3] I was referring to an observation made by Eugenio Montale (in *Inchiesta sul neorealismo*, ed. by Carlo Bo, Ed. Radio Italiana, 1951): "In France the resistance lasted very much longer and the phenomenon of collaborationism had a greater significance. Besides in France everything becomes literature, in a highly social sense: in France life enters into art while in Italy discussions will go on for centuries as to whether and how art can enter into life."

Thus the writer began again to write about the still warm ashes of the bombing, of bloodshed and of persecutions, of the sorrows of the world and of the offenses perpetrated against the spirit of man. He returned to a primordial vision of horror. But beside confession the internal stimulus was that of feeling himself engaged, in "revolt," and consequently he pursued an aim. Thus he felt himself being *antifascist* or a member of the *resistance*: he wrote in order to reveal and to purify himself. But the great and undifferentiated inspiration of art entered in very few books — of those books born of the impulse of *engagement*.[4] This is an observation that it is worthwhile to set forth now, now that also the myth of "engagement" of adherence to history and of Marxism has for all intents and purposes collapsed and now that commitment does not guide and surpass poetry — as should always be the case — but tries to be *only* a poetry of commitment, a poetry of consciousness and of ideas."[5]

Nevertheless rhetoric did not suit a person in the possession of Pavese's moral intransigence. In fact he never loaded his books with antifascism, with ideology, with outpourings that today might appear gratuitous or adolescent. In February 1946, he replied as follows to an inquiry conducted by the review *Aretusa*:

I don't think that the generic ingredients of the new will produce in me what are called renewals of content. I will not re-evoke anyone's life in the underground or in the jails. I shall not indulge in a homiletic poetry…. What can you do about it? It is not prescribed that the sorrowing human material of poor Italy and of poor Europe can be dealt with only from the springs of colloquial and circumstantial realism. For in substance this is the demand that is made when one insists upon knowing whether the events of the last years have had an influence. Some, further-

---

[4] In this sense, later in the aforementioned book, I pointed out the great importance of Pavese's *La casa in collina*.

[5] Giose Rimanelli, *Il mestiere del furbo* (Milan: Sugar, 1959) 58-59.

more, add that the matter has now assumed the gravity of a duty towards the new reading public: namely, to produce a realistic, objective spoken literature, so that an audience of millions can be brought into being.[6]

Pavese, in short, did not mince words when he had something to say, nor did he hide his sympathies. It is curious that *Il compagno* was written precisely in 1946, the year of this declaration. In this declaration Pavese makes an allusion to the fact that he was wholly imbued with the themes of his *Dialoghi*. ("Today as today, furthermore, I am navigating frankly in a neoclassical world of pre-Homeric myths."). It was in that year also that he tried the four handed experiment in narration, so to speak, with Bianca Garufi,[7] and wrote the poems, *La terra e la morte*. *Il compagno*, however, which was the first novel published after *La spiaggia*, re-kindled the neorealistic polemic, and testifies to the fact that Pavese, willy-nilly, responded to "the influence of the events."

Elsewhere I have written that Pavese's novels are not *Bildungs-roman*, that is to say novels of "education." This is true and *Il compagno*, therefore, must be viewed as an exception. It tells the story of a young man, Pablo, who after his contact with workers achieves a self-awareness to the point where he is convinced that fascism must be fought precisely by people like himself. Following this the protagonist reveals himself to be more of a man, not only because his educational search strengthens his relations with others but because it leads him towards political truth, allowing him to distinguish between historical fact and propagandistic distortion. Pablo belongs to the petit-bourgeois class, that is to say the most representative class of Italian society. The fact, further-

---

[6] *Letteratura americana e altri saggi*, 246.
[7] *Fuoco grande*, published posthumously, is an "exercise." The theme is still that of "return." But the torbid air that pervades it, and the narration which is broken and then re-joined has another sensibility. It is not a colloquy in a mirror, but of voices which never succeed in integrating themselves. It is a spurious work, which Pavese, for that matter, attempted without too much conviction. This is confirmed by the fact that it was never finished.

more, that the action unfolds towards the end of the Spanish Civil War—which constitutes the descending phase of the fascist parabola—might lead to the supposition that Pavese, by way of a typical character, had wanted to indicate symptoms of a growing political and ideological awareness on the part of the people. In fact, in the novel, opposition to the regime is manifested not in the name of an abstract and overly intellectualistic freedom, but above all as a reaction to economic exploitation. The fascists are immediately identified with the "signori." Lubrani, the so-called "littorian tower," "lives on the backs of the people."[8] The shows which he produces in his theatres serve the fascist dictatorship by presenting grotesque parodies of Jews, as if to take the mind of the spectator off his own social condition and, consequently, continue the oppression.

The novel is clearly divided into two sections. Pablo appears much more mature than his friends to us from the very first pages. He feels much more than they do the acute necessity of reacting against the surrounding ambience. His silent revolt culminates in his departure for Rome. Before all else, therefore, his problem at bottom is how to escape from the usual round of things and from that lethargic life around him: his parents' store during the day, the tavern with the guitar and his friends at night. "On certain days, thinking about how many people there are in this world, also poor devils that nobody knows, I used to be seized by a desire to take off, to jump on a train, so that I felt like screaming. The hell with the guitar! I would say. The hell with the grocery store! To live like Amelio. To live like everybody else" (364). Amelio is the model to imitate. But living with Linda, the stylish woman who had belonged to Amelio and who had then been attracted by Lubrani's money and sophisticated circles, does not solve anything for Pablo. If in Turin the truckdrivers had vaguely talked to him about the war in Spain, it is only in Rome, where the events of the other eleven chapters of the book unfold, that Pablo really begins to understand. Whereas before he had looked for a way out

---

[8] *Il compagno*, 377.

of a personal situation, now thanks to his contact with the Roman proletariat he finally knows the direction that he must take. He succeeds in identifying himself with the people and with his environment by way of active participation in the underground poltical movement. What had at first distinguished Pablo from the others was his skill with the guitar and his exotic name. But in Rome he stops playing and dedicates himself to work, and he sees his name almost as a destiny when he meets Scarpa, the communist who had fought in Spain. "How come you're called Pablo?" he asked me. "Were you down there?" "Me? Hell no. I was playing the guitar" (444). The distance between the individual and the collectivity is abolished. Forced by the authorities to leave Rome, Pablo is sure that now even in Turin he will be able to insert himself into society with other responsibilities. The fact that after a brief encounter he breaks definitively with Linda and leaves with Gina, the woman who is always in overalls, leaves no doubt on the importance of the Roman sojourn. For a long time, he no longer sees Carletto and his friends who oppose fascism only because it represents a political faction. In other words Carletto and his friends are bourgeois and remain bourgeois because they do not feel economic exploitation in the flesh. Without this all-determining experience, which also becomes a moral requirement, they remain theoreticians, people for whom antifascism is a way of killing time. In any case their success would not change the condition of the masses. Pablo, instead, compromises himself with the Reds, the men of action. Thus by disciplining his life with a precise moral orientation, he surpasses the final phase of his educational development.

2. *LA CASA IN COLLINA*

Il compagno is the work in which Pavese deals most exclusively with politics. And it is also the only one, perhaps, which has a happy ending. Without wishing to make a syllogism of it, it can very well be defined as a thesis novel. In fact it is not difficult to identify correspondences between the articles, which appeared in *L'Unità* (1945-47), and *Il compagno*, which was conceived and written precisely in that period. The title itself re-echoes the first of a series of dialogues written for the communist newspaper. For example, consider how Scarpa's words reflect the thought expressed in the article "Ritorno all'uomo": "I want to tell you one thing... There is this single difference between us two: What cost me months of sweat and wretched books and heart-searchings in order to make up my mind, you and your class have in your blood" (451). If Scarpa tries to understand the workers, Pablo tries to understand the intellectuals: "In order to trust those who study it is necessary to study them" (419), he says (and this assertison suggests another article entitled "Leggere"). The two characters represent the terms of a dialectic that is solved by means of political commitment. Pavese nevertheless manages to add the ideological dimension to the quotidian character of life, to affirm the uncertainties and disturbances of a period, and above all to think like the man in the street without forcing the rhythm of the narration. Nothing extraordinary occurs, the whole is sufficiently credible: I mean to say that there are no ferocious fascist repressions to demonstrate the heroism of the workers. It is not a book with a purpose or homiletic or populist in the now literary sense of the term. Yet by seeking artistic reasons only in the context of the novel or on the moral integrity of the writer one would be committing a wrong against Pavese. Now that twenty years have passed since that famous Italian postwar period, *Il compagno* cannot be accepted as the measure for the other works of Pavese's artistic maturity.

Il compagno, despite the honesty of the efforts of a critic like Franco Mollia, who includes this novel in a chapter of his essay on Pavese under the title "La maturità artistica nei racconti politici" (The Artistic Maturity in the Political Short Stories),[9] cuts itself off from the other works both in terms of theme and technique. *Il compagno* perfectly models itself upon the Lukacsian directive: historical characterization, typology, linear and descriptive development, etc. In this book the character and the story are limited in

---

[9] Francesco Mollia, *Cesare Pavese* (Florence: La Nuova Italia, 1963) 62.

135

time. Perhaps, this also formed part of Pavese's intentions: namely to be understood by his comrades. But if *Il compagno* is compared with the novels written from 1947 to 1950 it is lacking in universality, in short it does not go beyond a particular historical situation. In depth it is lacking in that mythic reference, or that countryside-city dimension which is so traumatic in the Pavesian record of human experience. There is only one level in this novel instead of the many levels we find in the other novels. Consider, on the other hand, the function of the political theme in books like *La casa in collina* and *La luna e i falò*. The events that are narrated occur in a precise historical moment: the days of the bombing raids, of the armistice, of the deportations and of the partisan struggle in the former, the polemics between the clergy and the communists, the tense atmosphere of 1948 in the other. At any rate Pavese repeats what he had already asserted.

In *La casa in collina*, for example, antifascism still signifies class struggle and the worker participates more actively than the intellectual or the bourgeois in the resistance. It also suggests that it is precisely individuals, like Corrado, who have arrived at maturity under fascism, and who now eagerly look back more towards the past than towards the future, are convinced of the futility of any commitment whatsoever and of any kind of participation in social movements. For this reason also the novel is "the history of a long illusion."[10]

In *La luna e i falò* the ideals of the resistance, now become propagandistic slogans, are decisively betrayed by the politicians. The two bodies of republicans, risen like a nemesis to bring to the surface a past soon superannuated, once more set forth and with a greater actuality the question posed at the end of *La casa in collina*: "And what about those who have fallen? What do we do about them? Why are they dead?" (131). This is a question that obviously still remains unanswered, indeed it is set aside by the political factions who are ready only to erect monuments, and to lead demonstrations. On the other hand Corrado's and Anguilla's prob-

---

[10] *Romanzi*, Vol. II, 10.

lem transcends politics and ideologies. Both find themselves in a historical matrix, in an ambience, as do all the characters. But above all they live in a personal dimension, in an exclusive reality, individualized by myths and by remembrances, which belongs to them and to nobody else. While *Il compagno* is distinguished from the other postwar works only by virtue of a certain narrative rhythm, these two novels, by way of structures and situation, present the totality of a world and of a style that is more typically Pavesian.

Let us take a closer look at *La casa in collina*. For Corrado solitude becomes a necessity which later the war itself will justify. He relives his childhood in the countryside: his reality is a lair, a refuge, a closed world which allows a certain self-sufficiency:

> Even now sometimes voices were heard breaking out, laughing in the distance, but the great darkness weighed upon and covered every thing, and the earth had again become wild, solitary, as I had known it as a boy. Behind the cultivations and the roads, behind the human things, under the feet, the ancient indifferent heart of the the earth brooded in the darkness, lived in deep ravines, in roots, in occult things, in the fears of childhood. One might say that under the grudges and uncertainties, under the desire to be alone I discovered myself a boy in order to have a companion, a colleague, a son. (11)

In his relation with reality, and therefore with others, Corrado tries to defend, to protect an unconscious order (the images, the earth enveloped in darkness, and adjectives like "wild," "ancient," "indifferent," suggest the Unconscious). Although the city folk crowd the countryside and thus disturb his private life, his seclusion, all is resolved by his encounter with Dino, who, as the narration progresses, becomes his counter figure, his other self. Cate, on the other hand, brings back old problems: "Are there any loves that are not selfishness, that do not desire to reduce man or woman to one's own convenience?" (55). When he discovers that Dino could be his son, Corrado asks Cate to marry him, but she refuses him, responding negatively to his entreaties. She knows that, for Corrado, the others serve only to reveal him to himself and that at any rate he would have married her only in order to liberate himself from the thought of having maltreated her in the past. But once he is liberated from the sexual problem, Corrado manages to live with greater calm, even though the doubt of paternity is not yet clarified.

The central problem of the book, therefore, is presented in these terms. After having reduced the city into debris, the war invades the countryside, corrupting its mythic quality: "From now on even solitude, even the woods would have a different taste. I became aware of this after a simple glance that I cast among the plants" (43). Following the transfiguration of the desolate landscape in which only the soldiers find a place, the cosmos is slowly transformed into chaos. Time intrudes into its staticness with ever increasing frequency. The blood that has been shed is in itself something wild and mythic in character. But the war reveals itself to be all the more irrational and inconceivable in that it becomes an extra-human determinism, an event external to the individual. Not only does it endanger his life, but it takes the individual by surprise, in the very roots of his psyche, suddenly taking away from him references, the order of his day-to-day life, estranging him in an anxiety-ridden provisional state. Nevertheless Corrado remains passive while the others, the younger ones, react (perhaps with the hope of building a new order). The evangelical call of the cock who crows "noisily and faraway" (93) symbolizes his betrayal. After hiding in a school, once more in a lair, when Dino runs away to rejoin the partisans, Corrado returns to the hills where he was born.

The reasons for this odyssey across the landscape soaked in blood are clear. Cate's arrest and Dino's flight had upset his past, his routine. Therefore Corrado hoped to find in the hills a world that was still intact, static as always, "like a room that has been closed" (117). But there is war and there are corpses also in the landscape of his childhood. He realizes that the dead were people with whom, perhaps, he would not have wanted to fight, human beings like himself, with their own past and their own solitude. All men must die sooner or later, but with a corpse at one's feet life and man assume a value that surpasses all contingencies. This is why Corrado says:

> I have looked on dead who are unknown to me, the dead of the Republic. It was seeing them that awakened me. If a stranger, a dying enemy has this effect, and one stops and is afraid to stride over his body, it means that even conquered, the enemy is still a human being, that having shed his blood, we must placate it, lend it a voice, justify whoever has spilt it. (130)

In this religiosity, which is more than Christian, was as a historical event and as a political fact remains an unresolved problem, but one of secondary importance. It is not this that counts. The real problem is that war reduces human life, the living and pulsating flesh, into an abstraction, into a statistic. The others, the enemy, become objects, the republicans and the Germans by turn. By identifying himself with the dead, by recognizing their spirituality and their reality as men, Corrado not only discovers the futility of war but arrives at the awareness that although separation and solitude are irrevocable presuppositions of the human condition, they become irrelevant obstacles at some moments. The myth is not abolished: the hill "remains still a country of childhood, of bonfires, of escapades, of games" (129). Corrado is not a sentimentalist even if he feels a sense of nostalgia in seeing the countryside change its countenance, nor is he one with respect to others. He knows that everyone must have a past, a hill, in his blood. That everyone has within himself a secret place that is inaccessible to others, and that perhaps a perfect human brotherhood is not possible. But he can accept man in his isolation, separated, as another himself, with only life as his undefended dignity.

The fact that Corrado remains anonymous for a great part of the narration, and that the theme is elaborated in the juxtaposition of two terms, the personal and the collective, also adds to the significance of this book. War, actually, assumes an ambivalent meaning: it intrudes like some objective factor between the individual and reality, and at the same time it sets into relief the ethical problem, namely one's relations with others. To take part in the resistance becomes almost like fighting war itself in order to re-establish order. On the other hand by discovering death Corrado has discovered man, and this awareness leads him towards a form of mysticism in which the absolute is human life. Many religious images recur in the book. The most functional and explicit is that of the "boy of wax crowned with thorns" (123), precisely at the end of the journey is inevitable, the young republican soldier has given his life in order to save the lives of others. "We learn through our eyes that it might well be ourselves in the place of these dead and it would be no different and that if we are alive, we owe it to this sullied corpse" (130). In this sense, the image correctly suggests a redemption, a rebirth. Perhaps Corrado will be compelled to engage himself or perhaps he will still remain among the vineyards. We do not know. Certainly, however, he is more responsible now and can view the past with a new sensibility.

3. POLI AND MOMINA

It would be necessary to consider *La luna e i falò* in relation to *La casa in collina*, and thus close a discussion. But first we must consider *Tra donne sole* and *Il diavolo sulle colline* which, although they do not suggest any abrupt change in the writer, nevertheless do give the impression that they constitute a laborious preparation for the grand final work. Pavese appears "engagè" under various aspects in *Il compagno*, *La casa in collina* and *La luna e i falò*. In addition to the historical characterization and also the ideological interest (*Il compagno*), he interprets his time in order to portray it in mythic formulations that re-echo the psychic rhythm of the characters.

But these two works, *Diavolo* and *Donne sole*, are extremely important because with them Pavese interprets, more than he describes an ambience, the mores of an era, even broadening his basic theme, namely the dualism city-countryside. Both Poli with his soliloquies and Momina with her cynicism represent at one and the same time a decadent bourgeoisie and a human condition. They live in an adult, urban civilization where the daily mechanization of life intensifies boredom leaving the individual time to think, to begin early to doubt the circumambient reality and to express judgments on life. Thus while some—the toughest-minded—put on the air of a morbid nihilism as a defense, for others the only way out is drunkenness or suicide. Rosetta, for example, does not kill herself for a specific reason but only because, being too sensitive, she simply cannot manage to adapt herself to the world of her friends which in the last analysis is the world of her life.

The fundamental theme of *Il diavolo sulle colline* and *Tra donne sole*, written between 1948 and 1949, is the conflict between two ways of life. In the two books the artificiality of city life, or at least of an urban social stratum, is compared to the simplicity of the proletariat or to the naturalness of country folk. In the first case the most obvious examples are Poli with his drugs, and Resina, the girl who prefers the swimming pool to the river, and rubs herself with suntan lotion the moment she is in her bathing suit. In the other the terms are sufficiently explicit: the distance between life and art, between appearance and reality is abolished almost in a Pirandellian sense by a group of pseudo-intellectuals, and the gestures, the acts of daily life, become theatrical in performance and speech: "Even now in this room, with our clothes, between these walls, we are part of a mise-en-scène that is ours to accept or reject" (284). And in another passage: "In fact I like this fantasy of reality for which the situations of art are devalued and become life" (291). Marionettes who watch other marionettes go through their motions, the characters of this desolate world are absolutely devoid of any human feeling, each one concerning himself with the role and the pose that he must assume. Thus Rosetta's suicide is finally assumed beforehand, as it were, and doesn't shock anybody, nor does Rosalba's suicide cause any remorse in Poli. To abstract things from their human immediacy, to look at facts coldly, are the laws of survival and are the symptoms of a morally sick society. Feelings become vice and perversion. In *Tra donne sole* there are allusions to a lesbian relation between Momina and Rosetta, while in the other novel Poli drags his mistress along with him only to excite himself, to use her as a drug, to pervert his nature: "The life they lead.... They become like women" (146), says a character speaking of Poli and of his friends. Clelia, with the moral firmness of a woman of the people, and Oreste, the only one of the three friends who would prefer to sleep at night instead of gallivanting around, that is to say, to follow the natural instead of the mechanical rhythm of life, represent the opposite condition. The city-people end up by acting irrationally precisely because they are too ratiocinative, too conscious of themselves.

If the parallel that has been established serves to demonstrate Pavesian uniformity, the themes obviously assume a different functional role in the respective works. *Il diavolo sulle colline* is a very complex novel and much more difficult than the other because it contains a greater number of symbols. The sea, the river, the pool, the vineyards are interconnected and counterposed to each other in order to heighten the inevitable contrast between the countryside and the city even more strongly, and above all in order to counter distinguish the two states of being. The characters of this novel are more conscious of their condition and, it could be said, conscious also of the value attributed to the symbols used. During their night walk the three students discuss themes such as wildness or destiny which, as has been seen, are fundamental in the Pavesian problem-complex. This awareness, this desire to act spontaneously and according to a fixed schema—to feel oneself involved in the action but remaining outside of it—not only reinforces the parallel with *Tra donne sole* by placing the emphasis on artificiality, but it becomes a premise for the thematic development of the theme. In other words Pavese not only wanted simply to conceptualize some symbols. Rather, by presenting them as concepts formulated by the characters he makes them doubly functional. The contrast city-countryside is seen from the point of view of the city-dwellers, and their very interpretation places their real position into bold relief.

But aside from the content, the discussions of the students are important because they help to effect distinctions between things and ideas. They are always started by Pieretto, the most sophisticated of the group, and are continued by the most timid person of the group, the narrating "I", ever on the defensive, who tries to contradict the comments of the other and to react against his free and easy tone while Oreste remains to one side or replies with a shrug of his shoulders. The students as well as Poli are convinced of the artificiality of the city-dweller's life. "How filthy are certain people who do everything wearing gloves. Even when they are making babies or millions" (142). The vacation at the seaside or in the country or in the hills—a kind of long city-dweller's *fiesta*—represents an attempt to shake off the superstructures imposed by an over-civilized, over-mechanized life in order to return to a more authentic life. "One comes to the country in order to feel free" (213), says Gabriella. But Pieretto, in truth, seeks the forbidden, the wild, which has always been the urban-intellectualistic conception of the countryside. At the seashore, for example, he often changes beaches in order to hide in the most deserted and desolate places. Later, in Oreste's vineyards, he hopes to find the virgin place, intact, outside history, which might correspond to some vague sensation of his. By looking for the uncontaminated place, in order to discover it for the first time and to give to it their configuration, Pieretto and the narrating "I" unconsciously are seeking to abolish time in order to look at things as in a new childhood. They are trying, that is to say, to identify myth without having lived it, to return *ab initio* while remaining in the present. In this sense the fact that they take sun baths in the nude at the bottom of the well, in order to tan themselves completely from head to foot, is sufficiently significant. The image is surrealist, but the return to the material womb, in the terrestrial uterus is a letting go of oneself that becomes or aspires to possession, nudism for them being a variation of wildness. In short, except for Oreste, the students as well as Poli would like to impose an urban concept on the countryside and to fuse the two opposites. This is why they always oppose the scientific to the primitive and to the mysterious

and they consider it paradoxical that a peasant should use a trac-
tor or chemical fertilizer or other modern equipment—in short
that he has tamed nature.

> I had a discussion in the vineyards with Oreste... on whether in
> the countrysides there exists a little corner, a brook-side, an un-
> cultivated patch of ground, where from the beginning of time
> the rain, the sun and the seasons follow each other unknown to
> man. Oreste said no, there is neither a gorge nor a grove of
> woods which the hand or the eye of man has not disturbed. (185)

What the others understand by countryside seems strange to the
peasant. When Pieretto says that the hoe is also a scientific in-
strument he does it with the air of one who has made a discovery,
while Oreste's father does not understand why at first the three
friends had decided to return to the hills on foot rather than take
the train. But machines are only a means and not an end. The important thing is that the peasants cultivate the soil and therefore
remain in contact with the seasons and the natural rhythm. A
bond exists between them and the earth of which city-dwellers are
aware but which they do not feel. The contrast between the order
and the staticness of the vineyards, Poli's villa surrounded by uncultivated terrain, with a pool and record-player and all the other
modern equipment, comes to represent time, the countryside in-
vaded by the city. It becomes a landscape with which Poli really
has no relationship. He had said to his friends: "My life...I see it
as though it were the life of another" (152). But he remains always
a spectator even after the return to the countryside because he is
out of place now, wherever he may go. In his case blood, which
should signify wildness, is the symptom of a contagious sickness
which destroys the organism. Hence the title of the book is clear.
Gabriella tries to corrupt Oreste ("the only one of us who is sincere and healthy" [219]), to separate him from his friends just like
the others try to transform the countryside, idealistically. It is precisely she who, from the chaos of chairs, the earthly paradise of

trunks, goes forth to meet the students as soon as they arrive at her husband's villa.

The levels of the Pavesian art, the individual and the collective, are usually connected with a paradigmatic return of the protagonists to the childhood setting. In *La luna e i falò* the return coincides with the reappearance of the bonfires on the hills; in *Tra donne sole* and *Il diavolo sulle colline*, it coincides with the carnival celebration and the feasts in preparation of the vintages, that is to say with archetypical events which are repeated cyclically in time. The return, however, does not become the central fact of *Il diavolo* because it does not co-involve the "I," and in a way that, instead of following a pattern, the plot and the narration are developed in the dialogue by way of symbolical allusions. Since in addition the novel lacks the constant recall of childhood, alluded to but not significantly re-linked to the progress of the story, it also lacks the psychic process. At the end of the book the "I" remains the character presented in the first pages, an adolescent waiting to come into man's estate, wavering between the countryside and the city, who defends the one when confronted by the other and vice versa. His friends, on the other hand, represent the two aspects of the dualism. More than anything else the return serves to illustrate the impossibility of a fusion between the two relations.

Poli, who is also physically sick, often talks about God, sin and death. But he talks about them in abstract terms as though he were in need of something that not even drugs can give him. If he seeks for answers, he seeks them beyond man. Oreste and his father do not talk along such lines or at any rate not with Poli's tone. They have answers, but in their blood, in the earth, in life itself. "Religion," declares Oreste's father "is not just a matter of going to church. Religion's a very difficult thing. It's a question of raising children, keeping a family, living in harmony with everybody" (197). The failure of the two civilizations to come together is confirmed by the encounter of the two friends who had become different in the course of time, the one in his own way linked to the hills, the other still separated from them, and by the brief and ambiguous relation between Oreste and Gabriella. The references

to vulgarized existentialist concepts, with which Pavese character-
izes a cultural stratum of the postwar period, form part of the
thematic of *Tra donne sole*. Nevertheless Momina, the typical exemplary of a generation prematurely aged and which perhaps had
never known the joy of living, is an even more negative character
than Poli. The latter, even for the sole fact that he takes drugs, is
conscious of himself and therefore more tragically alive: implicit
in his passivity is a spiritual search, albeit one that gets nowhere.
Momina makes peremptory judgments on reality without having
first suffered and paid in her own person. In other words while
Poli admits that his unhappiness may derive from himself ("I was
an old man who thinks himself a boy: now I know that I am a
man, a corrupted man, a weak man, but a man... I don't have any
illusions"[152]), Momina shakes off any responsibility whatsoever
and rails against existence, reality itself ("... she was telling me
how strongly she was seized by disgust at times – not a nausea
over this or that, over an evening or a season, but the aversion for
living itself, for everything and everybody, of the time that flits by
so swiftly and yet never passes" [219]).[11]

Before being the story of a group of girlfriends, however, *Tra
donne sole* is the story of Clelia. In this sense the novel repeats the
Pavesian theatrical rhythm: namely when the ambition to be
someone, to break the bonds with the environment, which corresponds to the ascendant phase of the traditional tragic protagonist, is about to be or is now appeased, the character becomes
aware of the futility of his efforts. Clelia realizes that her work is
very different from the fashionable world of mink coats which she
had dreamed about as a girl. She finds herself in an ambiguous
situation since she can no longer accept the life of the past represented by Becuccio, nor really belong to the decadent society of
the present. Bereft of any bonds with her childhood, all that re-

---

[11] Momina is a Sartrian character with a true awareness of the absurd. As such,
polemical reactions against a certain popularized existentialism are not lacking.
See: "... A certain Pegi, who had been shoveling snow on the avenues that winter, out of eccentricity the girls said, to engage himself the young man said"
(283).

mains to her is a social position as an awareness of fate. Clelia also becomes a symbol of the human condition even though she is not a complete and tragic figure like Anguilla.

4. *LA LUNA E I FALÒ*

In one of his most lucid criticisms, Geno Pampaloni, writes about *La luna e i falò* as follows: "From the very first moment it was immediately clear, even to the most inexpert of the critics, that the book had the air of being something final, a conclusion."[12] The novel, in fact, is a great elegy, a death song. Whereas with *La casa in collina* Pavese above all presents the ethical implications of a universal situation (the war, after all, could also be a pretext), in *La luna*, he deepens the relation between individual and reality. This is the most orchestrated of his novels, recapitulating, as it does, many themes and encompassing an entire epoch, from fascism to the postwar period. Anguilla, moreover, is a more complete character than either Pablo or Corrado because we can get a closer, more intimate look at him. Pablo lives in a certain present, whereas Corrado generically alludes to his childhood: that is to say, he does not tell about the particulars of his childhood because his origin is something that is well-defined. Anguilla, on the contrary, expounds his problem from the first pages of the book: he presents himself with the question: "Who can say of what flesh I am made?"[13] he returns to his native town in order also to answer this question. And this is why, after this attempt has also failed and after he re-evokes his past as though to convince himself that he belongs to a place, Anguilla lets it be understood that he will leave once more for America where "all are bastards," all are uprooted (390).

In a little more than two hundred pages he says more than, at times, he would have said in a novel three times as long. The contrast, for example, between the present and the past, implicit in *La casa in collina* in the contrast between countryside as landscape

---

[12] Geno Pampaloni, "L'ultimo libro di Cesare Pavese," *Belfagor* 5 (1950): 582-587.
[13] *Romanzi*, vol. II, 385.

and war as fragmentariness, but not developed in *Il compagno*, is elaborated in *La luna* in a context that is both individual and universal, summarizing the entire Pavesian cosmology. In the last analysis it is order which characterized the time before the war and which Anguilla regrets. At the Mora life had a natural flow ancient and eternal. "The beauty of those times was that everything was done according to the seasons, and every season had its own custom and its game, according to the work that had to be done and the harvests, and the rain or fair weather" (459).

Everybody had a job to do, a task, a rung in the ladder of social stratification. The wage-earners did not complain about their relations with Sor Matteo. Rather than a medieval hierarchy it would be more correct to speak of a matriarchy, a stage of civilization, a way of life and of thought which above all distinguishes agrarian societies. In almost all of Pavese's novels the peasants of the Langhe do things as a mass, they get drunk *en masse* at feasts etc. as though natural bonds ran between them, as though the earth was the mother of all.

Upon his return, Anguilla finds that the countryside has changed countenance: disorder and anarchy reign. The Cavaliere's share croppers have become idlers who do not cultivate the soil and who do not work in the vineyards, and the mistress treats Valino with all the traits of the exploiter without even paying him. In this sense there is a deep significance in the fact that Valino, after a visit, kills the mother and the sister-in-law before setting fire to the dairy-barn and hanging himself. He is a stranger, a man, too much attached to the values of the countryside, who now finds himself living in a society with different criteria. This is the reason why he discharges all the grudges against his family, that have accumulated over the years, against his relatives who, unconsciously, are the symbols of a time now vanished forever.

Sor Matteo's family, with all its vicissitudes, represents the disintegration of an epoch. With a name that seems ironical when she is alive, but explicit when she is dead—in the sense that she pays for and redeems the sins of a society—Santa is offered in sacrifice by the partisans in order to propitiate a new civilization in the frightening stake-bonfire at the end of the book.

The process from the past to the present assumes an even broader significance in relation to childhood and maturity. In fact for Anguilla "the Mora was like the world" (417). But he and Nuto, the only survivors of a vanished time, now find themselves in two opposed conditions. Having lived for a long time far from the countryside, being located in the city, Anguilla lives only in the present. His counter-figure, Cinto, another foundling, who has already been deprived of a home has no feeling for the collective myths and represents a future generation. On the other hand if there is an exemplary and almost perfect character in the works of Pavese it is most certainly Nuto. He too has his remembrances, but he is not eager to talk about them. "I wanted to amuse myself but I can't even with you," he says to Anguilla who asks him about Santa (434). Without ever having left his native town, Nuto had dramatically lived the transition from adolescence to maturity during the war. Nevertheless in his case the transition remains a continuity with the past. Always in contact with traditional symbols, he retains his bonds with others by way of his social commitment: "Nuto said that I was wrong, that I should rebel, that a bestial, inhuman life was still being lived on those hills, that the war had been to no purpose, that everything was as before, save for the dead" (420).

But it is not politics that binds Nuto to the others, but the moon, the bonfires, in short the earth. If Anguilla and Cinto represent an individualistic life, a civilization based on laws that separate people instead of uniting them, Nuto represents a new agrarian society which, through Santa, retains the fundamental qualities of the old one—an unwritten but nevertheless progressive morality, without which no relation with others would be possible and no community would be truly such. Like Pablo, in *Il compagno*, who gives up the guitar, Nuto also stops playing the clarinet at feasts. But, once again, he lives in a perfect equilibrium between the rational and the irrational.

As I have already pointed out in the introductory chapter, some critics have chosen to interpret Anguilla's (and Pavese's) nostalgia for a life that is schematized, on moralistic terms, on the basis of Freudian concepts, such as the *pleasure principle* and the *reality principle*. In this sense the mythic past would represent an amoral infantilism which is replaced by the adult age only with a historical clarification of events that have transpired and with the acceptance of social values. The return, supposedly, is a form of regression. But such an interpretation does not seem to take account of the various aspects of the Pavesian theme. The city, the rational society, does not solve problems because it is precisely in the urban ambience that the characters are most alone. It could be said that once the myths are clarified they try to preserve them intact, to create a fourth dimension, namely fate-freedom. Maturity is revealed precisely by way of an awareness of a tension between the city and the countryside, between the present and the past. Moreover, if the countryside becomes a wild landscape where blood is often shed and the forbidden happens, it is also true that the most open kind of comraderie—an unconscious communism— is practiced by the rustics and the young people because they live more intensely and more primitively. Nuto, besides, decisively has a social conscience, but at the same time he believes in the moon and in the bonfires. The myth does not signify escapism, indeed it strengthens the sense of duty. More than all else it represents an attempt to flee from the restraint of nature, of time, of the contingency of facts and objects, by opposing to it a humanized world where everything is necessary. This criticism, which stems from George Luckacs' view of realism in literature, and which aimed to link Pavese to the writers of his generation who came into prominence in the immediate postwar period, does not lead very far. I have already explained the nature of the relation between Pavese and neorealism. With *La luna e i falò* Pavese does nothing else but set forth what, in different forms, he had already asserted in *Feria d'agosto*. Reality is discovered in childhood through words, images, fables which had already at one time emotionally affected our intimate being through *signs*. These concepts, these categories which belong to the cultural heritage of an environment immediately assume a personal meaning. When a place, a thing more completely corresponds to the concept, when that is to say it affects us most intensely, it is abstracted from the surrounding reality and becomes a psychic reference, the prototype of a genre. Thus a particular hill symbolizes all hills etc. They do not subsist in our memory by way of some trauma or suggestions, but because up to a certain point, even without our knowing it, they interpret reality in terms of pre-established schemes. But with the advent of adulthood, having discovered his own individuality, his own subjectivity, having broken his bond with nature, man becomes aware of being separated from others, of being surrounded by an inexhaustible mass of matter, by objects that are totally irreducible to concepts. The schemes are no longer serviceable when finally we become aware of the irreversibility of time. It is in this period that questions which had never been necessary before begin to torment us, and doubts arise about existence itself. This is why, I repeat, Anguilla opens the story with a series of rhetorical questions. At least in *La luna e i falò* e *La casa in collina* the return precisely signals the onset of the crisis. There is no continuity between past and present, between the unconscious and consciousness. Anguilla remains separated from himself. He knows, however, that this is the human condition: "And yet life is the same and one day they will look at themselves going around in a circle and everything will have passed even for them" (481).

Reality in itself does not interest Pavese as it does the neorealists. Rather, he is interested in the relation between man and his feelings. What is lacking in neorealist novels, as well as in *Il compagno*, is a psychic inwardness, that emotive charge which in the works of Pavese's maturity is revealed in the most casual dialogues and also in the most banal details. The ontological measure is jousted within a masterly way in these novels, and reaches its apex in *La luna e i falò*. Here Pavese wanted to interpret an historical period, Italian society under fascism and in the aftermath of the war, by contrasting present and past, childhood and maturity. But he did not limit himself to this. Pavese interprets the eternal problem of the old and the new with the manner of the classic. In fact Aeschylus developed the same themes (a countryside-city dualism) in Oreste's cycle with the conflict between autochthonous deities and Olympian deities, between matriarchy and patriarchy. But in the tragedies the Furies finally become Eumenides, amid the transition toward a new epoch is ushered in with the reconciliation between the two opposite ways of life. In *La luna e i falò* the fusion remains impossible even though it is still necessary. But the levels of this fundamental configuration, linked together by various correspondences, assume a precise functional role. Finally the structure of the novel turns out to be almost perfectly symmetrical.

Pavese interprets history in terms of Vico's *cycles* and *recurrences*. One could properly assert that *Dialogues with Leucò* are a commentary on *The New Science*. This is the reason why the phenomenon of contrast is renewed in every generation in his novels. To the counter-position between two epochs, however, Pavese adds that between stasis and history. Political questions do not intrude in the daily rhythm at the Mora. Later, instead, the finding of the corpses of two republicans is enough to engender polemics and confusion. In this sense, Anguilla's return represents another attempt to abolish time.

5. CONCLUSION

How, then, are we to judge these five works of Pavese's maturity as novelist. From a purely literary point of view it must be noted how, in the course of the years, Pavese had enthusiastically rediscovered the classics. In Herodotus, in Plato, in the Greek tragedians he found a wholly modern and topical problem-complex. This is to say that in the correspondences between ancient literature and contemporary literature he also found the archetypical models, the universal themes, those psychic bonds that constitute the collective unconscious of a race, of the human species, and which are the fundamental and necessary substratum of any tradition whatsoever. All this re-confirms the validity of the theory of cyclical recurrences. At bottom man does not change his essence, his fate is always the same. Besides Pavese had consummately absorbed the culture of our time, beginning with the literary masters of the nineteenth century up to the great modern American writers. Donald Heiney has brilliantly explained the importance that the so-called *American Dream* assumed for Pavese, to which I would have little to add.[14] The essential thing, however, is that through his sensibility, he had examined, lived, and filtered the problems suggested to him by other writers. In short, by starting out anew from the beginnings, as with his poems, Pavese re-traversed the whole history of a genre and all the presuppositions of Western art, extracting there from a highly personal style in which — without setting forth a new voluminous human comedy — history, cosmology, ontology, thematic and technique, content and form, interpenetrates perfectly.

One thing is certain: in time Pavese will find a very precise place in the literature of this century. Some works, like *La luna e i falò* indubitably must be classified among the best fiction that has been written since the 1920s. These novels, beyond their commitment and moral justification, involve us more than so many others because Pavese has left his unmistakeable stamp on them. And it is not only a question of style, at least not in the sense that is usually attributed to the term. One says Dantesque, Proustian, Gidean, Kafkian etc. because Dante, Proust, Gide, Kafka expressed themselves in a considerably singular way, through concepts, images which, while representing a particular way of thinking and feeling, finally have become emblematic and proverbial. What occurs in these cases when the writer succeeds in grasping the most secret stirrings of the human spirit in their essentiality — is that the distances between him and the reader are completely obliterated. Time, space, culture are obstacles: but in a quiet room, in a library, a dialogue is conducted which at times is no longer interrupted. With complicated words or with simple words, but always there as a presence, the writer talks about himself or about others to the

---

14 Donal Heiney, *America in Modern Italian Literature* (New Brunswick, N.J.: Rutgers University Press, 1964) 171-186.

listener. In short, some writers, like some friends, require and obtain a more intense participation, but they give more.

In reply to some questions put to him by a cultural review Pavese said:

> I have the certainty of a fundamental and enduring unity in everything that I have written or will write. And I do not mean an autobiographical unity or one of taste which are inanities — but a unity of themes, of vital interests, the stubborn monotonousness — of him who has the certainty of having touched on the first day the real world, the eternal world, and can do naught else save revolve around the great monolith and detach pieces from it in order to work them and study them under all possible lights. [15]

By way of stylistic complexities, Pavese talks about life, death, about that which is of value and which remains. Perhaps, he is important also and above all for this.

---

[15] *Letteratura americana e altri saggi,* 248.

Chapter VIII

THE BURNING BRAND: A LIFE FOR THANATOS

1. THE EXTERNAL CAUSALITIES

Pavese's diary, *Il mestiere di vivere*, embraces an arc of fifteen years: the period of his maturity. From 1935 to 1950 the red line runs from his political banishment to his literary success to his suicide. At the beginning it is possible that it was born as a receptacle for notes on esthetics, destined only for the author as a guide to the developments of his poetics. Then, little by little, the notes took on a more personal tone and the writing of them became a trade, a job, a *mestiere*, an occupation, and also a refuge and a mirror for Pavese himself, his other self to whom he could tell everything, without lying.

Yet *Il mestiere di vivere* is not simply a journal. There are no references to the fashionable world or details to recount. Instead it is made up a series of *pensèes*, moments of an inner development which, upon being transferred to the page with immediacy, confirm that every word was in its time lived by the author and linked up with the unfolding of his life and of his literary work. Pavese was trying to justify himself vis-à-vis himself and others in daily reality.

A publisher's note in the first edition of *Il mestiere di vivere* states that the manuscript was found among Pavese's papers, complete with title and an analytic index: "1935-1950/ *Il mestiere di vivere* di Ce. Pavese." This suggests that Pavese himself had given some thought to its eventual publication and that thereby his private confession might become a public one. His drama, therefore, while still so different from that of an Andrè Gide or a Julien Green, takes its place among the human-intellectual speculations of the latter, the *Carnets* of Albert Camus and the *Diaries* and letters of Franz Kafka. It is another testimony of the intellectual and

155

of the man of our time seared by the irreconcilable conflict between feeling and reason, the conscious and the unconscious, life as action or life as a fate. In an entry of the *Diario* dated 14 July 1950, he writes frantically: "Stoicism is suicide. People are dying in battle again. If ever there is a peaceful, happy world, what will it think of these things? Perhaps what we think about cannibals, Aztec sacrifices, witchcraft" (364).

The first pages of *Il mestiere di vivere* are notes on the creative process. Pavese, not at all sure of what he wrote about his poetry in 1934, and later published as an appendix to the *Solaria* edition of *Lavorare stanca*, wanted to clarify and deepen his poetics. He wrote this part during the months of his political banishment to Brancaleone Calabro. However, his return to Turin effected the turn of the screw, the change. Here Pavese learned that a former girl friend of his university days, to whom he was emotionally attached, had been married only a day before his arrival. He was devastated by a moral and spiritual feelings of futility and failure, the more so because "[i]n spite of all my weaknesses, that lady managed to make me conform to discipline, to self-sacrifice, by her simple gift of herself to me."[1]

This relationship, however, is to be understood as an attempt on Pavese's part to plant himself in society, to normalize his existence which already for some time had been tormented with complexes of timidity, hedonism, solitude, and ideas of suicide. From some of Pavese's early poetry, or poetic undertaking, we see that even during his pre-university years he was tormented and tempted by the idea of suicide:

One December evening I walked along a deserted country path, my heart in tumult. I carried with me a revolver. When I was sure I was far away from any inhabited place. I pointed it at the ground and pressed the trigger. It leaped at the roar, a sudden leap that seemed to me to shake it as though alive in that silence. It truly trembled between my fingers at the sudden light which

---

[1] *The Burning Brand*, 48.

shot from its barrel. It was like the spasm, the last atrocious shudder, of one who dies a violent death. Then, I returned it, still hot, to my pocket, and I resumed the path. Thus, moving between the naked trees, the last illusion and fears will have abandoned me, and I'll place it against a temple to shatter my brain.[2]

No matter how much the poem reveals a romantic attitude, it is more than a romantic poem or an act of bravado. Words like, "tumult" in the heart, "last illusion," "fears," etc. express a felt state of mind, a struggle "of all the days, of all the hours against inertia, dejection, fear" (84). The failure of his love relationship, which struck him, like an enormous joke, induced Pavese to re-evaluate all his action, past and present. The introspections to which he fell victim, now began to assume an existential character. And since any misfortune "is either due to error, or comes out of our own culpable inadequacy,"[3] he tried to define himself and to discover within himself the causes of his problems.

In practice, these are examinations of conscience which will be repeated in the entire diary, and with greater frequency in the years from 1936 to 1940, years in which Pavese sought for the exact standards by which to measure himself: "The lesson is this: to build in art, or build in life, banish sensuousness from art as from life; exist tragically" (50). Pavese finds himself in an important phase of his life, in that key point in which life is woven into art, and the two spheres will never again be separated. Why banish *sensuousness*, and why exist *tragically*? These are not simple propositions. One becomes aware of the fact that, for Pavese, to live sensuously means to live instinctually, to abandon oneself, to events and to passions without posing questions to oneself. It means not to be really conscious.

Hedonists, in fact, approach life without reservations, totally exposed; they try to dissipate themselves in the pursuit of sensation or some absolute principle. It is for this very reason, perhaps,

---

[2] Davide Lajolo, *Il vizio assurdo*, 75-76.
[3] *The Burning Brand*, 64.

that they end up finding themselves always, or almost always, in a disarmed state in comparison to others: those who act according to a scheme, a moral code. The latter, not accepting the "act," or the "moment" as an end in itself, have the capacity to transform experience into consciousness. Placed before a hierarchy of values, in the end they choose among these values and construct their own lives on the basis of this choice. On the other hand, the man who lives sensuously or unconsciously is nothing but a boy who is not master of himself. Pavese considers himself an adolescent. He writes: "so far in life my tendency has been to advocate enjoying things as they are, rather than to agitate to reform" (30). But he who enjoys does not possess. And although childhood and adolescence are spontaneous experiences and authentic living, they remain the age of impotence because they are not translated into fullness.

Pitiless self-analysis, that constant self-auscultation are the phases of a process of spiritual maturation during which the passive "I," that gives, arrives at the point of transforming itself into an active "I" that selects and receives. For the moment Pavese rejected suicide because "it is no longer an action, only a submission."[4] To face problems, to live them or to try to resolve them, this is the problem of the virile man.

On the other hand, however, if becoming adult means immersing oneself in history, that is to say acceptance of the problems and the values of a whole society and make a self-adjustment, then Pavese becomes aware that he must struggle against an insurmountable obstacle. His struggle was waged between thought and feeling, reason and emotion, between the rational and the irrational. In other words, maturity coincides with the discovery of the "I," when man becomes conscious of himself. But if this knowledge comes "through a loving recognition" (146) which is still equivalent to a state of inferiority, no real contact with others has been established. We become aware of the fact that maturity—that is to say the mastery of our own feelings—is

---

[4] *The Burning Brand*, 52.

essentially separation, "is isolation that is sufficient unto itself" (142). In childhood, instead, "one feels the never-ending thrill of universal knowledge" (146), for the very reason that we believe in others, and establish friendship and love in the most absolute sense. It follows that if every person represents a monad, human brotherhood is a form of communion. In other words the adult desires to remain conscious, and the other person can be approached only if a kind of common agreement takes place between the two. The reason for this is that the morality imposed by society does not correspond to the reality of facts. It does not facilitate union: all that remains is a path in between leading to communication. Society, finally, falsifies and impoverishes the feelings by justifying a kind of behavior that is then translated into indifference. Hence, for Pavese, day-to-day practical life reveals itself to be only an accumulation of interests which favor the shrewd.

In this practical life (at least on the basis of some caustic observations), women would be the greatest practicants of this shrewdness. "If a woman does not betray you, it is because it does not suit her convenience" (116). "The practical way of life is a matter of shrewdness, nothing else. Like the high-minded shrewdness of the engaged girl who feels she ought not to give herself to her lover, lest he should jilt her" (105).

Obviously Pavese was still resentful of his unfortunate amorous experience with women. But it is not exactly a vendetta against the female sex; rather, it is a documentation of the failure of his dialogue with life. His search, which should have culminated in the awareness of the duties to be assumed, and which should have persuaded Pavese to participate in society, actually drove him still farther away from both prospects. No longer accepting the common morality, which had revealed itself to be an amalgam of shrewdness and hypocrisy, he built for himself a system based on the Christian principle of charity. "Kant's philosophy is senseless and gloomy: if God does not exist, everything is permissible. Morality is not enough; the only creed worthy of respect is compassion—charity to one's neighbor. The teaching of Christ and Dostoievsky. All the rest is nonsense" (94).

Pavese descended ever more deeply into his subconscious, making a god of it, like Boehme and Jung. In other words, Pavese, in rejecting a philosophy that denied the existence of God, rejected it above all because it denied an absolute value to every ethic, thus precluding every form of community to man and, consequently, of charity. Charity, Pavese discovers, reflects the tendency toward order and cosmology. Soon, however, he had to realize his mistake on this point too. Charity requires a conscious annihilation of the personality, and for him this was too high a price. He ran the risk of falling once more into that childish ingenuousness which he had desperately sought to overcome. On the other hand, the price he paid for remaining in his solitude was exceedingly high. "I spent the whole evening sitting before a mirror to keep myself company" (132).

With the passing of time Pavese succeeded in forgetting himself and assuaging the pain of memories, at least to the extent that it allowed him to achieve a certain calm and a certain orientation in his studies. He wrote his first stories, and seriously interested himself once more in ethnology. But perhaps work was only a pretext, a palliative. In 1940 he got himself involved in another love affair. Now he was better prepared and approached the obstacle with caution. This time the girl was Fernanda Pivano, a former student of his during the time of his temporary teaching post at the *Liceo Massimo D'Azeglio*. Lajolo describes her as "a young lady now fully developed, beautiful, much courted, loquacious, elegant and happy."[5] I met Signora Pivano in 1953 and I remember her as an elegant woman, intelligent, and of a slightly faded beauty. For this reason, perhaps, she was more intense, but I would not be able to say how happy she was. She inquired about my American background and my grandfather, a Dixieland jazzman who is described on the jacket cover of my first novel, and I couldn't help remembering Pavese who courted her without saying anything to her, who tried to win her intellectually, and who

---

[5] Lajolo, *Il vizio assurdo*, 252.

160

unexpectedly twice asked her to marry him, being refused on both occasions.

But this time it was not the woman's fault. Perhaps it had not been the woman's fault the first time either. Nor, perhaps, was it the fault of the American actress Constance Dowling the last time. I remember the third time I met Pavese in Rome in 1950, at a table in the Caffè Greco, and she was there. I had met her at a party about a month before at the home of an American actress, Lois Maxwell, because at that time I was frequenting motion picture people. With me was the poet Rocco Scotellaro, who knew Pavese better than I did. But that encounter turned out to be an embarrassing occasion for all concerned. The custom at the Caffè Greco, known all too well to its clientele, is that upon entering one went to sit at a table occupied by a "familiar face." Miss Dowling invited us to sit at their table, but Pavese remained silent, visibly annoyed.

We left quickly, and lost our way while strolling through those tangled little streets between Piazza di Spagna and Via del Corso. In the neighborhood of the Hotel d'Inghilterra, on Via del Leoncino, we again ran into Pavese and Miss Dowling, who were trying to make their way to the Corso. The woman greeted us with a cordial "Ciao" while Pavese darted a helpless glance at us. I blushed. I felt miserable. I thought that my chances of being published by Einaudi, then run by Pavese, were ruined because of that stupid incident, and Scotellaro felt the same: he, too, had a book in Turin, at the mercy of Pavese's acceptance or rejection.[6] "He must think that we're spying on him," said Scotellaro. "He's in Rome incognito, and he doesn't like gossip." I replied, "If that's

---

[6] Rocco Scotellaro was a protegè of Carlo Levi, the internationally known author of *Christ Stopped at Eboli*. Scotellaro, who was born in Lucania in 1923 and died in Naples in 1953, was at that time waiting for the publication of his first book of poems, *E' fatto giorno*, by Einaudi. That publication never materialized. The book was published posthumously, in 1954, by Mondadori (Milan).

the case why does he show up in the Caffè Greco which is always very crowded?" But evidently she had dragged him there.

At any rate, Pavese knew that the deficiency in communication was his failing, not the other's. The wound was reopened, but he had expected it. Now his suffering derived not so much from the failure in himself as from the fact that it once more revealed his weakness:

> The bitterest lesson of this new kick fate has given you is that you have not changed at all or *corrected* anything by your two years of meditation. You have even lost the consolation of thinking that you might still be able to get out of this slough through meditation.[7]

In short, he had tried to remain always fully aware of himself, to take the initiative, to be superior, but he had not succeeded and he had fallen once more into the usual error. The problem of the preceding years still remained with him: how to approach the others. Further, the alternatives, the possible solutions were still the same: stoic isolation or Christian annihilation. These failures with women have a considerable importance in themselves because they support the need for self-knowledge. To understand the reason for a sorrow is tantamount to fleeing from despair.

The years from 1940 to 1945 were decisive for Pavese the man and the writer. He moved to Rome in order to open a branch of the Einaudi publishing house there. He wrote his first long stories in Rome. He was drafted into the army but discharged because he suffered from asthma. After the armistice of September 8, Pavese took refuge in Serralunga instead of joining his Communist friends and taking part in the partisan struggle. He spent his time reading and meditating, and discovered his "method" in the vocation of the myth. He wrestled with himself between mysticism and ethnology, two things that revealed themselves to him as being incompatible. Up to then the ethical imperative of love had

---

[7] *The Burning Brand*, 196.

acted in Pavese as communion with the other. But in Serralunga love became an undoing of the personality which, after the act of mortification, becomes a regenerative force. These are the phases that lead to ecstasy: "We feel this same glow of divinity when suffering has brought us to our knees, so much so that the first pang can give us a sense of joy, gratitude, anticipation.... We reach the point of wanting pain (255).

The configuration of the myth made steady progress. For the mentality of primitive man, the gesture has the value of a rite, and as a symbolical expression it therefore presupposes another reality. For the ascetic, possessed by God, his vision—his world of essences, his life as a series of encounters that are continually repeated in the same way—is at times exhausting because it involves an extremely emotional participation. Revelation occurs by way of the senses. The mystic humbles himself, in short, he annihilates himself in the single desire to become one with the Absolute. It is the transport of St. Teresa of Avila, entirely permeated with a sexual imagery.

But Pavese believes that "any suffering that does not also teach you something is futile" (144). The myth, in point of fact, is a manifestation of the irrational, of the unconscious. It is an involuntary, childish manifestation that Pavese interprets by using Freud: the unconscious is the same as impotence. But if the fundamental encounter, which through repetition is transformed into myth, occurs during childhood—if the life of the adult remains pre-fixed in time, man is deprived of free will. Myth, having become consciousness, discloses fate. In a very important page of his diary Pavese wrote:

> As a child one learns to know the world not—as it would seem—
> by immediate initial contact with things, but through signs of
> things: words, pictures, stories. If anything in the world inspires
> a moment of ecstatic emotion, we find that we are moved be-
> cause we were previously moved by it; and we were moved be-
> cause, on some day or other, it seemed to us transfigured, de-

tached from everything else, by a word, a fable, a fancy that we correct with it. (229)

For clarity's sake one might say that man, as it were, makes himself *happen*, (unconsciously), and then re-discovers himself by way of analysis. The myth is a tribal archetype and at the same time an objectification of feelings. Hence it functions as a contact, as a form of communion between the "I" and the collectivity. The chief difference between myth and mysticism is that mystical experience is not translated into knowledge. God is unknowable, and at any rate He represents an extra-human dimension. No religion would manage to survive without the presupposition of faith. Pavese's thought is an assertion of faith in the real. He is a non-contemplative mystic who perceives the spiritual only through experience. It is from this experience that revelation — myth — is born from which he derives the ethic of fate. Thus he made the following entry in his diary: "This very suggestion that the subconscious may be God, that God lives and speaks in our subconscious mind, has exalted you" (276).

At the end of the war Pavese joined the Italian Communist Party. But his attitude remained ambiguous: after trying to assimilate religion and communism into his thinking, he was forced to reject them. God, if He exists, is too distant from us. And communism is history, it situates the Absolute in hope, in generations of struggles and sacrifices. On the other hand, Pavese does not know what to do with a reality that does not have a radical link with his essence, his subconscious etc.

Pavese achieved the status of a writer of the first rank in Italian literature following the publication of *Il compagno* and *La casa in collina*. And all people turned to him, all needed him. At that time I wrote him a letter (1948), requesting permission to use — if nobody else was — a typewriter belonging to the Einaudi offices in Rome in order to type a copy of one of my novels.[8] (Although he

---

[8] Rimanelli writes Pavese asking if he could use a typewriter in the Einaudi's Roman office on June 4, 1949. See *"Tiro al piccione* di Giose Ri-

had returned to Turin, Pavese was still officially responsible for the branch in Rome.) He replied promptly that he had no objection to my using a typewriter, but that the decision would have to be made by the new director of the branch, the critic Carlo Muscetta.

For those who knew him and for those who did not know him, Pavese was already a kind of myth. But he was increasingly more alone. "For you, home means the office, the cinema and your own clenched jaws" (228). It was in this state of mind that he met the American actress with whom he lived his last adventure. He wrote to Lajolo that "an unexpected lark from America" had arrived for him. And he added: "But she will soon go away, I feel it, I will hear her wings flap, without even having the strength to make an attempt, to utter a shout to call her back."[9]

2. THE INTERNAL CAUSALITIES

One day in 1952 I was guest at the house of Maria Livia Serini, on Via dei Quatto Venti in Rome, the Turinese young woman to whom Pavese was linked by a bond of affectionate friendship, and to whom, for about two years, he dictated a couple of his novels. It was a happy gathering, there had been much drinking, and now the group of friends was preparing to wind up the festivities at a restaurant in the Trastevere quarter. While the others were listening to records, I took *Dialoghi con Leucò* down from the shelves and read Pavese's affectionate dedication to Maria Livia. At first she said nothing, but then the expression of her face changed and she exclaimed: "Take the book, take all the Pavese you find. But let's not talk about him. It makes me mad and sad." From that day on our friendship was somewhat solidified in the remembrance of Pavese. We always talked about him. And at the end of every discussion she gave utterance to the question that still tormented her: "Why did he do it?"

---

manelli e il ritorno agli inizi: la corrispondenza completa tra lo scrittore molisano e l'editore Giulio Einaudi," 286.
[9] Davide Lajolo, *Il vizio assurdo*, 113.

Pavese did not kill himself for any woman. Perhaps he conceived of suicide as the ultimate expression of his very being, a gesture for which his life was but a preparation. It is also not enough to assert that the central problem of his life was an impossible maturity, or the lack of a bond with the *other*, the world of causes and effects. It is clear, on the other hand, that Pavese interprets life and reality dualistically. And an attentive reading of the diary confirms that he considered his task to be the clarification and possibly the reconciliation of the two extremes, sensuousness and existing tragically, extroversion and introversion.

For Pavese knowing was a form of arriving at the secret of knowledge. In order to reveal himself to himself, in a first phase he tried to objectivize himself. For example: "If only we could *treat ourselves* as we treat *other men*…"[10] "The art of putting ourselves in another man's place and so learning that each is concerned only with himself…" (120). But all this becomes still more evident if the myth is interpreted as a means and not an end. Once having unmasked his myths, and consequently reduced them to fate, Pavese transformed himself into a character. In fact, his tendency to use the second person to address himself, the third person to talk about himself to others, and finally his interest in dreams, were symptoms of a split personality. They concealed his need to *see himself* act. There was a cognitive process even in this seeing himself act. Only when fate emerges from it does freedom vanish.

What is fate? It represents the objectivization of an entire life, and therefore of the present. Pavese observed that fate is not things that happen according to a scheme. Rather, each of us, if he has the strength, interprets the things that have occurred, arranging them according to a meaning. For Pavese, each life is a closed world.[11] This is because each person creates his own fate which

---

[10] *The Burning Brand*, 126.

[11] In his *Death and Sensuality: A Study of Eroticism and the Taboo* (New York: Walker and Company, 1962) 12), George Bataille writes: "Beings which reproduce themselves are distinct from one another, and those reproduced are likewise distinct from each other, just as they are distinct

will be discovered in maturity. The mind (in childhood) decides the facts that will come into being, whereas man is free of every determinism. Nevertheless the man who has reduced the myths into consciousness is fatally separated from himself and from his world. In practice objectivization leads to alienation. "I am sad, useless, like a god."[12]

Hence Pavese's need for contact which in the years of maturity became an utter fixation. But the conjunction, the communion, never occurred:

> You are alone, and you know it. You were born to live under the wings of someone who would sustain and justify you, someone kind enough to let you play the fool and imagine yourself capable of remaking the world singlehanded. You never found anyone who could endure so much; hence your suffering when friends depart, not because of any tenderness for them; hence your resentment towards the one who has gone; hence the facility for finding a new ally — not out of cordiality. You are a woman, and like a woman you are obstinate. But alone you are not enough, and you know it. (305-306)

The arrival of Constance Dowling was another illusion, and Pavese knew it. But he gave himself up to it. This blonde woman, refined, precarious, vivacious and distant (there are so many like her in the United States, a cross between mother-father figure, hard work and fatalism), for him symbolized the past, his childhood, the dream of an America learned through literature, and so on. But by transforming woman into myth, which means letting go, a status of inferiority (i.e. impotence), he ended up by possessing nothing. And when he was in possession, that is to say,

---

from their parents. Each being is distinct from all others. His birth, his death, the events of his life may have an interest for others, but he alone is directly concerned in them. He is born alone. He dies alone. Between one being and another, there is a gulf, a discontinuity."
12 *The Burning Brand*, 317.

when woman is not myth—he felt himself absent, detached. Pavese, in short, would have liked to possess himself and woman at the same time; but he was too overcome by himself. His conquest, his maturity in the end constituted defeat.

3. *DEATH WILL COME...*

The poems after *Lavorare stanca* are connected with his diary *Il mestiere di vivere*, and they are all dated, with the exception of one—"La casa"—which still suggests the old style. These poems, therefore, are first of all to be interpreted in relation to that spiritual development which had been assuming specific contours in Pavese during the war years. But they are also important from a technical point of view. They represent a renewal of rhythms in comparison with those of 1934. Now the poet no longer invents characters, he no longer narrates, but expresses only his emotion. If in *Lavorare stanca* he presents the exterior life of the character and his relation to the landscape, thus falling into naturalistic description, with the poems of 1945 and of 1950 he gave up description, the images become epithets, attributes that transfigured the woman-goddess into a cosmic symbol:

> You are life and death.
> You came in March
> on the naked earth..
> your shudder endures.[13]

Instead of the epic-narrative, here we have lyrical poetry. Necessarily, the rhythm is different. It is no longer slow and calm, but impatient, dry, hammering. Words assume an importance they did not have in *Lavorare stanca*. They contain a violent emotional charge even without being onomatopoeic. They are metaphorical, mythic, hallucinatory words that have the same power of ineluctability and of hieratic evocation that we find, for example, in lita-

---

[13] *Poesie edite e inedite*, 183.

nies or in prayers. The poet's experience is in the present, but he literally creates the woman while seeking her name.

A group of poems written in 1945 opens with the following lines:

> Red land black land,
> you come from the sea,
> from the parched green,
> where are ancient words
> and blood-red toil
> and geraniums among stones... (168)

Here the recurrent images constitute a leitmotif even if a story is not being unfolded, and we glimpse a certain but almost imperceptible structure in them. Pavese, however, defines woman from the time of the very first poems. The designation "you come from the sea" immediately discloses the mythic level. It is Aphrodite who is being defined. She is continually being associated with the earth, the countryside, the process of nature which renews itself cyclically but remains the same in repetition. Woman is immobilized. She becomes an archetype

> of seasons and crushed dreams
> which on the moonlight reveals
> as very old, like
> the hands of your mother,
> the pot of the brazier. (164)

She is something that no one has ever possessed, who is self-sufficient, who has no need of others. But at the same time, for the "I" she is something more, an intimate myth, his entire childhood.

> You are the closed cellar,
> hardened by the earth,
> where the barefoot child
> entered one day

and thinks of it always. (168)

But the woman is dark, like the cellar—and impenetrable, inscrutable. As long as they are lovers they will always be enemies, because one will try to possess the other. The complete union will be effected only in death, beyond human individuality.

Two poems from the collection of *La terra e la morte* probably do not belong to this group, or at least not to that theme of sentimental adventure. They are "Tu non sai le colline" (You don't know the hills) and "E allora noi vili" (And so we cowards). In the first poem the "I" defines his hills; in the second, perhaps, the war, a collective experience.

They are autobiographical poems, written in Rome from October 27 to December 3, 1945. Pavese was under the influence of another infatuation, the third one in his life. All three were important. On November 27 he wrote in his diary:

> It came to you for the third time, that day. It is dawn, a dawn of scattered cloud, pale mauve. The Tiber has the same color. Sadness, but not overbearingly so, ready to be cheered by the sun. Houses and trees, everything's sleeping. I watched the dawn a while ago, from her side windows. There was haze, stillness, and a human warmth. Astarte-Aphrodite-Melita is still sleeping. She will wake in a bad mood. For the third time, my day has come. The keenest pang of my grief is to know that grief will pass. Now it is easy to feel humiliated. What next?[14]

The woman sleeps at dawn because "for you the dawn is silence," while the poet has spent a sleepless night. The thought is clear: the woman who sleeps is self-sufficient, she is free, there is no one yet who tames her by possessing her, nor is she interested in possession. For Pavese this constitutes reflection: "What a great thought it is that truly *nothing is due to us*. Has anyone ever promised us anything? Then why should we expect anything?" (283).

---

[14] *The Burning Brand*, 282-283.

The other group of poems, *Verrà la morte e avrà i tuoi occhi* (Death will come and it will have your eyes), in a certain sense repeats Pavese's experience of 1945. They are sustained by the same meter, and images and words are used there as in the first poems. They are a reflection of the mythic return. This time, too, Aphrodite has "come from the sea." And Pavese on March 9, 1950 noted: "My heart throbs; I tremble, I cannot stop sighing. Is it possible at my age?" (359).

The difference is that this time the woman is "life and death." The encounter which occurred in March coincided with germination and had the meaning of a rebirth. For Pavese it was an awakening, a hope with a question mark: "Yet I feel confident and [incredibly] serenely hopeful" (360). He knows that it will not last, but he snatches at every mad idea that it might last. Meanwhile the poems are suffused with a tender light, and this atmosphere surrounds the woman who has become spring, who transforms night into morning, who is "sweet fruit," "clear water," "anemone or cloud." But at the same time she is a "fierce root."

> Your light step
> has re-opened the pain. (167)

Communion is impossible.

Pavese's suicide is usually interpreted as a symbolical gesture in terms of these poems. It does not seem to me, however, that this idea of sacrifice, the consummation of a rite of union with the woman-goddess-mother, is valid. The thought of suicide had accompanied Pavese from the time he was eighteen. Lajolo writes:

> At eighteen he had already written (in a letter to a friend): *Pavese è morto*, Pavese is dead. And if shortly afterwards he declared that he must return to the struggle, it was only to dedicate the rest of his life to poetry. His struggle, he explained, consisted solely in persevering in order to reach the heights of "the solitude of geniuses." The "blows and kicks" were not an excuse for resignation; and for this reason the final poetry, anticipated in

the pre-university poetry, death returns as the protagonist, that same death before which he will immolate himself, evoking it once more in the final, most desolate lines:

Death will come and it will have your eyes —
that death that is with us
from morning to night, sleepless,
deaf, like an old remorse
or an absurd vice.

It is the same "absurd vice," Lajolo concludes, that tortured Pavese in these early days and crept into his blood like a disease. It was his syphilis—as he wrote—a kind of suicide fever which, barely expulsed, quickly returned, incurable.[15]

Obviously, Pavese had managed to overcome the many crises because, in point of fact, he had succeeded in transforming the woman into a "means" of a cognitive process. This process came to an end in 1950. In order to go forward Pavese would have had to deny himself—that is to say, to accept the emptiness of a de-mythified life. It was this that he was afraid of. Clearly, he knew that the fate which hovered above him was sterility. Therefore suicide came to represent a choice—the only way of escaping from fate. And it also represented a gesture of deep, infinite resignation.

The diary is important for the complete understanding of the man and the writer. But by itself it is still an "object" that sears. One feels almost a sense of self-righteousness in reading it, like watching another perform an obscene act. It wounds us in our pride as "sane" people. Our narcissism lies in this. So we wreak our revenges. It is called masochism and taking pleasure in the sorrow of another. And it is forgotten that this man, through his suffering, has not limited any one's freedom, and that on the contrary he took upon himself the sufferings of others, and he has given us poetry.

---

[15] Davide Lajolo, *Il vizio assurdo*, 89.

By killing himself, Cesare Pavese has asked only that too much gossip not be indulged in over his case. But now his case, as such, is past. With the passing of years, it is he as a whole being who remains, grown monolithic. And this might suffice because it constitutes the envy of the gods. But by remembering him, and by studying him, we have also learned how to respect him.

APPENDIX

The following letters were exchanged between Hon. Davide Lajolo, a deputy in the Italian Parliament, Elio Archimede, literary editor of the Asti weekly *La nuova provincia*, and myself. They are documents that underline the intentions of this study of Pavese, on how it came into being. It also gives an idea of the Italian public's interest in the personality of Cesare Pavese.

℘

Milan
November 3, 1960.

Dear Rimanelli:

When I wrote the book on Pavese I not only had in mind what you wrote in your book of literary criticism namely that Pavese was worthy of a comprehensive study — but I wanted also to consult with you.[1] I looked for you in Rome, but you were already in the United States.

I also wanted to ask you if you had any unpublished material or remembrances concerning Pavese. Unfortunately, it was not possible because of your sojourns in America. Did you see the book? I hope it has filled the gap a little.

The book has enjoyed a great success. It is already in its second edition, and the critics have been favorable, even the most difficult ones, without dragging in the author's political party affiliation. Why don't you write a review about the book?

Our friendship was alive and kicking even during our last encounter on the train, do you remember? Even though you write

---

[1] Lajolo's book is entitled *Il vizio assurdo* (*An Absurd Vice*). It is the most complete and affectionate biography of Pavese, and also contains many and varied critical insights. The book of literary criticism to which Lajolo refers is my *Il mestiere del furbo*, an ironic paraphrase of Pavese's book entitled *Il mestiere di vivere*.

for a weekly that is not tender with the Communists,[2] I think that you can write a review of the book. Your views, be they positive or negative, would interest me. Notwithstanding I made an effort to be objective and I believe I have been sincere. Above all, in having demonstrated that I was fond of Pavese, just as he was.

Will you answer?

Affectionately,
Yours, Lajolo

⌀

New York
November 24, 1960[3]

Dear Ulisse:[4]

If I were still writing for that weekly that is "not tender with Communists," I would have certainly reviewed your book on Pavese. That magazine gave me the freedom to write about anything I liked. Perhaps for this reason, they attributed critical pieces to me that were not mine, which I didn't like.

I left that magazine after the publication of a harshly critical survey of Italian contemporary letters, precisely when I could have used the name of A.G. Solari. And when I left I issued a public statement that you didn't read, since that position had become superfluous for someone who does not want protection nor did he conduct his critical battles for blackmail purposes. I also left Italy, because if you have to call it quits you need to disappear. I'm in New York, not in Canada, where I am a professor. Your letter found me here, and I am most grateful to you for having written me, because it has brought me two joys: to learn that you have

---

[2] The newspaper referred to by Lajolo is *Lo Specchio* of Rome, for which I wrote a weekly column.
[3] This letter and the accompanying syllabus were not in Rimanelli's original manuscript. See *Rimanelliana*, 104-108.
[4] Ulisse was the *nom de guerre* that David Lajolo assumed during the years of struggle waged by the Italian Resistance.

written "a book" on Pavese, and to be able to tell you that, also on my behalf, the friendship and the esteem for you are very much alive.

You know that it was Pavese who pulled me out of a hole; the Pavese who was not always tender with young writers; the Pavese who was both timid and presumptuous; the Pavese who wore death; the Pavese who did not know how to love. And that is the same Pavese who was tender with young writers; the Pavese who was attentive and understanding; the Pavese who knew above all how to love. He came to retrieve the manuscript at my home, in Via dei Serpenti in Rome, in a subletted room, where there were whores and cats, personally taking it out of a cardboard suitcase that I kept under the bed. If it still interests you, this is how it went: he had come to Rome a few days before Easter of 1950, or '49, with that girl.[5] In those days, I held two jobs: at the same time that I was deciphering the Calabrian manuscripts of Padula for Muscetta, I was typing Jovine's *Le terre del Sacramento*. One day I didn't have any money, not even to pay for dinner, and Jovine, by an oversight, had forgotten to pay me. I then stole a book: *Prima che il gallo canti*. I wanted to sell it, but could not find anyone who would buy it. With that book in hand, I went to Via Uffici del Vicario to see if at least Muscetta could pay me. And he did. I thought that I needed to return the book to Jovine. I then saw Pavese, in the middle of a lounge, perfectly alone. Five minutes later I saw him again at the bar Giolitti. He offered me and a friend of mine who worked at the Einaudi office a coffee. I showed him his book and told him the story of the theft. He responded: "I've never stolen, not even books." However he signed his autograph (generic) on that book, and I had to buy another copy for Jovine. He then asked me what I was doing. I told him that I was working in my own way towards a degree in the Faculty of Letters and Philosophy, that on Saturday I boxed, during the week I wrote theses at the National Library for students who had no desire to write

---

[5] The "girl" referenced here is Constance Dowling. The encounter in Rome would have been during Easter of 1950. Just before Constance Dowling's departure for America in early April of that year, Pavese went to Rome in the hope of defining their relationship.

them on their own and that, additionally, I now was working for Jovine and for Muscetta. For Muscetta I had even edited part of the glossary of the comedies of De Filippo. I told him that I also wrote, and that I had written, but in '47, a novel on the fascists of the Salò Republic. He liked it when I told him I had been one of them and that I had written a novel. He said "send it to me," using the polite form. Yes, he said it definitely in the polite form. I didn't send it to him but I thought about sending it to him. Then he returned to Rome a few months before the Strega Literary Prize, again with that girl.[6] He was with her when I ran into him at the Caffè Greco, in a corner away from the "action." I was with Rocco Scotellaro. Pavese didn't recognize me, but he did recognize Rocco. The girl recognized me. We had seen each other many times before, in via del Babuino. Pavese then said: "And the novel?" "It's in the suitcase," I replied. The girl said: "Why don't we go and get it?" Rocco was left on foot, as Pavese paid for a taxi. Afterwards, I remained in my room as they went off with the book.[7] And I never saw Pavese again. A letter arrived about a week later. He liked the book and wanted to publish it. I even received a contract. They printed it in the series "Coralli." When Pavese died the book was in proofs. And then they didn't want to publish it any longer. Bruno Fonzi told me that it had been Calvino.[8]

That's it.

I wrote a piece on Pavese in 1954 that appeared in the *Gazzetta del Popolo*.[9] When I was in Turin, I conducted an investigation of the night schools. I found a teacher who spoke to me about a mysterious Pavese. Pavese had been, for a certain period of time, a

---

[6] Pavese was accompanied to the Strega Literary Prize ceremony by Constance Dowling's sister, Doris, in July of 1950.

[7] The dates and circumstances of the encounter with Pavese described in this letter differ from those recounted in the opening section (I. The External Causalities) of this volume's closing chapter.

[8] For the actual events surrounding Rimanelli's novel, *Tiro al piccione*, see "Tiro al piccione di Giose Rimanelli e il ritorno agli inizi: la corrispondenza completa tra lo scrittore molisano e l'editore Giulio Einaudi": 270-325.

[9] Rimanelli's essay, "Ricordo di Pavese," appeared in the *Gazzetta del Popolo* on September 2, 1955.

teacher in one of Turin's night schools for tired seamstresses and laborers.

Now I'd like to read your book. Perhaps I can recommend that it be translated here in America. Maybe this book of yours will make him known in America, where he is not known; however, there are some young people here who love him, young intellectuals, poets, and artists, a small group whom I have met; and some of Pavese's poems have been translated by these young intellectuals and published in experimental magazines.

I'm teaching at New York University, and in the most progressive college of America, Sarah Lawrence College. At the University I'll be teaching a course on Pavese (you can see it in the attached syllabus), at the College my female students are studying him. In fact, I will request your book for some University libraries; however, I don't know the name of its publisher and how much it costs.

If you send me a copy, I'll write to you about the book, what I think about it, once I have read it.

In the mean time, best wishes, for the book and for your nomination as a member to Parliament. I don't know if you'll find yourself well at Montecitorio. But you always do things well.

Affectionately,
Giose Rimanelli

[Below is course information referenced in the above letter to Lajolo]

NEW YORK UNIVERSITY
GRADUATE SCHOOL OF ARTS & SCIENCES

ITALIAN: LA LETTERATURA ITALIANA CONTEMPORANEA
Prof. Giose Rimanelli
A Bibliography presenting more recent and current titles:

FEBRUARY

ASPETTI DELLA LETTERATURA ITALIANA TRA LE DUE GUERRE
G. Ravegnani, *Uomini visti*, 2 vols (Mondadori, Milano)
G. Rimanelli, *Il mestiere del furbo* (Sugar, Milano)

TOZZI E IL ROMANZO MODERNO

Tozzi, *Tre croci*, romanzo (Vallecchi, Firenze)

E. De Michelis, *Saggio su Tozzi* (Vallecchi, Firenze)

ALVARO E LA PROVINCIA

C. Alvaro, *Gente in Aspromonte*, romanzo (Bompiani Milano)

G. Pullini, *Narratori italiani del Novecento*

JOVINE E LA LOTTA DI CLASSE

F. Jovine, *Le terre del Sacramento* (Einaudi, Torino)

MARCH

LAMPEDUSA E IL ROMANZO STORICO

G. Tomasi di Lampedusa, *Il Gattopardo* (Feltrinelli, Milano)

MORAVIA E IL ROMANZO POPOLARE

A. Moravia, *La Ciociara* (Bompiani, Milano)

D. Fernandez, *Il romanzo italiano e la crisi della coscienza moderna* (Lerici, Milano)

VITTORINI E L'UOMO

E. Vittorini, *Conversazione in Sicilia*, romanzo (Bompiani, Milano)

PAVESE E IL MITO

C. Pavese, *La luna e i falò*, romanzo (Einaudi, Torino)

C. Pavese, *La letteratura americana e altri saggi*, (Einaudi, Torino)

L. Piccioni, *Letteratura leopardiana e altri saggi* (Vallecchi, Firenze)

APRIL

PRATOLINI E L'ITALIA

V. Pratolini, *Cronaca familiare*, romanzo (Vallecchi, Firenze)

CALVINO E LA SATIRA CAVALLERESCA

I. Calvino, *Il cavaliere inesistente*, romanzo (Einaudi, Torino)

REA E LA SCUOLA SALERNITANA

D. Rea, *Una vampata di rossore*, romanzo (Mondadori, Milano)

MORETTI E IL NEOREALISMO
U. Moretti, *Gente di Babuino*, racconti

MAY

C. E. GADDA E I DIALETTALI
C.E. Gadda, *Quer pasticciaccio brutto de via Merulana*, romanzo (Garzanti, Milano)
P.P. Pasolini, *Ragazzi di vita*, romanzo (Garzanti, Milano)
B. Fenoglio, *La malora*, romanzo (Einaudi, Torino)

CONCLUSION
G. Rimanelli, *Una posizione sociale*, romanzo (Vallecchi, Firenze)
L. De Stefani, *Passione di Rosa*, romanzo (Mondadori, Milano)
G. Berto, *Il cielo è rosso*, romanzo (Longanesi, Milano)

(NOTE: Class reports should not exceed 25 minutes in duration.)

∅

Rome
December 2, 1960

Dear Rimanelli:

Your new role also shows that you are a clever and resourceful man. I have seen your teaching program: it's excellent. An excellent thing for Italian culture.

I will have a copy of the book sent to you immediately and I will be very grateful to you if you can be of some help in having it translated in the United States.

I like you as much as ever and I embrace you.

Yours,
Ulisse

∅

Vancouver
February 7, 1964

Dear Ulisse:

Don't be surprised. I'm still around, even though I have not written you since 1960 to today, when we started our epistolary to each other. The last letter that I wrote you, in response to one of December 2, 1960, bears the date of March 22, 1961. I have the carbon copy, and among other things I then told you that I had passed on *Il vizio assurdo* to Dutton publishers — who returned it to me about a month later adducing the reason that it would be difficult to market it. In those days only a few knew Pavese, at best ten or so professors. The *Diario* came out in the United States in December 1961 (with the title *The Burning Brand*) as also did *La casa in collina*. From that time only four books of Pavese have been published in America but there has been no book on Pavese. I continued my efforts on behalf of your biography. But *Il vizio assurdo* has always run smack up against the absurd American vice of weighing things in terms of the "foreseeable" profit from the sale of a consumer's item and not in terms of the "unforeseeable" profit that would accrue from the marketing of a commodity, that is a qualitative entity in itself. To this day your book encounters difficulties. It runs into them because Pavese's work also runs into such difficulties since the Italians have not known how to validate it and protect it. The Italian character is defeatist, and when it suspends polemics it becomes indifferent. But it is useless to lament further. Tommaso Campanella was more farseeing. Do you remember his *Poesie filosofiche*? "Italy, tomb of her lights, of foreigner's candlesticks."

Your book is still a valuable source of documents and of psychological interpretations. I have not given up the idea of being able to see it published some day not only in the United States but everywhere. As regards the United States, however, Pavese can be brought to the attention of the serious reading public only by way of critical studies. Joyce had the critics behind him. Today his books are published and republished because they are required reading in the universities and along with those books hundreds of books of Joycean criticism and interpretation are also published and republished. The French and the Anglo-Americans are excellently organized on the critical front regarding their writers. Theirs is a culture in movement. Our literary critics instead, are still scholastic even if they pretend to be secular. Indeed, the parish priests are always on the scene. By reflection the Italian criticism that is written in America also shows traces of that which is written in Italy. In the universities the number of writers of the post-Renaissance who are the subject of study can be counted on one's fingers. Whole cycles are forgotten. The discouraging word is this: now and then there are good books, but there is no active movement of ideas.

Pavese, obviously, belongs to the band of those few contemporary writers who warrant critical study. But he remains an isolated event among those few. Major criticism makes no reference to Pavese, because there is lack of effective comparative studies. I could cite you a dozen of specialists on contemporary Italian literature who work on a comparative basis. Among them are Lewis, Cambon, Della Terza, Bergin, Beall, Cecchetti, Slonim and Fiedler. (Together with Cambon one of the most committed scholars was Renato Poggioli. Unfortunately he died too soon, to the misfortune of Italian studies and to the sorrow of his friends). On Pavese, however, there exists nothing at all, save for an article by Fiedler and an excellent essay by Professor John Freccero (limited only to *La luna e i falò*). As if for sheer irony the first book on Italian literature, which was published recently, written in order to fill a gap and at the same time in order to interest the American reader in our modern literary history, hardly mentions Pavese's name!

Now there is in preparation a collection of critical essays on Italian classics of all times (about thirty volumes in all, I believe). Upon being invited to participate I included Pavese. It will be a study of about 200 pages which I will embark upon most eagerly. But this is only a first step. It might be possible, once the ice is broken, to publish also *Il vizio assurdo*.

In the end the purpose of this long, chatty letter has been to pass on some good news to you. You were so fond of Pavese and you devoted one of your books to him. I, who was also fond of him, even though I could never consider myself a friend of his, will devote a book to him which I hope will turn out to be at least as important as yours. Your suggestions on this book (which I will start to write around May or June) would be most valuable to me, as would also the unpublished material that may possibly be in your possession. I must still mentally organize the contents of the book, and know exactly therefore what can be used or not. I'll be more explicit later. Meanwhile this letter constitutes a resumption of our dialogue – if you haven't forgotten me.

Ciao. Yours
Rimanelli

∅

Rome
February 11, 1964

Dear Rimanelli

You can imagine if I have forgotten you! I am glad to have received your letter and the items of news. Those on Pavese are always of interest to me. Good luck with your book! I am certain it will be a notable achievement. I don't know whether you know it but a "Mollia" and a "Mondo" have come out in Italy but neither of the two is worth much.

As regards the material I put all that I have in the book. On the other hand, in these last few months I have been trying to collect other letters in order to prepare Pavese's complete epistolary. I don't know whether I'll succeed, sooner or later. In any case, if you will write me, I will gladly give you the things that could be useful to you. Since I am quite mad and I like the work of being a writer, which helps me also to make politics more digestible, I have written a play on Pavese's problems: the man of interrupted dialogues.[10] Nobody has seen it yet. If it should go over it could be another contribution to inducing discussion on Pavese and to fur-

---

[10] Diego Fabbri and Davide Lajolo, *Il vizio assurdo. Dramma e dibattito*, Milan: Rizzoli (1974). Subsequently, Mariacristina Faraglia edited another edition of the play that includes correspondence between the two authors and critical essays: *Il vizio assurdo. Il testo teatrale, il carteggio, saggi critici e testimonianze*, Rome: Nuova Cultura (2004).

thering knowledge about him also among those who need the stage in order to get to know a writer.

Now please don't let another two years go by before you come to life and answer my letter.

Yours,
Davide Lajolo

∅

Asti
February 21, 1964

Dear Sir:

Our weekly *La nuova provincia*, resuming one of the most serious traditions of the Italian province, wishes to devote a page to cultural problems in each issue.

Bearing in mind our modest possibilities, and above all our commitment not to concern ourselves generically or presumptuously with the great problems, we count on establishing study centers on personalities and issues which are of particular interest to our province and to our region.

These study-centers will revolve around our cultural page and will be of interest to civic organizations, which in some way are linked to the personality or the issue that we propose for study.

In view of the recent initiatives surrounding the name of Cesare Pavese (the unveiling of a bust in Santo Stefano Belbo, the Canelli literary and journalistic prize), we have proposed "Cesare Pavese" as our first subject of study. For this purpose we would be pleased to publish the letter which, on February 7, 1964, you sent to Davide Lajolo, and which provides a very interesting picture of the state of Pavesian studies in the United States. We would be grateful, furthermore, if you could furnish us with other news about your interest in Pavese and about the awareness regarding Pavese in North America.

With many thanks,
Elio Archimede

∅

Vancouver
February 27, 1964[11]

Dear Mr. Archimede:

I have received your letter of February 21, and I hasten to reply. You may, if you wish, publish my letter to Lajolo regarding Pavese. Indeed I am glad that your newspaper is undertaking to publicize Pavese's name now and as much as it can. It also should be done by other Italian newspapers, and especially by the teachers in our universities who still deal gingerly with contemporary literature, since they do not have enough trust to defend it, and consequently establish it. The "Case of Pavese," as such, is already slightly different: several Ph.D. theses have already been written on Pavese but there is some doubt about as to how effective they have been. Pavesian criticism, not counting that in the newspapers which is always occasioned by some topical event, is still minimal and not at all satisfactory.

You ask me why I am interesting myself in Pavese. It's an accident. I was asked to write a book and I immediately thought of Pavese. Before all else I am bound to Pavese for a sentimental reason. Davide Lajolo was driven to write that tribute to Pavese, which became an impassioned biography, a clarification, an offertory and a critical query, for a reason that was first of all sentimental and personal, and only later of a critical character. It is the same with me, but I cannot guarantee its success as a venture in criticism. Others will judge this. The sentimental reason is that Pavese got his hands on one of my novels, accepted it and had it printed by Einaudi. Then, following his death, it was returned to me in galley-proofs with no explanation. In short, an offspring born and dead before he even had a chance to open his eyes. It

---

[11] This letter has been modified in parts by Rimanelli from the original that was first published in the Spring of 1964 in *La nuova provincia* and subsequently in the collection *Terra rossa terra nera*.

was later published by Mondadori with the help of Vittorini and Remo Cantoni. That novel is entitled *Tiro al piccione*, and in its time it created quite a stir.

This is the previous history. But Pavese's writing, save for the *Dialoghi con Leucò* and *La luna e i falò*, was pretty much alien to me in Italy. I had little feeling or understanding for it. My literary education had been different, and my preferences were of a different sort. Pavese had no influence whatsoever on me. I must admit, however, that I was so absorbed in myself at that time that I found reading his books hard work, consequently I read them superficially. Things changed later. I happened to find myself lying still in a hospital bed in Mexico City for about a week. There I read and studied *Lavorare stanca*. It contains all of Pavese, that is to say, all his essential themes are to be found in it. The fact of being in Mexico signified participation in the *fiesta*, that is to say in a cosmic experiment in disorder, a journey into the unconscious which brings one back to the beginnings and hence to a new start, a re-vivification. Thus it was the Mexican *fiesta* which offered me a clear view of the myth about which Pavese had always talked, and it clarified for me the significance of Nuto's clarinet, of those orgiastic dances on the threshing floors and in the hills, of this sudden madness of Valino, the meaning of blood and of human sacrifices, of words pronounced with murmurings, which tell tales by touching lightly upon a story and imply other stories and still other symbols.

It is well known that Pavese had deeply immersed himself in anthropological studies. It is wrong, however, to assert — as Moravia asserts — that "Pavese's ideas are those of a critic, of a literary man, or in other words a reflection *on* the works and *after* the works, not *through* the works and *before* the works." One must first settle accounts with *Lavorare stanca* before judging Pavese's works. The *Diario* can also be taken as a reflection on the works and after the works, but it clarifies and does not add ideas to the works. In short, before having understood these things on a critical and creative plane, Pavese had lived then within himself, thus the Langhe, Asti, Canelli, Santo Stefano, the whole of Piedmont, for him (and also for us) ceases to be mere geographical references and become part of that mythic history which belongs to the history of mankind. If it is true, as Moravia says, that Pavese's ideas are more than work summed up as a whole because it bears traces of a certain literariness which is never felicitous nor truly resolved into poetry, then we should apply the same judgment, summing up, also to the work of Joyce and Thomas Mann who, like Pavese, were professional men of letters, and they too drew abundantly on mythology and anthropology, as well as making use of symbols and thematic recurrences. The truth is that Pavese's poetry, and consequently all his work, offers — as do for that matter all great literary works — diverse planes and levels, they are strata piled upon strata, like those very ancient stones that bear the marks of their different formation. The successive strata never cancel out the previous accumulations, they only hide them.

By virtue, therefore, of the quality of his writing and of his views, Pavese appears to some like a writer portraying social facts, to others like a difficult stylist concerned with intellectual considerations of form. To others still he is an artist who has elaborated archetypes. There was a time, for example, when naïve critics saw in *Moby Dick* merely a philological concern often ending up in riddles and charades. But great works harbor secrets that the psychology or the style or the realism which they contain are not always sufficient to clarify. They have a mythic time that renders the past present or the present already past, and nevertheless sacred, actual, unpetrified, because they constantly offer a new way to explain reality.

Therefore a study of Pavese would have to be conducted not only in a comparative key, but comprehensively by pursuing an investigation along the various directions that his poetry suggests. In order to do this, it is obvious, and above all necessary, to individuate and isolate, and above all to establish clearly the relations between Pavese and realism, Pavese and existentialism, Pavese and his contemporaries, Pavese and America etc. Now it seems possible for everybody to recognize direct American influences on Cesare Pavese's poetics especially in the relation Pavese-America. This is fine. It must be made pointedly clear, however, and one must insist upon it that America had acted upon Pavese only as a pretext, as a dimension of memory. We must bear clearly in mind that we have all had fathers and professors and books that have held colloquy with our souls, often changing it — but at a certain moment we have learned to walk by ourselves, to think with our own brains, and to suffer in our own flesh. Hence one does not arrive at Pavese, as it were but one could very well begin from him.

As regards "Pavese in America" my letter to Lajolo is rather explicit. If Pavese's name is not as well-known as that of Silone and of Moravia, it is, however, known by specialists. A strange phenomenon is being actualized, not only in the United States but in all Europe. Cesare Pavese is one of those writers who conquers a public little by little. He belongs to that tiny band of writers of modern *weltliteratur* to which belong the Prousts, the Joyces, the Faulkners and the Lowrys (if we may paraphrase a judgment of Maurice Nadeau re-echoed later by the excellent translator Giorgio Monicelli), whose first works initially found only a small number of admirers and later, in the course of time, faithful followers ever growing in numbers. Pavese's fate is still and always time. And time works in his favor. In Italy Lorenzo Mondo's study constitutes a good point of departure. Fernandez has already discussed him in France, a study on Pavese has been published in Germany, and one is in preparation in Spain. In America recently, thanks to the interest in Italian literature shown by young and talented scholars, a new process of cognition with respect to Italian literature has been set in motion. Italian literature is emerging from its restricted zone of the campus, important as it may be. Italian poets and prose-writers are being translated more assiduously, and make their appearance in newspapers and periodicals. The *Dialoghi con Leucò* will soon be published in translation, and it is hoped that this will soon be followed by a translation of *Lavorare stanca* which has already been prepared by Carlo Golino.[12] Suggestions for studies of other contemporary writers are also being considered, and it is to be hoped that after this Pavese others will be published, for example, on Svevo, Gadda, Moravia, Vittorini, Pratolini, Rea, Cassola, Berto, Tozzi, Calvino and Jovine.

---

[12] To our knowledge, this volume of the translation of *Lavorare stanca* remained unpublished.

This is what I can provide as information for the moment even if it is not all.

Cordially,
Giose Rimanelli

BIBLIOGRAPHY

WORKS BY CESARE PAVESE

Lavorare stanca (poetry 1931-1935) *Solaria*, Firenze, 1936; new edition (including poetry 1936-40) Einaudi, Torino 1943.

Paesi tuoi (1939) Einaudi, Torino, 1941.

La spiaggia (1940-41) *Lettere d'Oggi*, Roma, 1942. New Edition, Einaudi, Torino, 1956.

Feria D'agosto (1941-44) Einaudi, Torino, 1946.

La terra e la morte (poetry 1945) review *Le Tre Venezie*, Padova, 1947. New edition (including the poems *Verrà la morte e avrà i tuoi occhi*) Einaudi, Torino, 1951.

Dialoghi con Leucò (1945-46) Einaudi, Torino, 1947.

Il compagno (1946) Einaudi, Torino, 1947.

Prima che il gallo canti (1938-39) Einaudi, Torino, 1949 (including *La casa in collina* and *Il carcere*).

La casa in collina (1947-48) Einaudi, Torino, 1949 (including *Prima che il gallo canti*).

La bella estate (1940) Einaudi, Torino, 1949 (including *Il diavolo sulle colline* and *Tra donne sole* under the title *La bella estate*).

Il diavolo sulle colline (1948) Einaudi, Torino, 1949 (including *La bella estate*).

Tra donne sole (1949) Einaudi, Torino, 1949 (including *La bella estate*).

La luna e i falò (1949) Einaudi, Torino, 1950.

Verrà la morte e avrà i tuoi occhi (poetry 1950) Einaudi, Torino, 1951 (including also *La terra e la morte*).

La letteratura americana e altri saggi (essays and articles 1930-50) Einaudi, Torino, 1951.

Il mestiere di vivere (diaries 1935-50) Einaudi, Torino, 1953.

Notte di festa (1936-38) Einaudi, Torino, 1959.

Fuoco grande (with Bianca Garufi, 1946) Einaudi, Torino, 1959.

Racconti (1936-44) Einaudi, Torino, 1960 (including *Notte di festa*, *Feria d'agosto* and about twenty previously unpublished short stories and fragments).

Romanzi (complete novels) Einaudi, Torino, 1961. Two volumes.

Poesie edite e inedite (1931-1950, complete poems) Einaudi, Torino, 1962.

AMERICAN AND ENGLISH PUBLICATIONS OF WORKS
BY CESARE PAVESE

The Political Prison (includes *The Political Prisoner* and *The Beautiful Summer* translated from *Il carcere* and *La bella estate* by W. J. Strachan) Peter Owen Limited, London, 1955.

The Moon And The Bonfires (*La luna e i falò* translated by Marianne Ceconi) Farrar, Straus, New York, 1953.

Among Women Only (*Tra donne sole* translated by D. D. Paige) Noonday, New York, 1953.

The Devil In The Hills (*Il diavolo sulle colline* translated by D. D. Paige) Noonday, New York, 1954.

The House On The Hill (*La casa in collina* translated by W. J. Strachan) Walker, New York, 1961.

The Burning Brand (*Il mestiere di vivere* translated by A. E. Murch with Jeanne Molli, Introduction by Frances Keene) Walker, New York, 1961.

Dialogues With Leucò (*Dialoghi con Leucò* translated by William Arrowsmith and D. S. Carne-Ross) The University of Michigan Press, Ann Arbor, 1965.

Appendix

Translations by Cesare Pavese

SINCLAIR LEWIS: *Il nostro signor Wrenn* (Bemporad, Firenze, 1931)
HERMANN MELVILLE: *Moby Dick* (Frassinelli, Torino, 1932)
SHERWOOD ANDERSON: *Riso nero* (Frassinelli, Torino, 1932)
JAMES JOYCE: *Dedalus* (Frassinelli, Torino, 1932)
JOHN DOS PASSOS: *Il 42 parallelo* (Mondadori, Milano, 1935)
JOHN DOS PASSOS: *Un mucchio di quattrini* (Mondadori, 1937)
JOHN STEINBECK: *Uomini e topi* (Bompiani, Milano, 1938)
GERTRUDE STEIN: *Autobiografia di Alice Toklas* (Einaudi, Torino, 1938)
DANIEL DEFOE: *Moll Flanders* (Einaudi, Torino, 1938)
CHARLES DICKENS: *David Copperfield* (Einaudi, Torino, 1939)
GERTRUDE STEIN: *Tre esistenze* (Einaudi, Torino, 1940)
HERMANN MELVILLE: *Benito Cereno* (Einaudi, Torino, 1940)
GEORGE MACAULAY TREVELYAN: *La rivoluzione inglese del 1688-89* (Einaudi, Torino, 1941)
CHRISTOPHER MORLEY: *Il cavallo di Troia* (Bompiani, Milano, 1941)
WILLIAM FAULKNER: *Il borgo* (Mondadori, Milano, 1942)
ROBERT HENRIQUES: *Capitan Smith* (Einaudi, Torino, 1947)

In 1954 Michelangelo Antonioni directed a film from *Tra donne sole* entitled *Le amiche*.
From *Il compagno* Sergio Velitti has written a play called *Storia di Pablo* which was performed at "Piccolo Teatro" of Milano, March 20, 1961.

APPENDIX

CRITICISM ON PAVESE

DAVIDE LAJOLO: *Il vizio assurdo. Storia di Cesare Pavese.* Il Saggiatore, Milano, 1960.
FRANCO MOLLIA: *Cesare Pavese*, Rebellato, Padova, 1960.
GIUSEPPE TREVISANI: *Cesare Pavese*, Trevi Editore, Milano, 1961.
LORENZO MONDO: *Cesare Pavese*, Ugo Mursia Editore, Milano, 1962.
Terra rossa terra nera, edited by Laurana Lajolo and Elio Archimede, *Presenza Astigiana*, Asti, 1964.

Paesi tuoi (1941)

VIVIANI Alberto: *Il libro italiano*, Roma, May 1941.
VILLA Emilio: *Il libro italiano nel mondo*, Roma, May 1941.
BIGIARETTI Libero: *Lettere d'oggi*, Roma, May-June, 1941.
PRATOLINI Vasco: *Domani*, Roma, June 12, 1941.
ROBERTAZZI Mario: *La sera*, Milano, June 14, 1941.
PANCRAZI Piero: *Il corriere della* sera, Milano, July 8, 1941. (reprinted in *Scrittori d'oggi*, IV, Laterza, bari, 1946).
GALVANO Eugenio: *Primato*, Roma, July 15, 1941.
DAL FABBRO Beniamino: *Primato*, Roma, July 15, 1941.
ALICATA Mario: *Oggi*, Roma, July 19, 1941.
BELLONCI Goffredo: *Il giornale d'Italia*, Roma, July 20, 1941.
ROSSI Alberto: *Gazzetta del popolo*, Torino, July 25, 1941.
BONICELLI Vittorio: *Cronaca prealpina*, Varese, July 26, 1941.
BENCO Silvio: *Il popolo di Trieste*, Trieste, July 31, 1941.
CERCHIARI Luigi: *Il bosco*, Milano, July 31, 1941.
DE MICHELIS Eurialo: *Nuova Italia*, Firenze, July-August 1941.
ROSATI Salvatore: *L'Italia che scrive*, Roma, July-August 1941.
BIGIARETTI Libero: *La tribuna*, Roma, August 6, 1941.
BORLENGHI Aldo: *Corriere emiliano*, Parma, August 24, 1941.
RICCI Romeo: *Raccolta*, Roma, August-September, 1941.
DELLA PONTI Sandro: *L'ora*, Palermo, September 2, 1941.
VIGLIANI Luigi: *Leonardo*, Firenze, September-October, 1941.
PELLICANO Piero: *Vita italiana*, Roma, October 1941.
DAL FABBRO Beniamino: *Lettere d'oggi*, Roma, October-November 1941.
VALTORTA Franco: *La festa*, Assisi, Nobember 23, 1941.
CALLEGARI Giampaolo: *Meridiano di Roma*, Roma, December 21, 1941.
BENEDETTI Gino: *Il popolo di Bresca*, Brescia, December 23, 1941.
AZZALI Ferrante: *Il telegrafo*, Livorno, December 27, 1941.

LETTORE Ugo: *Domus*, Milano, January 1942.
GATTO Salvatore: *Torino*, Torino, February 1942.
CECCHI Emilio: *Nuova antologia*, Roma, March 1, 1942.
COMI Umberto: *Sentinella fascista*, Livorno, April 1942.
GADDA CONTI Piero: *Stile*, Milano, May 1942.
SUSINI Giuseppe: *Meridiano di Roma*, Roma, July 2, 1942.
CASINI Giorgio: *Signum*, Treviso, September 25, 1942.
PUCCINELLI Elvio: *Darsena nuova*, Viareggio, March 1, 1946.

La spiaggia (1942 and 1956)

BENCO Silvio: *Il popolo di Trieste*, Trieste, April 2, 1942.
GORGERINO Giuseppe: *Corriere padano*, Ferrara, April 5, 1942.
FRATELLI Arnaldo: *La tribuna*, Roma, April 18, 1942.
BOCCHI Lorenzo: *Gazzetta di Parma*, Parma, April 26, 1942.
ROBERTAZZI Mario: *La sera*, Milano, April 30, 1942.
BIANCHI Pietro: *Settegiorni*, Milano, May 2, 1942.
CHIAVARELLI Lucio: *Roma fascista*, Roma, May 7, 1942.
TOFANELLI Arturo: *Tempo*, Milano, May 21, 1942.
APOLLONIO Umbro: *Il popolo di Trieste*, Trieste, May 28, 1942.
MARUSSI Garibaldo: *Vedetta d'Italia*, Fiume, June 3, 1942.
SUSINI Giuseppe: *Meridiano di Roma*, Roma, July 2, 1942.
BUCCICO Rocco: *Meridiano di Roma*, Roma, August 30, 1942.
CAMILLUCCI Marcello: *Architrave*, Bologna, September 30, 1942.
BERGEL Lienhard: *Lo spettatore italiano*, Roma, October 10, 1955.
VACCARELLA Giovanni: *L'ora*, Palermo, October 21, 1942.
VILLAROEL Giuseppe: *Il popolo d'Italia*, Milano, July 3, 1943.
PORZIO Domenico: *Oggi*, Milano, August 23, 1956.
BO Carlo: La stampa, *Torino*, October 2, 1956.
BERTACCHINI Renato: *Convivium*, n. 2, 1957.

Lavorare stanca (1936 AND 1943)

CONTINI Gianfranco: *Libera stampa*, Lugano, June 30, 1944.
DIONISOTTI Carlo: *La nuova Europa*, Roma, August 26, 1945.
CAVALLARI Alberto: *L'Italia libera*, Milano, September 1, 1945.
VILLA Emilio: *L'unità*, Roma, November 14, 1945.
GUERRINI, Tito: *Cosmopolita*, Roma, March 14, 1946.
GIANNESSI Ferdinando: *Paesaggio*, Pisa, April 1946.
RUSSI Antonio: *La strada*, Roma, April-May, 1946.

ASSUNTO Rosario: *L'Italia che scrive*, Roma April-May 1946.
CALVINO Italo: *Agorà*, Torino, August 1946.
RISI Nelo, *Domus*, Milano, October 1946.
ALTEROCCA Bona: *Torino*, Torino, October 15, 1949.
RIZZARDI Alfredo: *Archi*, Bologna, June 1951.
FRATTINI Alberto: *Momenti*, Torino, November-December 1951.
BORLENGHI Aldo: *Libera stampa*, Lugano, February 12, 1952.
ANTONIELLI Sergio: *Aspetti e figure del Novecento*, Guanda, Parma, 1955.
PAUTASSO Sergio: *Questioni*, Torino, July-September 1956.
BARBERI SQUAROTTI Giorgio: *Questioni*, Torino, January-April 1959
    (reprinted in *Astrazione e realtà*, Rusconi e Paolazzi, Milano, 1960).

Feria d'agosto (1946)

PIAZZESI Gianfranco: *Inventario*, Firenze, January-February 1946.
DEL BUONO Oreste: *Costume*, Milano, January-February 1946.
SCHACHERL Bruno: *Il mondo*, Firenze, February 16, 1946.
FALQUI Enrico: *Risorgimento liberale*, Roma, April 18 1946.
PIZZORUSSO Arnaldo: *Paesaggio*, Pisa, April 1946.
LIVI Augusto: *Società*, Firenze, April-June 1946.
BADANO Nino: *Il popolo*, Torino, May 19, 1946.
GUERRINI Tito: *Avanti!*, Roma, June 23, 1946.
PUGLIESE Giuseppe: *Il gazzettino*, Venezia, June 23, 1946.
ANDREUCCI Domenico: *Gazzetta delle arti*, Roma, July 15-August 21, 1946.
CAPASSO Aldo: *Maestrale*, Reggio Calabria, July 28, 1946.
MICHEA Nicolò: *Osservatore letterario*, Trieste, December 2, 1946.
SAMONÀ Carmelo: *Presenza*, Messino, December 1946.
ANDREUCCI Domenico: *Il garibaldino*, Forlì, February 26, 1947.

Dialoghi con Leucò (1947)

CALVINO Italo: *Bollettino d'informazioni culturali Einaudi*, 10 November
    1947.
UNTERSTEINER Mario: *Educazione politica*, Milano, November-December
    1947.
BADANO Nino: *Il popolo*, Torino, December 3, 1947.
MAZZOCCHI Muzio: *L'Italia socialista*, Roma, December 9, 1947.
TALARICO Elio: *L'espresso*, Roma, January 20, 1948.
RISI Nelo: *Milano sera*, Milano, February 7, 1948.
DE ROBERTIS Giuseppe: *Tempo*, Milano, Februrary 7, 1948.

CALVINO Italo: *Publishers monthly*, Milano, February 1948.
CIAFFI Vincenzo: *Sempre avanti*, Torino, March 7, 1948.
BORLENGHI Aldo: *Corriere del Ticino*, Lugano, April 30, 1948.
VARESE Claudio: *Nuova antologia*, Roma, May 1948.
INVREA David: *Il ponte*, Firenze, August 1949.
FORTI Marco: *Il nuovo corriere*, Firenze, April 21, 1951.
SOBRERO Ornella: *Inventario*, Milano, January-June 1955.
PELLEGRINI Alessandro: *Belfagor*, September 30, 1955.
PREMUDA Maria Luisa: *Annali della Scuola Normale Superiore di Pisa*, Pisa 1957, vol. XXVI, fasc. III-IV.

Il compagno (1947)

CALVINO Italo: *L'unità*, Torino, July 20, 1947.
BADANO Nino: *Il popolo*, Torino, July 27, 1947.
VIGORELLI Giancarlo: *Oggi*, Milano, August 3, 1947.
EMANUELLI Enrico: *L'europeo*, Milano, August 3, 1947.
MONTI Augusto: *Mondo nuovo*, Torino, August 10, 1947.
CAJUMI Arrigo: *La stampa*, Torino, August 21, 1947.
DEL BO Giuseppe: *Avanti!*, Roma, August 31, 1947.
TALARICO Elio: *L'espresso*, Roma, September 5, 1947.
PRISCO Michele: *La fiera letteraria*, Roma, November 3, 1947.
DE ROBERTIS Giuseppe: *Tempo*, Milano, November 29, 1947.
FALQUI Enrico: *Il mondo europeo*, Roma, December 1, 1947.
VALLI Carlo: *Gazzetta veneta*, Padova, January 27, 1948.
RUSSI Antonio: *Italia socialista*, Roma, January 1, 1948.
FALQUI Enrico: *Il mattino di Roma*, Roma, January 18, 1948.
CAPASSO Aldo: *Adamo*, Brescia, February 1948.
BASSANI Giorgio: *Lo spettatore italiano*, Roma, April 1, 1948.
BUCCICO Rocco: *Gazzetta del mezzogiorno*, Bari, June 22, 1948.
DE SECLY Luigi: *Gazzetta del mezzogiorno*, Bari, August 26, 1948.
CAMPESE Luigi: *La selva*, Benevento, August 31, 1948.
PUCCINI Dario: *L'Italia che scrive*, Roma, October 1948.
FERRATA Giansiro: *Libera stampa*, Lugano, November 10, 1948.
RASTELLI Dario: *Fronte democratico*, Cremona, November 12, 1948.

Prima che il gallo canti and La casa in collina (1949)

ALTEROCCA Bona: *Il nostro tempo*, Torino, December 11, 1948.
CALVINO Italo: *L'unità*, Torino, December 30, 1948.

MAYERÙ Paolo: *Corriere di Napoli*, Napoli, January 7, 1949.
DE ROBERTIS Giuseppe: *Tempo*, Milano, January 15, 1949.
CECCHI Emilio: *L'europeo*, Milano, January 16, 1949 (reprinted in *Di giorno in giorno*, Garzanti, Milano, 1954).
GROSSO Augusta: *Il popolo*, Torino, January 16, 1949.
CAJUMI Arrigo: *La stampa*, Torino, January 19, 1949.
BO Carlo: *Omnibus*, Milano, January 20, 1949.
DEL BO Giuseppe: *Avanti!*, Milano, January 22, 1949.
BIGIARETTI Libero: *Mondo operaio*, Roma, January 27, 1949.
FERRATA Giansiro: *L'unità*, Milano, February 9, 1949.
BANTI Anna: *L'illustrazione italiana*, Milano, February 20, 1949.
BOCELLI Arnaldo: *Il mondo*, Roma, February 26, 1949.
BORLENGHI Aldo: *La fiera letteraria*, Roma, February 27, 1949.
PUCCINI Dario: *L'Italia che scrive*, Roma, February 1949.
FALQUI Enrico: *Il tempo*, Roma, March 18, 1949.
BADANO Nino: *Sicilia del popolo*, Palermo, March 20, 1949.
GORGERINO Giuseppe: *Il tempo di Milano*, Milano, March 26, 1949.
LUPO Valeria: *La fiera letteraria*, March 27, 1949.
ROMANO Lalla: *La rassegna d'Italia*, Milano, March 1949.
PAMPALONI Geno: *Comunità*, Ivrea, March-April 1949.
PICCIONI Leone: *Il popolo*, Milano, April 3, 1949.
LOPEZ Guido: *L'umanità*, Milano, April 12, 1949.
DEL PIZZO Giovanni: *L'elefante*, Roma, April 14, 1949.
CAPASSO Aldo: *La bussola*, Torino, April 20, 1949.
PEIRCE Guglielmo: *Lavoro*, Roma, April 25, 1949.
BONFANTINI Mario: *Gazzetta del popolo*, Torino, April 26, 1949.
LOPEZ Guido: *Gazzetta di Parma*, Parma, May 5, 1949.
TOZZI Luigi: *Gazzetta di Mondovì*, Mondovì, May 28, 1949.
VARESE Claudio: *Nuova antologia*, Roma, May 1949.
VIRDIA Ferdinando: *L'Umbria*, Perugia, June 7, 1949.
BORLEGHI Aldo, *Il progresso d'Italia*, Bologna, September 16, 1949.
GRIECO Giuseppe: *Giornale di Brescia*, Brescia, October 2, 1949.
CIBOTTO Gian Antonio: *La fiera letteraria*, Roma, October 20, 1949.
CIOBOTTO Gian Antonio: *Gazzetta veneta*, Padova, October 23, 1949.
MELE Angelo: *Sud letterario*, Napoli, October-December 1949.
MAGNI Maria: *Giornale del popolo*, Bergamo, December 30, 1949.
FORTINI Franco: *Letteratura/arte*, Firenze, January-February 1950.
VOLPINI Valerio: *Ricerca*, Roma, August 1, 1950.
DUVIGNAUD Jean: *Nouvelle Revue Francaise*, Parigi, June 1953.
LA CAVA Mario: *Comunità*, Milano, December 1956.

La bella estate, Il diavolo sulle colline, Tra donne sole (1949)

BORLENGHI Aldo: *Avanti!*, Milano, December 30, 1949.
GIGLI Lorenzo: *Gazzetta del popolo*, Torino, December 30, 1949.
CAJUMI Arrigo: *La stampa*, Torino, January 18, 1950.
PICCIONI Leone: *Il popolo*, Milano, January 19, 1950.
DE ROBERTIS Giuseppe: *Tempo*, Milano, January 21, 1950.
CECCHI Emilio: *L'europeo*, Milano, January 22, 1950 (reprinted in *Di giorno in giorno*, Garzanti, Milano, 1954).
DE MICHELI Mario: *L'unità*, Milano, January 28, 1950.
BONFANTINI Mario: *Gazzetta del popolo*, Torino, February 7, 1950.
BRUNO Francesco: *Risorgimento*, Napoli, February 8, 1950.
GROSSO Augusta: *Il popolo*, Torino, February 12, 1950.
GRIECO Giuseppe: *Il giornale*, Napoli, February 15, 1950.
DAL SASSO Rino: *L'unità*, Roma, February 25, 1950.
BOCELLI Arnaldo: *Il mondo*, Roma, March 4, 1950.
MARINESE Lorenzo: *Il progresso d'Italia*, Bologna, March 7, 1950.
PADOVANI Paolo: *Avanti!*, Roma, March 14, 1950.
TOZZI Luigi: *Il rinnovamento liberale*, Torino, April 15, 1950.
SERGI Pina: *Il nuovo corriere*, Firenze, April 15, 1950.
SOLDINI Adriano: *Gazzetta ticinese*, Lugano, April 27, 1950.
PICCIONI Leone: *Giornale del lunedi*, Trieste, April 30, 1950.
SOLDINI Adriano: *Corriere del Ticino*, Lugano, May 12, 1950.
BOTTA Guido: *Delta*, Napoli, May 1950.
PUCCINI Dario: *Bollettino del centro edizioni sociali*, Milano, May-July 1950.
TOZZI Luigi: *Gazzetta di Mondovì*, Mondovì, June 3, 1950.
DEL BUONO Oreste: *Milano sera*, June 6-7, 1950.
MARIANI Guido: *Il Vesuvio*, Napoli, June 17, 1950.
DELLA MEA Luciano: *Avanti!*, Milano, June 24, 1950.
FRANK Nino: *Mercure de France*, Parigi, July 1, 1950.
CIBOTTO Gian Antonio: *Alto Adige*, Bolzano, July 13, 1950.

La luna e i falò (1949)

CAJUMI Arrigo: *La stampa*, Torino, May 26, 1950.
CAMERINO Aldo: *Il gazzettino*, Venezia, May 27, 1950.
LAJOLO Davide: *L'unità*, Milano, May 30, 1950.
DEL BUONO Oreste: *Milano sera*, Milano, June 7-8, 1950.
VIRDIA Ferdinando: *La voce repubblicana*, Roma, June 11, 1950.
PRISCO Michele: *Idea*, Roma, June 12, 1950.

GROSSO Augusta: *Il popolo*, Torino, June 18, 1950.
PICCIONI Leone: *Il popolo*, Roma, June 20, 1950.
FALQUI Enrico: *Il tempo*, Roma, June 20, 1950.
BORLENGHI Aldo: *Quarta dimensione*, Milano, June 23, 1950.
DE ROBERTIS Giuseppe: *Tempo*, Milano, June 24, 1950.
LOMBARDO RADICE Lucio: *Vie nuove*, Roma, June 25, 1950.
MELE Angelo: *Il sud letterario*, Napoli, June-August 1950.
BRUNO Francesco: *Idea*, Roma, July 5, 1950.
CHIRI Enrico: *La voce della giustizia*, July 8, 1950.
GRIECO Giuseppe: *Omnibus*, Milano, July 9, 1950.
RICHELMY Tino: *La serra*, Ivrea, July 14, 1950.
LOMBARDI Olga: *La fiera letteraria*, Roma, July 23, 1950.
PORZIO Domenico: *Oggi*, Milano, July 27, 1950.
TOZZI Luigi: *Gazzetta di Mondovì*, Mondovì, July 29, 1950.
ALICATA Mario: *Rinascita*, Roma, July 1950.
PASOLINI Desideria: *Lo spettatore italiano*, Roma, July 1950.
BARGIS Piero: *Avanti!*, August 6, 1950.
DE ROBERTIS Giuseppe: *Il nuovo corriere*, Firenze, August 9, 1950.
BRUNO Francesco: *Poesis*, Roma, August 15, 1950.
BARTOLUCCI Giuseppe: *Avanti!*, Roma, August 22, 1950.
TESI Oreste: *Inventario*, Milano, estate 1950.
CASNATI Francesco: *Il popolo*, Milano, September 3, 1950.
CIBOTTO Gian Antonio: *Gazzetta veneta*, Padova, September 5, 1950.
SOLDINI Adriano: *Libera stampa*, Lugano, September 5, 1950.
FRATELLI Arnaldo: *Paese-sera*, Roma, September 7, 1950.
PAMPALONI Geno: *Belfagor*, Firenze, September 1950.
PUCCINI Dario: *L'Italia che scrive*, Roma, September 1950.
FORTINI Franco: *Comunità*, Ivrea, September-October 1950.
MAGNI Maria: *Giornale del popolo*, Bergamo, October 10, 1950.
MALLOGGI M.: *Corriere tridentino*, Trento, October 26, 1950.
VARESE Claudio: *Nuova antologia*, Roma, October 1950.
VOLPINI Valerio: *Coscienza*, Roma, November 5, 1950.
JAHIER Piero: *Il ponte*, Firenze, November 1950.
DAVIDSON Basil: *New Statesman*, London, April 14, 1951.

Verrà la morte e avrà i tuoi occhi (1951)

BELLONCI Goffredo: *Il giornale d'Italia*, Roma, April 13, 1951.
BO Carlo: *La fiera letteraria*, Roma, April 15, 1951.
CAMERINO Aldo: *Il gazzettino*, Venezia, April 15, 1951.

APPENDIX

MILANO Paolo: *The New York Times Book Review*, April 19, 1951.
BOCELLI Arnaldo: *Il mondo*, Roma, April 21, 1951.
GRAMIGNA Giuliano: *Settimo giorno*, Milano, April 26, 1951.
DELLA MEA Luciano: *Avanti!*, Roma, April 28, 1951.
TIBALDUCCI Gino: *Portici*, Bologna, April 1951.
PORZIO Domenico: *Oggi*, Milano, May 10, 1951.
GIGLI Lorenzo: *Gazzetta del popolo*, Torino, May 11, 1951.
TOZZI Luigi: *Gazzetta di Mondovì*, Mondovì, May 12, 1951.
GRIECO Giuseppe: *Omnibus*, Milano, May 20, 1951.
DI GIACOMO Vittorio: *Il quotidiano*, Roma, May 22, 1951.
FALQUI Enrico: *Il tempo*, Roma, May 22, 1951 (reprinted in *Novecento letterario*, Vallecchi, Firenze, 1954).
SCHIPPISI Ranieri: *Libertà*, Piacenza, May 24, 1951.
MENECHINI Dino: *Messaggero Veneto*, Venezia, June 30, 1951.
GROSSO Augusta: *Il popolo*, Torino, May 29, 1951.
MARTINI Silvano: *Alto Adige*, Bolzano, June 2, 1951.
DE ROBERTIS Giuseppe: *Tempo*, Milano, June 2, 1951.
BRUNO Francesco: *La giustizia*, Roma, June 6, 1951.
MARVADI Umberto: *Idea*, Roma, June 24, 1951.
MENECHINI Dino: *Messaggero Veneto*, Venezia, June 30, 1951.
PAMPALONI Geno: *Il ponte*, Firenze, June 1951.
RIZZARDI Alfredo: *Archi*, Bologna, June 1951.
ROMANÒ Angelo: *Humanitas*, Brescia, June 1951.
SPAGNOLETTI Giacinto: *Paragone*, Firenze, June 1951.
LUSARDI Bruno: *La gazzetta di Modena*, Modena, July 30, 1951.
SOLDINI Adriano: *Libera stampa*, Lugano, July 31, 1951.
BOMBACI Sebastiano: *Pensiero letterario*, Milano, July-August 1951.
RICHELMY Carlo: *Orizzonti*, Roma, August 9, 1951.
BOSELLI Mario: *Il lavoro nuovo*, Genova, August 28, 1951.
CAMILLUCCI Marcello: *Idea*, Roma, September 16, 1951.
GARELLI Cesare: *La giustizia*, Roma, September 16, 1951.
MANACORDA Giuliano: *Il paese*, Roma, September 23, 1951.
FRATTINI Alberto: *La via*, Roma, November 17, 1951.
MELE Angelo: *Corriere del giorno*, Taranto, November 20, 1951.
ANTONIELLI Sergio: *Belfagor*, Firenze, November 30, 1951.
BALDACCI Luigi: *Letteratura ed arte contemporanea*, Vicenza, November 1951.
BORLENGHI Aldo: *Letterature moderne*, Bologna, November-December 1951.
RIVA Franco: *L'ordine*, Como, January 4, 1952.
VOLPINI Valerio: *Idea*, Roma, March 9, 1952.
RIVA Franco: *Gazzetta di Mantova*, Mantova, April 10, 1952.
SOLMI Sergio: *Lo spettatore italiano*, Roma, March 1953.

La letteratura americana e altri saggi (1951)

CALVINO Italo: Prefazione a *La letteratura americana e altri saggi*, Einaudi, Firenze, 1951.
CAJUMI Arrigo: *La stampa*, Torino, January 2, 1952.
DUSE Gastone: *L'unità*, Genova, January 15, 1952.
GIGLIO Tommaso: *Milano-sera*, Milano, January 18, 1952.
LAJOLO Davide: *L'unità*, Torino, February 5, 1952.
CRAVERI CROCE Elena: *Lo spettatore italiano*, Roma, February 1952.
VARESE Claudio: *Nuova antologia*, Roma, June 1952.
FORTINI Franco: *Comunità*, Milano, June 1952.
D'AGOSTINO Nemi: *Belfagor*, Firenze, November 30, 1952.

Il mestiere di vivere (1952)

CAJUMI Arrigo: *La stampa*, Torino, September 24, 1952.
BO Carlo: *La fiera letteraria*, Roma, September 28, 1952.
ANTONICELLI Franco: *Stampa-sera*, Torino, October 6, 1952.
GIGLI Lorenzo: *Gazzetta del popolo*, Torino, October 9, 1952.
LAJOLO Davide: *L'unità*, Torino, October 11, 1952.
MONTALE Eugenio: *Il corriere della sera*, Milano, October 11, 1952.
FABBRETTI Nazareno: *Il quotidiano*, Roma, October 12, 1952.
CERRUTI Franco: *Il popolo di Roma*, Roma, October 28, 1952.
DE FEO Sandro: *Il corriere della sera*, Milano, October 30, 1952.
PICCIONI Leone: *Giovedì*, Roma, November 13, 1952.
GIRARDI Enzo Noè: *Vita e pensiero*, Milano, December 1952.
PORTINARI Folco: *Aut-Aut*, Milano, December 1952.
PAMPALONI Geno: *Comunità*, Milano, December 1952.
MONDRONE Domenico: *La civiltà cattolica*, Roma, January 17, 1953.
GRAMIGNA Giuliano: *Inventario*, Milano, primavera 1953.
CITATI Pietro: *Belfagor*, Firenze, May 3, 1953.
GERRATANA Valentino: *L'unità*, Torino, October 22, 1953.
MILA Massimo: *L'unità*, Torino, Ocotber 22, 1953.
MORAVIA Alberto: *Il corriere della sera*, Milano, December 22, 1954.
BERGEL Lienhard: *Lo spettatore italiano*, Roma, October 10, 1955.
PELLEGRINI Alessandro: *Belfagor*, Firenze, September 30, 1955.
RAVEGNANI Giuseppe: *Uomini visti*, Mondadori, Milano, 1955, vol. II.
INGHILES Paolo: *Testimonianze*, Firenze, December 1960.

Notte di festa (1953)

VIRDIA Ferdinando: *Giovedì*, Roma, June 12, 1953.
DE FEO Sandro: *L'europeo*, Milano, July 12, 1953.
MANACORDA Giuliano: *Il paese*, Roma, July 22, 1953.
CECCHI Emilio: *Il corriere della sera*, July 24, 1953 (reprinted in *Di giorno in giorno*, Garzanti, Milano, 1954).
DE ROBERTIS Giuseppe: *Tempo*, Milano, September 8, 1953.
SOBRERO Ornella, *Il presente*, Caltanissetta, autunno 1953.
LONGOBARDI Fulvio: *Aut-Aut*, Milano, September 1953.
FORTI Marco: *Paragone*, Firenze, December 1953.
GIANNESSI Ferdinando: *Letterature moderne*, Bologna, January-February 1954.
VARESE Claudio: *Nuova antologia*, Roma, June 1954.

Fuoco grande (1959)

GIGLI Lorenzo: *Gazzetta del popolo*, Torino, June 24, 1959.
BO Carlo: *La stampa*, Torino, June 25, 1959.
Anonimo: *L'espresso*, Roma, June 28, 1959.
Anonimo: *Vita*, Roma, July 2, 1959.
MILANO Paolo: *L'espresso*, Roma, July 5, 1959.
VIRDIA Ferdinando: *La fiera letteraria*, Roma, July 12, 1959.
BOCELLI Arnaldo: *Il mondo*, Roma, July 14, 1959.
PICCIONI Leone: *Il popolo*, Roma, July 21, 1959.
RAGO Michele: *L'unità*, Roma, July 28, 1959.
SALINARI Carlo: *Vie nuove*, Roma, September 2, 1959.

Racconti editi e inediti (1960)

ANTONICELLI Franco: *La stampa*, Torino, February 9, 1960.
SALINARI Carlo: *Vie nuove*, Roma, February 20, 1960.
RIMANELLI Giose: *Rotosei*, Roma, February 26, 1960.
VERGANI Guido: *Visto*, Milano, February 27, 1960.
PICCIONI Leone: *Il popolo*, Roma, March 3, 1960.
ZAMPA Giorgio: *Corriere della sera*, Milano, March 3, 1960.
VIRDIA Gerdinando: *La fiera letteraria*, Roma, March 20, 1960.
MAURO Walter: *Il paese*, Roma, March 24, 1960.
CAMERINO Aldo: *Il gazzettino*, Venezia, March 29, 1960.

TONDO Michele: *Gazzetta del mezzogiorno*, June 30, 1960.
FALQUI Enrico: *Giornale di Sicilia*, Palermo, September 19, 1961.

Poesie edite e inedite (1962)

GIANNESSI Ferdinando: *La stampa*, Torino, January 9, 1963.
MONDO Lorenzo: *Gazzetta del popolo*, Torino, January 16, 1963.
RAGO Michele: *L'unità*, Roma, January 16, 1963.
BOCCELLI Arnaldo: *Il mondo*, January 1, 1963.
VISANI Mario: *L'avvenire d'Italia*, Bologna, January 18, 1963.
FERRATA Giansiro: *Rinascita*, Roma, January 19, 1963.
ZUCARO Domenico: *Avanti!*, Milano, February 27, 1963.
COSTANZO Giuseppe: *Il ponte*, Firenze, June 1963.
CICCIARELLI Tullio: *Il lavoro nuovo*, Genova, September 1, 1963.
SALINARI Carlo: *Vie nuove*, Roma, September 12, 1963.
CROCI Giovanni: *Cooperazione*, Lugano, May 9, 1964.

Sull'opera poetica di Pavese

SPAGNOLETTI Giancinto: *Antologia della poesia italiana*, Vallecchi, Firenze, 1946, and Guanda, Parma, 1949.
ANCESCHI and ANTONIELLI: *Lirica del '900*, Vallecchi, Firenze, 1953.
ANTONIELLI Sergio: *Aspetti e figure del '900*, Guanda, Parma, 1955.
BORLENGHI Aldo: *Tra ottocento e novecento*, Nistri Lischi, Pisa, 1955.
CRAVERI CROCE Elena: *Poeti del '900*, Einaudi, Torino, 1960.

Sull'opera e sulla figura di Pavese

CAJUMI Arrigo: *La stampa*, Torino, August 29, 1950.
CECCHI Emilio: *Paragone*, Firenze, August 1950.
BOCELLI Arnaldo: *Il mondo*, Roma, September 9, 1950.
DE LAURENTIS Lanza: *Rassegna di cultura*, Roma, September 1950.
ANTONICELLI Franco: *Il ponte*, Firenze, November 1950.
FALQUI Enrico: *Tra racconti e romanzi del novecento*, D'Anna, Messina, 1950.
GIRARDI Enzo Noè: *Vita e pensiero*, Milano, April 1951.
GRIECO Giuseppe: *Omnibus*, Milano, May 20, 1951.
LEGGERI Giuliano: *Nuova antologia*, Roma, November, 1951.
VARESE Claudio: *Cultura letteraria contemporanea*, Nistri Lischi, Pisa, 1951.
MANACORDA Giuliano: *Società*, Roma, June 1952.

APPENDIX

MUSCETTA Carlo: *Società*, Roma, June 1952.

PICCIONI Leone: *Lettura leopardiana e altri saggi*, Vallecchi, Firenze, 1952.

PRAMPOLINI Giacomo: *Storia universale della letteratura*, U.T.E.T., Torino, 1952, vol. VI.

BARBERI SQUAROTTI Giorgio: *Archivio glottologico italiano*, Firenze, January 1953.

PICCIONI Leone: *La fiera letteraria*, Roma, February 22, 1953.

DAL SASSO Rino: *Rinascita*, Roma, December 1953.

MUSCETTA Carlo: *Letteratura militante*, Parenti, Firenze, 1953.

PICCIONI Leone: *Sui contemporanei*, Fratelli Fabbri, Milano, 1953.

GUIDETTI Armando: *Questioni*, Torino, April 1954.

DEVOTO Giacomo: *Profilo di storia linguistica italiana*, Firenze, 1954.

FALQUI Enrico: *Novecento letterario*, Firenze, 1954.

ANTONICELLI Franco: *La stampa*, Torino, February 9, 1955.

BOCELLI Arnaldo: *Il mondo*, Roma, May 10, 1955.

SERONI Adriano: *Leggere e sperimentare*, Parenti, Firenze, 1957.

BARBERI SQAROTTI Giorgio: *Questioni*, Torino, January-April, 1958.

GUGLIELMI Guido: *Convivium*, Roma, January-February 1958.

REPETTO Arrigo: *Presenza*, Milano, August-September 1958.

BELLONCI Maria: *Il punto*, Roma, September 6, 1958.

SPAGNOLETTI Giacinto: *La nuova narrativa italiana*, Guanda, Parma, 1958.

PICCIONI Leone: *Successo*, Milano, March 1959.

BO Carlo: *La stampa*, Torino, July 5, 1959.

BARBERI SQUAROTTI Giorgio: *Dizionario enciclopedico*, U.T.E.T., vol. IX, Torino, 1959.

RIMANELLI Giose: *Il mestiere del furbo*, Sugar, Milano, November, 1959.

FERNANDEZ Dominique: *Il romanzo italiano*, Lerici, Milano, January 1960.

SALINARI Carlo: *La questione del realismo*, Parenti, Firenze, May 1960.

LAJOLO Davide: *L'Europa letteraria*, Roma, June 1960.

PILLON Cesare: *Vie nuove*, Roma, July 8, 1960.

BO Carlo: *L'europeo*, Milano, August 8, 1960.

DEL BUONO Oreste: *Epoca*, Milano, August 16, 1960.

CITATI Pietro: *Il giorno*, Milano, August 16, 1960.

ANTONICELLI Franco: *La stampa*, Torino, August 22, 1960.

GORIA Giulio: *Paese-sera*, Roma, August 22, 1960.

VOLPINI Valerio: *Gazzetta del popolo*, Torino, August 27, 1960.

GRISI Francesco: *La fiera letteraria*, Roma, September 11-18, 1960.

MILANO Paolo: *L'espresso*, Roma, September 11, 1960.

PICCIONI Leone: *Il popolo*, Roma, September 14, 1960.

FALQUI Enrico: *Il tempo*, Roma, October 21, 1960.

BOCELLI Arnaldo: *Il mondo*, Roma, November 1, 1960.

TEDESCHI Giuseppe: *La fiera letteraria*, Roma, June 9, 1961.
GRISI Francesco: *Incontri in libreria*, Ceschina, Milano, 1961.
GORINI Mario: *La fiera letteraria*, Roma, January 7, 1962.
PAMPALONI Geno: *Terzo programma*, Roma, September 1962.
GRISI Francesco: *Italia cronache*, Roma, January 9, 1963.
PIGNOTTI Lamberto: *Paese-sera libri*, Roma, February 15, 1963.
PENTO Bortolo: *La fiera letteraria*, Roma, February 25, 1963.
SAPEGNO Natalino: *La stampa*, Torino, May 23, 1963.
SPRIANO Paolo, *Rinascita*, Roma, August 24, 1963.
FERRERO Ernesto: *Gazzetta del mezzogiorno*, Bari, September 15, 1963.
FONTANELLI Giorgio: *Avanti!*, Roma, August 27, 1964.
TONTO Michele: *Annali della facoltà di lettere*, Bari, 1962.

INDEX

Gadda, Carlo Emilio 181, 189
Gallimard Editore 109
Garufi, Bianca Maria 132, 191
Gentile, Giovanni 129
Gide, Andrè (gidean) 153, 155
Giachino, Enzo 9
Giese, Rachel xxxv
Ginsberg, Alan 82
Ginzburg, Leone 128
Gobetti, Piero 128
Golden Bough 55, 100
Golino, Carlo L. xii, 189
Gozzano, Guido 83, 84, 85
Green, Julien 155
Guardini, Romano 109

Hegel, G.W.F. (hegelian) 111-112,
   129
Heiney, Donald xxii-xxiii, 85, 153
Herodotus 152
Homer 41, 48, 85, 96, 113, 115,
   132

Iliad 41, 96
Inchiesta sul neorealismo 130
Italian Quarterly ix, xxi, xxxv

James, William 38
Jovine, Francesco 128, 177-178,
   180, 189
Joyce, James xix, 17, 25, 115, 182,
   188-189, 193
Jung, C.G. (junghian) 32, 112,
   116, 160

Kafka, Franz 153, 155
Kant, Immanuel (kantian) 159
Keene, Frances xxiii, 192
Kierkegaard, Soren 14
King Lear 21

Lajolo, Davide xi, xii-xiv, xviii-
   xxi, xxiii, xxxv, 3, 58, 110,
   127-128, 157, 160, 165, 171-
   172, 175-176, 179, 181-186,
   189, 194, 199, 202, 205
Lajolo, Laurana xii, xxxv, 194
Landolfi, Tommaso 4
Leaves of Grass 79-83, 85
Leopardi, Giacomo 3, 25
Levi, Carlo xxv, 128, 161
Lèvy-Bruhl, Lucien 29
Lewis, R.W.B.183
Lewis, Sinclair 193
Locke, John 38
Longanesi, Leo 4, 181
Loriggio, Franco xxxv
Lotze, Rudolf Hermann 14
Lowry, Malcolm 189
Lukacs, George (lukacsian) 135

Mallarmè, Stephane 75
Malinowski, Bronislaw 30
Malraux, Andrè 19
Mann, Thoma 112, 188
Marx, Karl (marxism) 112, 128-
   129, 131
Maxwell, Lois 161
Melville, Herman xvii, xix-xx,
   14-15, 188, 193
Mestiere del furbo (Il) xvi-xvii, xx,
   xxvii-xxviii, 131, 175, 179,
   205
Mila, Massimo 76, 83, 202
Milano, Paolo xxiv-xxv, 201, 203,
   205
Moby Dick xix, 14-15, 188, 193
Mollia, Franco 23, 135, 184, 194
Mondadori, Albert xii, xiii
Mondadori Casa Editrice xii, 4,
   76, 161, 179-181, 187, 193, 202

SAGGISTICA

Taking its name from the Italian—which means essays, essay writing, or non-fiction—*Saggisitca* is a referred book series dedicated to the study of all topics and cultural productions that fall under what we might consider that larger umbrella of all things Italian and Italian/American.

Vito Zagarrio
 The "Un-Happy Ending": Re-viewing The Cinema of Frank Capra. 2011. ISBN 978-1-59954-005-4. Volume 1.
Paolo A. Giordano, Editor
 The Hyphenate Writer and The Legacy of Exile. 2010. ISBN 978-1-59954-007-8. Volume 2.
Dennis Barone
 America / Trattabili. 2011. ISBN 978-1-59954-018-4. Volume 3.
Fred L. Gardaphè
 The Art of Reading Italian Americana. 2011. ISBN 978-1-59954-019-1. Volume 4.
Anthony Julian Tamburri
 Re-viewing Italian Americana: Generalities and Specificities on Cinema. 2011. ISBN 978-1-59954-020-7. Volume 5.
Sheryl Lynn Postman
 An Italian Writer's Journey through American Realities: Giose Rimanelli's English Novels. "The most tormented decade of America: the 60s" ISBN 978-1-59954-034-4. Volume 6.
Luigi Fontanella
 Migrating Words: Italian Writers in the United States. 2012. ISBN 978-1-59954-041-2. Volume 7.
Peter Covino & Dennis Barone, Editors
 Essays on Italian American Literature and Culture. 2012. ISBN 978-1-59954-035-1. Volume 8.
Gianfranco Viesti
 Italy at the Crossroads. 2012. ISBN 978-1-59954-071-9. Volume 9.
Peter Carravetta, Editor
 Discourse Boundary Creation (LOGOS TOPOS POIESIS): A Festschrift in Honor of Paolo Valesio. ISBN 978-1-59954-036-8. Volume 10.
Antonio Vitti and Anthony Julian Tamburri, Editors
 Europe, Italy, and the Mediterranean. ISBN 978-1-59954-073-3. Volume 11.
Vincenzo Scotti
 Pax Mafiosa or War: Twenty Years after the Palermo Massacres. 2012. ISBN 978-1-59954-074-0. Volume 12.

Stephen J. Belluscio
  Garibaldi M. Lapolla: A Study of His Novels. ISBN 978-1-59954-125-9. Volume 27.
Antonio Vitti and Anthony Julian Tamburri, Editors
  The Representation of the Mediterranean World by Insiders and Outsiders. ISBN 978-1-59954-113-6. Volume 28.
Philip Balma and Giovanni Spani, Editors
  Translating for (and from) The Italian Screen: Dubbing and Subtitles. ISBN 978-1-59954-141-9. Volume 29.
Antonio Vitti and Anthony Julian Tamburri, Editors
  The Representation of the Mediterranean World by Insiders and Outsiders. ISBN 978-1-59954-142-6. Volume 30.
Anthony Julian Tamburri, Editor
  Interrogations into Italian-American Studies. The Francesco and Mary Giambelli Foundation Lectures. ISBN 978-1-59954-143-3. Volume 31.

www.ingramcontent.com/pod-product-compliance
Lightning Source LLC
Chambersburg PA
CBHW031942010726
47493CB00007B/2044